Unconditional Freedom

'A carefully argued case for basic income as central to a democratic transformation of society. Basic income must be seen not just as an anti-poverty policy but as a means for achieving both individual socio-economic independence and collective self-government. [It] can thus be seen as vital for solving a political problem, which also demands the appropriate universalist policies and structure of rights to uphold unconditional freedom for everyone.'
—Carole Pateman, political theorist, Distinguished Professor Emeritus of Political Science UCLA

'Casassa's path-breaking work throws new light on how we understand work, freedom, and emancipation in today's highly precariatised and insecure world. He is provocative and equally tender in his treatment of the human condition in our particular moment of capitalist evolution, painstakingly sketching what true emancipation looks and feels like, and what role a basic income could play in the process. A must-read for students and teachers, policymakers and activists who are keen to make this world a better place for all of us.'
—Sarath Davala, Sociologist, Chair, Basic Income Earth Network

'This is a very important and timely book. The focus on "social power" adds a new and much needed societal dimension to research and debate about basic income in an age of economic and political upheaval. This excellent book ... is a must-read for anyone wanting to gain a broader perspective on basic income reform.'
—Louise Haagh, author of *The Case for Basic Income*

'An ethical defence of basic income constructed on the value of republican freedom, an important proposal in an era of rentier capitalism that allows plutocrats to pocket more and more wealth. We need a new system of distribution with basic income acting as an anchor.'
—Guy Standing, author of *The Corruption of Capitalism*

'Casassas firmly retraces the Republican case for basic income to its traditional left-wing origins of combatting structural domination and unequal social power. A timely antidote to those propagating the myth of basic income as a trojan horse of the right!'
—Jurgen De Wispelaere, Visiting Professor, Götz Werner Chair of Economic Policy & Constitutional Theory, University of Freiburg

'A useful, militant book, useful because it clearly, rigorously and skilfully sets out the basic principles of the universal basic income, and militant because it doesn't hide its position, which I'd describe as radical.'
—Daniel Raventós, author of *Basic Income: The Material Conditions of Freedom*

Unconditional Freedom

Universal Basic Income and Social Power

David Casassas

Translated by Julie Wark

First published in Spanish in 2018 as *Libertad incondicional* by Editorial Paidós.
This English language edition is arranged via Red Rock Literary Agency Ltd. and
Oh! Books Literary Agency.

English edition first published 2024 by Pluto Press
New Wing, Somerset House, Strand, London WC2R 1LA
and Pluto Press, Inc.
1930 Village Center Circle, 3-834, Las Vegas, NV 89134

www.plutobooks.com

British Library Cataloguing in Publication Data
A catalogue record for this book is available from the British Library

ISBN 978 0 7453 4863 6 Paperback
ISBN 978 0 7453 4865 0 PDF
ISBN 978 0 7453 4864 3 EPUB

This book is printed on paper suitable for recycling and made from fully
managed and sustained forest sources. Logging, pulping and manufacturing processes are expected to conform to the environmental standards of the country of
origin.

Typeset by Stanford DTP Services, Northampton, England

Simultaneously printed in the United Kingdom and United States of America

Something must be wrong with work, or the rich would have hogged it.

Mario Moreno (Cantinflas)

When nothing is done, nothing is left undone.

Lao Tzu

Man is at last compelled to face with sober senses his real condition of life and his relations with his kind.

Karl Marx and Friedrich Engels

Contents

Acknowledgements

Like any other item produced by humans, this book is the result of a social or collective effort, which wouldn't have been possible without clues and references from the past, as well as those garnered from the work and presence of the people I have around me. It's therefore impossible to begin without recognising this unburdensome debt.

Jurgen De Wispelaere, Andrés Di Masso, Antoni Domènech, Ion Fernández de las Heras, Iratxe Fernández de las Heras, Marina Garcés, Eduardo González de Molina, David Guerrero, Bru Laín Escandell, Julio Lucena de Andrés, Edgar Manjarín, María Jesús Marqués, Julio Martínez-Cava, Jordi Mundó, Juanma Pericàs, Daniel Raventós, Sebastià Riutort and Matías Zarlenga read and commented on parts of the book, giving advice that has certainly contributed to improving it.

Daniel Raventós, Jurgen De Wispelaere and Simon Birnbaum are the people with whom I've spent most time writing about and/or discussing the matters that appear in this book. Their influence as co-authors of earlier texts is clearly visible. Being aware of this as I was writing has enabled me to revisit and enjoy again spaces and moments, many of them truly diverting, in which these jointly produced texts and discussions were – and are still being – produced.

Over the years, I've enjoyed the company of a large group of women and men with whom I've been able to analyse and discuss, at greater or lesser length, the ideas I present here. While I balk at considering this a 'privilege', neither do I want to take it for granted that that's just how things are, so I feel really fortunate in this. Besides the people I have mentioned so far, they include Julio Leónidas Aguirre, Nuria Alabao, Rodrigo Amírola, Marco Aparicio, Jordi Arcarons, Pilar Arcidiácono, Christian Arnsperger, Francisco Báez Urbina, Lucía Baratech, Borja Barragué, Xosé Manuel Beiras, Joan Benach, Sara Berbel, Ángeles Bermúdez, María Julia Bertomeu, Pablo Blanco, Hernán Borisonik, Rafael Borràs Ensenyat, Yannick Bosc, Àlex Boso, David Bravo, Bob Brecher, Keith Breen, Carlos de Castro, Mònica Clua-Losada, Toni Comín, Benjamin Coriat, Richard Dagger, Sarath Davala, Federico Delgado, Juan Delgado, Xavier Domènech, Santiago Eizaguirre, Ángel Elías, Andrea Fumagalli, Laura Garcés, Gato, Florence Gauthier,

Luca Gervasoni, Anca Gheaus, Rodrigo Gil, Rudy Gnutti, Sandra Gonzélez-Bailón, Iñigo González-Ricoy, Axel Gosseries, Alex Gourevitch, Adoración Guamán, Julio César Guanche, Jordi Guiu, Louise Haagh, Christopher Hamel, Yayo Herrero, Lisa Herzog, Michael Howard, François Hudon, Hyosang Ahn, Andrés Imperioso, Pere Jodar, Luis Juberías, Michael Krätke, Hans Laguna, Irkus Larrinaga, Lena Lavinas, Carmen Lizárraga, Oriol Llauradó, Rubén Lo Vuolo, Pablo López Álvarez, Germán Loewe, Rubén Martínez, Roberto Merrill, Min Geum, Jaume Montés, Leticia Morales, Rommy Morales, Sara Moreno Colom, Jorge Moruno, Alejandro Nadal, Pierre-Yves Néron, José Antonio Noguera, Claus Offe, Fabienne Orsi, Carole Pateman, Cristian Pérez Muñoz, Philip Pettit, Gerardo Pisarello, Mònica Plana, Xavier Pedrol, Lluís Pérez Lozano, Gala Pin, José Manuel Chico 'Pin', Jorge Pinto, Juan Ponte, Carme Porta, Hervé Pourtois, Marc Pradel, Enric Prat, Paco Ramos, Sergi Raventós, César Rendueles, José Luis Rey, Mauricio Rifo, Bernat Riutort, Thiago Rocha, Corina Rodríguez Enríquez, Adriana Sabaté, Tomeu Sales Gelabert, Celestino Sánchez, Txema Sánchez, Daniel Sánchez Saumell, Clara Serra, Beatriz Silva, Héctor Sin, Ramon Souto, Guy Standing, Carlos Abel Suárez, Maciej Szlinder, Aina Tarabini, Javier Tébar, Lluís Torrens, Ailynn Torres Santana, Laura Tuero, Camil Ungureanu, Iñaki Uribarri, Philippe Van Parijs, Yannick Vanderborght, Peter Wagner, Fábio Waltenberg, Julie Wark, Daniel Weinstock, Stuart White, Karl Widerquist, Erik Olin Wright, Jean Wyllys, Pablo Yanes, Almaz Zelleke, my friends and fellows from the Basque trade union ESK, those from the Fundación de los Comunes, those at the Chilean Fundación SOL and those who gave rise and furthered the Catalan socio-political group 'Inflexió'. Carles Navarrete and Juanjo Boya encouraged me to write this book and also helped with ideas and suggestions to make sure I wouldn't take too long to finish it. Julie Wark has not only been an excellent translator, but by making it her own, she has helped to breathe new life into this book. David Castle and the Pluto Press team have warmly welcomed the English edition of this book, which has helped to make the adventure much more meaningful.

The undergraduates of Economic Sociology, of Social Movements, and of Introduction to Sociology at the University of Barcelona, and the postgrads of Economic and Philosophical-Political Analysis of Contemporary Capitalism, jointly organised by the university and the political review *Sin-Permiso*, have been among the first with whom I've discussed many of the ideas developed here and they've frequently suggested surprisingly fertile ways of understanding them and formulating them with greater precision. I'm not sure how much they realise this.

Theoretical reflection and sociopolitical intervention go together and lead to points that make sense when they settle into spaces and organisations that permit and foster a sharing of political aspirations and concerns. This book wouldn't be what it is, or the author what he is, if he hadn't been able to participate in the political and cultural project that is the backbone of the political review *SinPermiso*, the Red Renta Básica, the Basic Income Earth Network and the Observatori dels Drets Econòmics, Socials i Culturals (Observatory of Economic, Social, and Cultural Rights) in Barcelona. Moreover, the Grupo de Investigación en Ética Economicosocial y Epistemología de las Ciencias Sociales (Research Group in Economic and Social Ethics, and Epistemology of the Social Sciences) at the University of Barcelona, and the Spanish research projects on 'Political Freedom, Property Rights, Commons and Public Policy Understood as Fiduciary Relationships' (PGC2018-094324-B-I00) and 'Political Philosophy, Economics, and Ethics of Fiduciary Relationships: Freedom, Property, Commons and Public Policy' (PID2021-123885NB-I00) have provided a supportive background for bringing this project to light.

The process of writing the book was shaken by the terrible shock of the sudden premature death of my friend and mentor Antoni Domènech. But he has left the security and warmth of knowing I'll find, day after day, an audacious, creative way of thinking, always questing and with strands and more strands that keep fertilising the many kinds of intellectual and political scenarios that Toni seems to have left us to go on discovering and recognising over time. Thinking now, without Toni, means to keep discovering him, every day, which is the same as saying that it is, as always, being with Toni.

Finally, *Atxe* and, above all, Iratxe has understood and inspired this book, before and after it was written, and this has also helped me to keep understanding it better. Intelligent in managing the compass of personal and political spaces and times, Iratxe has taught me that it's also about learning to stray beyond the compass, with or without giddiness, and to try and grab life by the horns, and make it more ours. This book is dedicated to Iratxe and the courageous determination with which she's able to get a fix on the world and get it moving.

To conclude, this book has been written for and with the immense majority, those of us who are living in regimes of conditional freedom. I hope it's true that we're living in times of a slow, sometimes exasperatingly slow and erratic, but also unstoppable democratic revolution. This should ensure that freedom – which we can't decipher or experience unless we've previously thought about and struggled for its material and symbolic conditions of possibility – should come to be something to which we all have fully unconditional access.

Introduction: Cap and Life

'Going cap in hand', they say, isn't right. Scrounging, the story goes, is an affront to the hardworking; an offence to society, to its moral infrastructure; disastrous for the scrounger himself, who tends to collapse into a mournful state of lethargy. Lethargy of action, lethargy of the social bond. All quite disgraceful. A calamity.

That's how it is. Going cap in hand isn't right. But hang on. What's this going cap in hand all about? Let's look back a bit and dive into the origins of the expression, to the world of the nineteenth- and perhaps the early twentieth-century factories. This was the era of day labour, of the wages the foreman paid the workers for a single day's toil. And this was, of course, a time of utmost vulnerability for the now totally proletarianised working class. It was the time of Karl Polanyi's 'great transformation' of capitalism, mediating between the world of access to (and enjoyment of) certain still available common goods, usually on the local scale, and the gestation of the first public welfare and support systems, still a long way off. At the cusp of this 'great transformation' riding on the back of the 'great dispossession' of material and immaterial means of existence – an openly 'bloody expropriation', in the words of Marx – there was only one thing: *day labour*. And a day without work could be a day without basic provisions – a day without dinner.

But was day labour really all there was? In fact, there was something else too: the *cap*. In those days of blue smocks for men and long black dresses for women, the cap was a means of (re)creating bonds of solidarity among the proletarian masses. If anyone fell ill, some workmate, neighbour or relative would announce it at the factory; when pay time came, the absent worker's cap would be placed in an agreed-upon spot so that the others, on their way out, would drop in some of their own wages. Something like a full day's pay would then reach the ailing worker's house; basic provisions, a meal, could be supplied. As E. P. Thompson pointed out, the working class was not reduced simply to mere passive spectators of their own ruin, of the process of dispossession that was implacably pushing them into underselling their labour power. The proletariat was also a class that knew 'how to make itself', one that knew how to (re)think 'customs shared in common', seeking and finding mechanisms, not only to soothe the open wound but also – who knows – to start rewriting the script of its own history. With what mechanisms? The cap, for starters.

But, in this life, prepositions matter. They also matter when constructing 'metaphors for everyday life', as George Lakoff and Mark Johnson (1986) tell us: metaphors always loaded with political intention. In this heartless, factory-driven nineteenth century no one talked about going 'cap *in* hand'. The working class used the cap to construct forms of sociability and mutual aid that would allow them to pool their resources – the daily *wage*, the daily *wages* – so that everyone could, simply, live. This, then, is living 'cap *to* hand': finding ways to combat poverty and recover, if not a great deal of freedom, then at least some relief. Functioning *with* caps, operating *through* them, was still a long way from socialising the means of production and thus doing away with the dispossessing dynamics of capitalism. At most, what was socialised was wages. But it was a way of creating a popular culture that sought to give new, immaterial meaning to – and here I draw on E. P. Thompson's term – the 'material abode' of the capitalist enterprise, to make of it less harsh of a space. If possible, one with cracks which might allow for a gradual rehearsal of non-capitalist life.

Living with the cap *to* hand – and never the begging cap *in* hand – the proletariat escaped, at least partially, a destiny that was frequently presented as inescapable, and turned into a class that 'was making itself', becoming aware of its own nature, a class that, albeit cautiously, organised forms of struggle that would make it possible to walk back along the path towards a world held in common. So, the cap had to be demonised. Just as women, who had occupied and dwelled in those common lands, and – as Silvia Federici describes – nourished them with their own practices and wisdom, were accused of witchcraft in the (late) medieval and pre-industrial world, the struggle for hegemony of language in the battleground of the symbolic – which is crucial for settling the conflict between materially clashing classes – pushed capitalism's apologists, who were also protecting their own 'customs in common', to malign the cap. 'They go cap *in* hand', it was said. And the expression was born. A matter of prepositions.

Today we can't distance ourselves from this story. What public-common mechanisms can we turn to in the current circumstances, not only to soothe the open wound but also to imagine and live the kind of lives we choose for ourselves? With a special focus on the sphere of work – of *different kinds of work* – it would be a good idea to ask ourselves how we can interpret and give new meaning to the 'material abode' we find ourselves in, so old and yet so new. What caps do we have or might we have today? With what modern devices can we equip ourselves to make the domain of work – which reaches into all the times and spaces of our lives – compatible with human freedom and dignity?

Today, too, those of us who must work in order to live are a class made up of people who need to revolt against any metaphysical assumption of inevitability of human trajectories and orders: history is still unwritten. Those of us who must work in order to live are, in other words, a class that, today too, must 'make itself' and think about itself in terms of agency. And thinking about ourselves in terms of agency is the same as interpreting ourselves, not only as victims of a history hegemonised by powerful 'de-creators of the Earth' – as the Spanish philosopher Manuel Sacristán put it – but also as bearers of democratising moral intuitions and strivers in a permanent attempt to organise struggles that are as contingent as you want but aimed at dignifying our labours and our days.

Hence the basic income proposal, a cash allowance that is sufficient to cover the basic needs of existence, which the public authorities grant on an individual basis (so beneficiaries are people and not households), universally (granted to the entire population) and unconditionally (granted independently of any other sources of income or any other personal circumstances). But basic income is not some ubiquitously valid, universally effective, trans-historical cure-all. On the contrary, it must be examined as one (central) part of a set of mechanisms *with* which we can operate at present to endow ourselves with the power of negotiation and of creating our own lives. Like the nineteenth-century caps, basic income works as a 'rescue' for people in situations of privation and social vulnerability, which are often acute. But, like the nineteenth-century caps, this 'rescue' is also the embryo of multiple and multiform sociopolitical processes through which the (re)proletarianised working classes can once again try to 'make themselves' and, on that basis or thanks to it, construct social orders capable of laying the foundations for their own dissolution as proletarian or subaltern classes. Can a basic income help us deproletarianise and become free workers? In other words, could today's *caps* manage to free us not from *work* but from contemporary *day labour*, that is, from all freedom-limiting forms of wage-earning work?

This isn't just a book about basic income, though it revolves around basic income to explore paths, practices and institutional mechanisms that working populations might use, and are already using, in order to reappropriate their own lives. In this regard, basic income mustn't be revered and fetishised. But it can act as a kind of beacon. Indeed, the unconditionality in the conception of basic income suggests that our lives aren't for sale, and that there are big red lines that we can ensure aren't crossed. Basic income can become a promising starting point from which to imagine a whole cartography of sociopolitical landscapes embodied in material settings and symbolic devices, which we need for thinking about ourselves and acting as free subjects and collectivities. What we have, then, is a task that, at a very basic level, includes basic income but also goes beyond it.

But let's take it step by step. The route that starts from here crosses four fields of reflection, with many overlaps, which we should outline. Each corresponds to one of the four parts into which this book is divided. Here is a first approximation.

(DIS)ORDER

Is it possible to construct social *orders* in which 'self-made classes' can self-dissolve? Could the idea of *order* be appealing for emancipatory political projects? One of the most usual – and fatal – errors of this and last century's emancipatory traditions has been rejecting those terms and values that were part of the axiological heritage of the popular movements of the modern and early contemporary eras. These ideas and concepts were not only disputed but were also on occasion usurped by liberalism and even by the openly conservative world. We only need to think of values and projects such as freedom, democracy, the individual, self-interest, enterprise, property, the free market and, finally, order. All of them have been and are, far too often, anathematised and eventually repudiated. Why is this? The answer is tragically simple. Because they were warped and withered to a *reductio ad absurdum*, voided of any sense, by the intellectual and political traditions of utilitarianism, liberalism and neo-establishmentarianism (where 'establishment', in this book, refers to that of the post-feudal, Catholic-thinking, hierarchical elite of the late nineteenth and early twentieth centuries), all of them ill-disposed to accept any idea of social transformation along democratic lines.

In this reality, one of the most common – and politically fatal – errors of emancipatory traditions has been their diehard, strictly defensive encapsulation within a supposed bastion of their inherent values, and the corresponding surrender of the old, degraded values to the degraders or, in other words, utilitarianism, liberalism and neo-establishmentarianism, as well as Stalinism of whatever stripe. The fact is, *their inherent values* – equality, the commons, the state, self-management – are indeed their own. But it's no less true that the cast-off concepts and projects belonged to those emancipatory traditions, and still do, which means they can only be understood and practised with a minimum of sense when mass movements of democratic vocation embrace them as their own and fill them with content. Hence, instead of a merely hard-line strategy, we need to devise a Trojan horse path of infiltration which, without neglecting a defence of our own values, makes it possible to venture into the heart of darkness of lost values – the values that were handed down to us – to recover them, restore them and get them circulating in the bosom of newly emancipatory sociopolitical projects. And this isn't too far from the idea of order. As the geographer Élisée Reclus – who was associated with the mid-nineteenth-century group led by Anselme Bellegarrigue around what is considered to be the first anarchist newspaper, *L'Anarchie, Journal de l'Ordre* – remarked, disorder resides in each and every nook and cranny of capitalism, while anarchy is the 'highest expression of order'.

Order, yes. But what order? Needless to say, there are plenty of notions of order and some of them totally exclude any project of reclaiming our lives. So, what order then? Or to be more precise, what order requires the presence of which caps? And what role might a measure such as basic income, among all the possible caps, play at the core of such conceptions of the social order? Here are three interpretive frameworks from which we can draw a few conclusions.

First of all, there is no need for any caps when appeals are made to the elitist logic of exemplariness and docility. The model boss – *patron, pater* – and omniscient technocrat expert are *paternal* figures who can offer a guide, an order (vertical, of course) to orient our actions and situate us in the niche that is accorded to us in the social body. As Ortega y Gasset said, societies are 'invertebrate' when the elite neglects its functions and simply doesn't do its job. Then again, an adequate process of selection of 'the best' – the *aristoi* in Greek – will permit an *aristocratic* consolidation of the true mainstays around which we can all accommodate ourselves, tamely and placidly complying with the division of goods, tasks and social positions that are being dispensed. So, caps aren't needed because there will always be people who take charge of supervising the fates of those below them. And these people will supervise things on condition that the underdogs explicitly and clearly renounce any pretension of leaving their lowly status or of making social life horizontal. There is no need for caps, then, because the great protective mantle of those who exercise power in the heart of a rigorously verticalised, tenaciously classist society is hovering over us.

On other occasions, the process becomes cruder because those at the bottom resist such tutelage. The fighting starts or, rather, becomes visible, emerging from the darkness of an apparent previous social calm which had tried to hide it but hadn't dissolved it. In these cases, the handful of those who are, or aspire to be, at the top – the 'economic monarchs' in Roosevelt's words (and all sorts of other mandarins) – set out (as Adam Smith detailed so well, suggesting something more like the visible fist than the 'invisible hand') to righten and strengthen the vertical structure, using violent means if necessary. 'There's class warfare, all right, but it's my class, the rich class, that's making war, and we're winning', said the famous American investor Warren Buffet while the crisis unleashed in 2008 was still gestating.[1] In these cases, the elite gets sincere. Not so long afterwards, the Spanish minister of justice warned: 'Governing means, at times, distributing pain.'[2] The message, then, is crystal clear, and one should be grateful for that at least: there is no need for caps, no need for basic income, because capitalism's carrot-and-stick system is perfectly capable of *ordering* subjects, resources and activities along class lines and, most notably, reproducing that order over time – from top to bottom, with no room for dissent. The bulk of elitist political thought, whether indulgent or severe, though always paternalistic and top down, has gone through very different periods and historical junctures, fascism among them; and has come down to us today via the figure of the 'expert' who knows what's best for everyone in social organisms that need no caps. If everything stays calm, no cracks will appear.

Second, there is no need, either, for any kind of caps, including basic income, when the presence of conflict is simply denied, when the presence, here and now, of a vertical and verticalising resolution of the conflict inherent to the world we live in is questioned, or when the idea that the world has *some kind of intentional order* is contested or even rejected. At the beginning of the eighteenth century, the satirical Anglo-Dutch writer Bernard Mandeville (1997 [1724]) presented, with cunning humour that few seem to have picked up, the fanciful story of a prosperous hive that owed its well-being to the fact that its bees lived in a *(dis)orderly* fashion, devoted to their 'private vices' and utterly indifferent to what the other bees were doing and the consequences their own actions might have on their environment. Then, decades later, the liberal tradition took the jest seriously. It could be said that, in some ways, most of classical doctrinaire liberalism, which was codified at the beginning of the nineteenth century, 'solves' the question of immanent conflict in a world of scarce resources and clashing interests simply by denying the existence of this conflict, which is to say denying the presence of bonds of dependence and power relations when any kind of social relation is shaped, and when any kind of contract is signed. These relations, these contracts, are the result, they say, of strictly free, voluntary decisions.[3]

To quote Abba Lerner's portrayal of neoclassical economics, the liberal world becomes the world of 'solved political problems' by denying the presence of any such problems. If there is no power, if there is no conflict, then there is no need to think politically about the social order because there is no *society* whose structuring needs to be seen as a problem to be dealt with politically (or as Thatcherite neoliberalism would have it, *there is no such thing as society*). The liberal world, then, takes Mandeville's joke seriously. Social life doesn't harbour power relations whereby 'someone' somehow *orders* things vertically, horizontally or however because it's the result of the erratic interaction of bee-individuals laden with sets of desires and inclinations springing from their own preferences, capriciously navigating a social magma with no known defining structure or direction. And this, after all, is nothing but a form of denialism – a 'sociological denialism', if you prefer – because we know, without a doubt, that the capitalist social structuring, like that of any other human society, rests on a vast, diverse set of absolutely political *relationalities* aimed at solving the problem of access to finite resources and opportunities in social settings characterised by the presence of conflicting interests.

Although the liberal tradition takes Mandeville's joke seriously, it doesn't necessarily conclude that the world is pure chaos. The liberal story ends with a mind-boggling conceptual pirouette which consists in stating (let's say metaphysically) that it is precisely the absence of a defined social structure that ends up giving rise to a *certain order*. After all, without obstacles getting in the way, needs, whatever they might be, are met with the utmost efficiency. There exist, so the story goes, autogenous social orders that are thus because individuals behave like bees in Mandeville's hive. Each one blindly does what leads to order, which is an emergent property of a strictly non-intentional nature. If there are no intentions, then there is no need to turn intentions into institutions. In particular, there is no need for caps, including basic income, because in such an environment, any cap would create hindrances and obstacles getting in the way of the world's self-generating process.

So much for the myth. The really existing history of the (neo)liberal world has taken different directions. This isn't a matter of conceptual pirouettes. Property rights have worked with a view to stabilising an order that has lurched too much and too often. And given all this teetering and staggering, the really existing (neo)liberalism, which is patently jumpy and less trusting in the spontaneous resorts announced in the myth, hasn't hesitated to resort to paternalistic-verticalist thinking and praxis in order to intentionally contain the social advance of all the democratising or horizontalising projects that have been organised. The liberal-organicist implant thus puts down its roots.

Third, it's at this point that we need to talk about the republican social ontology – or the republican description of how social life works – and the idea of order that has always been part of democratic republicanism: a clarification of the importance of expressing this third vision of society and social justice in 'democratic republican' terms will immediately be offered. There is a need for caps because social life is defined by unequal access to external resources, and this generates social positions of privilege and subordination and, through them, undisguised conflict. There is a need for caps because the world is split into social groups with clashing interests. As John Millar (1990 [1771]), an outstanding follower of Adam Smith and prominent member of the Scottish Historical School, noted, we humans situate ourselves in social ranks whose differences have, not metaphysical, but historical and perfectly detectable origins that are politically open to all sorts of remedying.

Take for example an employment contract. Is the *(con)tract* a *tract* (in the etymological sense of *tractatus*, which is related with treatment) arising from *cooperation* between equals who strive *conjointly* to institute something new or, on the contrary, does it mean a manifest *imposition* by certain favoured actors? Sociologically informed and informative republican social ontology (which is a long way from the ingenuousness, in the best of cases, and frequently open negationism of the (neo)liberal world) has made it clear on more than a few occasions since Aristotle's times that those who come to sign (waged) employment contracts tend to do so as dispossessed people, which is why they have no choice but to comply with the conditions imposed upon them. Hence, by delegating their will to those who contract them, they become true 'part-time slaves', as Aristotle put it, or people who are subjected to the many forms of *wage slavery*, to use the concept that Marx employed 23 centuries later. Those who enter into the domain of employment because of a lack of alternatives are, then, semi-slaves who are swallowed up in a brutal labyrinth that offers very few exits.

It's interesting to note at this point that if the world of wage labour is conceived like this, and if one also embraces a democratising thrust for all of social life and assumes that nobody should be left by the wayside, then it should be concluded that it is necessary to devise – intentionally, of course – institutions geared to a horizontalising of social ties, to shaping and putting into practice a less *pater-filius* and more fraternal social *order*. In his inquiry into the vestiges of the idea of fraternity, Antoni Domènech showed how this notion was historically set in motion in order to demand horizontal arrangements of resources and opportunities, allowing everyone to be brought into politically mature civil existence. The idea is very simple: non-excluding forms of property and control of resources, and the popular culture that is annexed to them (i.e., what E. P. Thompson referred to as the 'moral economy of the crowd'), must allow all of us to hold our heads high, to stand tall without fear of walking on a tightrope, and enable us to *co-decide* freely the kind of life we want to live, starting with the domain of work. There is a need, then, for institutions that can horizontalise social relations. Disdaining them, neglecting them and, in the end, abandoning them – for this is the (neo)liberal project – tips us into pure brutality. Consciously rejecting them to vertically delegate decision-making power to others – and this is the elitist classist project which is in no way incompatible with the (neo)liberal plan – infantilises us in both civil and political domains.

The debate about basic income is here to stay. Basic income doesn't pressure us to go cap *in* hand, which, according to the old apologists for capitalism, is what the tattered caps of the nineteenth century permitted. Basic income *is* also a cap, one of all those caps which, brought together, can equip us materially and symbolically to enter the worlds of work, which are the worlds of our lives, so we can live in them with all the possibilities opened up by horizontal orders. Uncertain and hard to govern as they may be –but indisputably ready for spontaneity and freely chosen courses of action too – horizontal orders, in whatever form they take, tend to confer higher levels of freedom.

FREEDOM

Not long ago I met up with a friend – one of those friends you don't see very often but whom it's nice to seek out from time to time when you have a quiet moment, to catch up on things and chat about everything and nothing. 'What I can say about the recession years is that I've been lucky enough to never lose my job,' he said at one point in the conversation. 'Lucky.' Yes, it's lucky. The way things are, it would be enormously frivolous to urge people to 'leave their jobs' unless this 'leaving' took place in a context of well-planned and shared projects. It seems logical, then, that we're happy because the door isn't closed to the main channel through which income flows today: employment. And I was happy that my friend hadn't been sacked.

But the world of employment is a huge and sometimes opaque black box that we can't judge if we don't open it and observe the mechanisms operating inside it. There were lots of things my friend didn't say. Can he choose what to do and why? Can he decide how and at what pace? Can he determine with whom and where? And what other kinds of jobs, remunerated or not, does carrying out *his* job allow him to do? And still more, what kinds of interferences in his life, and with what degree of arbitrariness, did he have to put up with in all these years of keeping his job? What kinds of self-censorship has he resorted to in order to adapt to what's expected of him or what he thinks is expected of him? There are too many questions without answers, because we tend not to ask ourselves these things. And the fact is that political and social theory establishes a clear distinction between two related concepts with an abyss between them: *well-being* and *freedom*. One enjoys well-being when one has the resources that make it possible to satisfy a range of needs, but one is free when one defines and controls the paths through which such resources are obtained. Can we respond to these questions in a way that shows that we're at the helm of our (working) lives? I don't know, because my friend didn't tell me, whether he was *lucky* enough to enjoy years of working freely or whether he had to resign himself, which is no small thing, to certain doses of well-being mediated by his job.

This book is committed to an idea of freedom in which the socioeconomic independence of individuals and groups plays an essential role. Firmly rooted in the republican tradition, this notion of freedom tells us that my friend should be able to look the person who contracts him in the eye without having to bow and scrape because of being socioeconomically dependent on this employer – or *some* employer – in order to survive. To put it a little differently and in Marxist terms, can my friend live and feel that he is living without asking 'permission' from the person who contracts him? Obviously, this is not about my friend enjoying a kind of personal independence that leads him into isolation and an atomised existence but, rather, about his being able to avoid, at any moment or in any corner of his life, living at someone else's mercy and to keep weaving a truly desired interdependence that doesn't destroy his sense of autonomy or self-determination, his capacity to control the decisions that shape his own life and permit some genuine forms of human flourishing (Roberts, 2017).

But hang on a second. Why 'republicanism'? Why resort to this intellectual and political tradition? And what exactly is to be understood by 'republicanism'? And how is such republicanism linked to an emancipatory understanding and transformation of the realms of production and work? To start with, it should immediately be stressed that republicanism has nothing to do with the kind of (neo)liberal conservatism that is upheld by the US Republican Party or by many Latin American right-wing parties and political movements calling themselves 'republican'. The political grammar these parties and movements exhibit is closer to the liberal 'isonomic' idea of freedom as simply 'equality before the law' – which, as I explore later, disregards the question of the socioeconomic conditions of freedom – than to the building blocks of the republican tradition. Also, 'republicanism' should not be equated with any form of romantic nostalgia for the greatly cherished Spanish Second Republic of 1931-9 – including all Brigade-based anti-fascist international solidarity vis-à-vis this regime and the republican cause during the Spanish Civil War (1936-9) – or for other events and sociopolitical scenarios in other territories at any other point in time. Without denying the obvious connection of political episodes such as the Spanish Second Republic with the longstanding republican tradition of thought and action, what should be stressed here is that democratic republicanism is the ethical and political mould that shapes most contemporary emancipatory traditions – starting with socialisms, in plural. As explained by Antoni Domènech (2004) and other members of a mainly Barcelona-based school of republican scholarship, and as recently pointed out by those who nourish the perspective of the 'radical republicanism',[4] the main intuitions, social practices and institutions that can be found within the plebeian republican tradition shaped a political humus that cultivated many of the seeds of modern and contemporary rebel social and political movements, which is the reason why one can talk about a 'social(ist) republicanism' or even sustain that 'socialisms' are, to a large degree, the result of an updated democratic republicanism.[5] Let's see why.

According to the reconstruction that I make of all this, the general idea is quite straightforward. The republican tradition states that the exercise of individual and collective freedom – and citizenship – requires the (unconditional) enjoyment of sets of (im)material resources guaranteeing one's social existence. Social life is made up of conflict because it harbours diverging – sometimes clashing – interests within social settings that are characterised by the scarcity of resources, and any dissimilar access to these resources places resourceless individuals and groups in positions where they lack bargaining power and therefore experience social vulnerability with respect to other social actors, which prevents them from making genuine choices and pursuing their own life plans.

This is why (neo)republican theorists have always called and keep calling for the political introduction of social and institutional scenarios guaranteeing relevant degrees of socioeconomic independence, making sure not only that social actors are not actually interfered with in any arbitrary manner, but also that they have been freed from the mere possibility of being arbitrarily interfered with by others. But a big question mark still needs to be solved. Is everybody living in a given society invited to enjoy such freedom as the absence of the mere possibility of being arbitrarily interfered with? When the answer to this question is an unequivocal 'yes', then we are faced with forms of 'democratic' or 'plebeian republicanism'. But if the answer to this question is 'no' – because it is assumed, for instance, that it is not morally problematic that poor people, women, slaves and foreigners or immigrants lead unfree lives – then we are faced with forms of 'oligarchic republicanism'.

But what do socialisms have to do with all this? The emergence of socialisms cannot be understood if we have not previously mapped an interesting crossroads that marks European social and political life at the end of the eighteenth century and during the first third of the nineteenth century. During the French Revolution, equating freedom and citizenship with access to resources was commonplace. This is why the main aim of the left wing of the French Revolution – think of Robespierre or Thomas Paine – was to universalise freedom by universalising access to landed property through an agrarian reform guaranteeing either individual access to small plots of land or the collective sharing of communal spaces set at a municipal level. This was the democratic or plebeian form republicanism took at that time. On the contrary, late eighteenth-century French anti-democratic republicanism stated that it was not a moral or political problem if a large part of the population – those who had been born without any property and/or could not pay taxes above a certain threshold – were to be considered 'passive citizens', that is, individuals and groups that could be excluded from the exercise of freedom and full citizenship.

And what was the historical result of the dispute between democratic and oligarchic republicanism in revolutionary France? On closer inspection, the consolidation of capitalism and its attendant liberal culture is explained not so much by the victory of some kind of republicanism – democratic or oligarchic – but by the substitution of both types of republicanism by a novel political tradition that adopted a radically different notion of freedom: liberalism, which was codified at the beginning of the nineteenth century through the extension of Napoleonic Civic Codes. In effect, the liberal idea of freedom as 'mere' equality before the law or 'isonomy' completely disregarded the question of the material and symbolic conditions of all those lives that had to be led in the world that was ruled by such a law. Can individuals and groups build an interdependence that, thanks to social positions guaranteeing the absence of despotism and domination, respects the autonomy of all parties? This is something for which historical liberalism – and contemporary neoliberalism – shows utter disinterest. In fact, liberalism – and contemporary neoliberalism – openly denies the moral and sociopolitical relevance of this question, because its social ontology, that is, its description of how social life works, describes a world without any conflict among private actors where these private actors limit themselves to voluntary sign – or to voluntarily refraining from signing – contracts of all sorts. Socioeconomic backgrounds don't matter. In fact, it could also be said that they do not exist.

Hence the rise of socialisms. In a nutshell, socialist actors and thinkers – and the name of Karl Marx is especially relevant here – say no, that enough is enough, that all this amounts to a big fraud that must be stopped. Indeed, Marx makes it explicit that he sees himself as the heir to the left wing of the French Revolution (Domènech, 2004), that is, the democratic republican wing that has been defeated not by oligarchic republicanism but by the great liberal legal fiction or *fictio iuris*, according to which we are free just because, on paper, no one forces us to do anything. For this reason, Karl Marx, like so many other socialists, proposes to restore the old republican link between freedom and access to resources and sets out to think and fight for fully inclusive, democratic ways of interpreting and universalising it in and for the industrial world of the nineteenth century. Oligarchic republicanism may have been barbaric because it excluded large social majorities from the exercise of freedom, but at least it was honest and told the truth: whoever lacks resources cannot be free, cannot be a citizen. On the contrary, socialisms stress, liberalism obliterates the structural mechanisms that block the extension of effective freedom among the great social majorities and devalues the notion of freedom by affirming that we are free just because, on paper, nobody forces us to do anything. No. Contemporary political thought (socialists say) must once again tell the truth – those who do not own or control resources are not free – and democratic political action must be oriented towards achieving tools so that such resources are available to all. Here is the great socialist contribution to the rescue of plebeian republicanism.

Hence the centrality of property within the socialist tradition. Just as the left wing of the French Revolution – think again of Paine and Robespierre – understood that the guarantee of republican freedom lay in popular access to ownership or control of land, Marx and the bulk of socialisms suggest that the economic, social and demographic circumstances of the nineteenth century require a link between republican freedom, on the one hand, and ownership or collective control of the 'means of production' on the other hand; that is, of the many paths through which we produce material and immaterial goods and services and establish social relations and spaces for human coexistence. Hence the emphasis placed on cooperatives and/or on forms of public ownership of productive resources subject to popular control and scrutiny (Roberts, 2017). According to Marx – and Adam Smith, by the way – capitalist despotism rests on vast processes of dispossession of the great social majorities that turn markets, starting with labour markets, into structurally inevitable realities where the losers live at the mercy of the proprietor, which undermines the possibilities for the working classes to deploy their creative capacities and self-fulfil, and to lead elementally free lives. This is the reason why Marx himself assures us that capitalist despotism must be replaced by the 'republican and beneficent system of the association of free and equal producers'.[6]

All of this should allow us to get closer to societies where we can receive resources 'according to the needs' of our freely chosen life projects and, thanks to this, contribute 'according to (something close to) our capacities' – evidently, I am reworking the famous characterisation of possible communist societies that Marx offers in his *Critique of the Gotha Program* of 1875. Needless to say, measures like basic income that allow unconditional access to resources, given the bargaining power they would confer on all parties involved, can be part of contemporary strategies to reinterpret and put into circulation this type of relationalities (Van Parijs, 2013).

Let us close this excursus on the relationship between republicanism and socialism(s) by returning to the starting point: republican or effective freedom is not possible if social actors do not enjoy relevant levels of socioeconomic independence, if they cannot live without having to ask permission on a daily basis from those who managed to get hold of exclusive forms of property, if they cannot look the others in the eye. In effect, looking people in the eye with a steady pulse means being able to negotiate, and to negotiate if we're establishing a social relationship – signing a contract, say – or if we're not. And to negotiate, if we do go ahead and sign, the terms of the relationship or the terms of the contract. All things considered, this has clear similarities with the matter of divorce. The right to divorce doesn't mean you're obliged to get divorced, but it does allow for divorce if the relationship deteriorates and, most importantly, it offers both parties the chance of getting their voices heard and credibly signals that there is a practicable way out that they can take, which increases both sides' bargaining power. Could my friend make, unmake and remake, or enter, leave and recreate relations – of work, in this case – in keeping with his desires and needs, together with other equals chosen by him? Or did he become some stranger in a strange land, a machine-like mercenary, killing for no reason?

But the task of making, unmaking and remaking, individually and collectively, is something that requires resources: resources without conditions, or with the most minimal conditions only. This is why the greater part of the republican tradition took on a marked *propertarianist* character. In effect, as I have just shown, republicanism establishes a strong link between freedom and the guaranteed presence of (im)material resources which, in antiquity and through to the eighteenth century, were almost exclusively associated with landed property and that, nowadays, must take revamped forms. In any case, without resources, without a basic income, for example, decisions can be freely made – even slaves made free decisions when it suited their owners to let them do so – but there would certainly be no situations of social invulnerability guaranteeing that all of us could act, throughout our lives, as true, free, decision-making subjects or, in other words, people who can and do tend to make decisions freely. Republican freedom, then, requires the control of resources by those who deserve to lead a free existence. And in the contemporary world, in which the condition of citizen has become universalised, on paper at least (since the legal systems of states tend to establish that all of us are called to lead a free existence), mechanisms are needed to 'universalise property', to universalise the unconditional enjoyment of resources. Can basic income play this role today and help us to devise and introduce positions of social invulnerability for everybody?

Dubious contrasts are often raised between what Isaiah Berlin called 'positive freedom' (freedom *to*) and 'negative freedom' (freedom *from* or *in the face of*), and these contrasts somehow re-embrace the opposition that Benjamin Constant established between a romanticised, hyper-exigent and, in the end, impracticable 'freedom of the ancients' and a comfortable, convenient 'freedom of the moderns' that relegates individuals to the private sphere while pressing them to delegate sovereignty and agency to their representatives in the public sphere. A proper understanding of republican social ontology, that is, of the republican picture of social life (the world is replete with power relations) and of the political precepts managed by republicanism (it is necessary to have public powers that unmake these power relations and institute autonomous and democratic forms of power) can help us to see the meaninglessness of Berlin's and Constant's contrasts which, at bottom, are products of an unabashedly anti-democratic mindset. Freedom is not *either* negative (freedom *from*, freedom *in the face of*) or positive (freedom *to*). Freedom is always oriented to action, the possibility of materially or immaterially making or creating a world. In this sense, freedom is always freedom *to*. What happens is that the sociological consciousness of the republican tradition warns us that this freedom *to* is frequently constrained by social actors who are able to interfere arbitrarily in our lives to the point of coercively imposing on us courses of action that have nothing to do with us: did anyone, perhaps, ask my friend what job he wanted to do and how? When this is the case, freedom *to* needs the presence of freedom *from* or *in the face of* the mere possibility of arbitrary interference. Hence, these 'freedoms' are two sides of the same coin. You can't start walking anywhere when the only path is a quagmire that third parties have turned into private hunting grounds.

This is why not only universal, unconditional and guaranteed resources are needed (e.g. a basic income), but also equally conceived in-kind benefits. In some sense, what is being defended here are the principles of universality and unconditionality in public – state or self-managed – arrangements concerning *any kind of resource* that is deemed necessary for a free life. The right to divorce mustn't come into play when one's life is *already* shattered. The right to a reset can't become effective when we're *already* bogged down in a mire of forms of dependence, including precariousness and poverty traps. Republicanism advocates an *ex ante* disposal of resources precisely because it aspires to safeguard (negatively, if you will) the chances of the whole population's taking paths (hence positively) that are truly practicable. And there can be no possible *ex ante* disposal of resources if we don't embrace the principle of unconditionality that shapes, for example, the basic income proposal.

Freedom can't be thought of from the standpoint of *(re)distributive* justice. Freedom is an end in itself that can't be tied to social ups and downs that might invite *ex post* forms of assistance. Distributing resources *ex ante*, which is to say *predistributively*, constitutes the core strategy of democratic republican constitutionalism, that is, the undivided sets and waves of civic, social and economic rights that modern and contemporary emancipatory social and political movements managed to embed into fundamental laws and constitutions, from the revolutionary Mexican Constitution drafted in the State of Querétaro in 1917 to that of the Weimar Republic and the bulk of post-1945 Western European constitutions – I do not enter now into whether these constitutions were and are fully applied or not. Freedom isn't something you have to lose so you can later beg for resources to survive the shipwreck and, in the best of cases, partially recover. Freedom cannot be at stake. Freedom, simply, can't be wrecked.

Hence, basic income would seem to be one more piece in a wide-ranging political project of (re)constructing society, civil(ised) society, because, however much Thatcherite neoliberal denialism insists on the contrary, there is certainly a thing we can call *society*. And this something can be a suffocating liberticidal hell in which the only option is trying to divorce. But it could also be a kinder place where we can subsist, and even live decently. In any case, it will always be an intentionally *ordered* space (autogenic orders don't exist) the structure of which we must debate and recreate. Freedom for everyone, or relevant degrees of it, depends on this debating and recreating. This, then, gives rise to the need for instruments such as basic income which, thanks to their *ex ante* unconditional nature, let us make our voices heard and equip us to weave, horizontally of course, a world in common.

AGENCY

In the mid-1990s there was a famous Spanish television ad where a group of people tried to persuade a man who looked like a spoilt brat, the capricious owner of a board game called Scattergories, not to leave with his game when things didn't go his way. In this game they had to find words starting with a certain letter, then fit them with minimal definitions given on cards. The ad was so successful that two phrases which appeared in it – *aceptamos barco* (we accept boat) and *aceptamos pulpo* (we accept octopus) – have become common usage in Spanish today. The owner of the game forced his friends who wouldn't or couldn't stop playing to 'accept boat as an aquatic animal' and 'accept octopus as a pet' because, if they didn't, he was going to flounce off with his game. 'It's *my* game and it's going with me', he threatened. It was his game and he made or changed the rules as he pleased. So now, when people say *acepto barco* or *acepto pulpo* they mean that they don't like the methods or criteria being used to settle some question, but they accept these methods, criteria and results because they have no alternative.

To return to the question of democratising work, *all kinds of work*, we understand here that *democracy in the realm of work* means the capacity of individual and collective agency with regard to determining what jobs are to be done, why they're being done and how to do them. The fact is that exercising this capacity has interesting similarities with deciding about the games we might want to play and the rules that might order them. Are there people who can capriciously decide what game will be set out on the table and who has the ability, like the game owner in the ad, to capriciously change the rules and exclude anyone who disagrees with their arbitrary regulation? So, with regard to reflecting on (and practising) democracy in the spheres of work, there are two big decisions we have to make. First, what game are we playing? And, second, what rules do we establish for playing the game we've chosen? Of course, underlying these two questions there is also a third one concerning the democratic (or not) nature of the environment we live in: who makes these decisions? Just a few, the *oligoi*, which would take us into an openly *oligarchic* game? Or everyone within, of course, the limits established by the ever present information and coordination costs?

Basic income is a measure that can take both questions – or, better said, the exercise of answering them – within the reach of us all. And it aspires to do this, as we have seen, without anathematising the institutions and practices traditionally associated, too hastily perhaps, with the capitalist universe: markets, private property, individual initiative and entrepreneurship, etc. There are two reasons for this, one strategic and the other substantive. *Strategic*: 'gifting' these concepts, practices and institutions to politically alien traditions of thought, without having pondered them at length and from an emancipatory standpoint, only strengthens the field of action of the adversary camp and erodes the leeway that is actually ours. Moreover, we have seen that a Trojan horse strategy of (re)conquering previously and thoughtlessly discarded projects and courses of action can be extremely fertile in normative political terms. *Substantive*, and this is probably more important: concepts, practices and institutions such as markets, private property, individual initiative and entrepreneurship, duly pondered and defined, were situated and can (or perhaps *must*) be situated again at the heart of political projects for democratising all social life today, including work. Isn't it true that the famous 'moral economy of the crowd' with which, according to E. P. Thompson, the working classes of modern Europe resisted the advance of capitalism, sought to regulate a world in which free *proprietor* artisans could be *entrepreneurs* of their own projects in non-excluding *commercial* domains?

Hence, the proposal of contemplating a basic income and the possible processes of democratisation of work we find here isn't tied to any particular institution or social practice. Making such a commitment would be an exercise in blind idealism and also irresponsible in overlooking the always unpredictable consequences of human action and the changeable nature of the social settings in which we move. The validity of social practices and institutions is an entirely contingent matter. What will be found in these pages is an unconditional and not at all contingent call for practising the twofold democratising exercise I referred to above: we need to be able to decide what game we're playing, and we also need to be able to decide how to play the game we've chosen. The democratisation of work – or in other words with Kantian echoes, the processes of self-determination of our lives – can't be far from this double endeavour. Let's look at this in more detail.

A moment ago, I presented the power of negotiation as a condition of effective freedom. Now we must wonder: power to negotiate exactly what? In the sphere of wage labour we need to ask if the labour relations satisfy us or if we should threaten with or act upon our right to divorce. Basic income doesn't force anyone to leave wage-earning work but, by unconditionally guaranteeing our existence, it allows us to think about whether we want to keep playing this game and with these rules or whether, on the contrary, we choose to bring about a change in the rules – better salary, better working conditions – and maybe even a change of game. Perhaps we are tired of accepting an 'octopus as a pet'.

The domain of self-management and cooperativism holds out an alternative to wage labour. For some time now, writers such as Erik Olin Wright have been stressing that one of the possible ways left open by the decommodification of labour power, if we opted for that, would be the construction of cooperative work centres in which, perhaps, the processes of co-determination of working relations and conditions, or the rules of the game, would be encouraged. But no one is unaware that setting out on new productive paths can be an arduous task when what we have before us is a narrow defile full of risks and very often connected with the presence of social actors who are ill-disposed to let us escape from the usual games, *their* usual games, or allow us to play in equal conditions. 'It's *my* game and it's going with me', said the bratty man in the ad. Is it not true that powerful markets of goods and services often impose omnipresent entry barriers that aim to turn them into private and depriving spaces? The possibility of setting out (on something), cooperatively or not, is a long way from being a right today. Setting out today is a privilege reserved for a few social actors with real resources for playing this game. Can basic income, by guaranteeing our existence, do away with entry barriers? Can basic income therefore enable access to the game of setting out on one's own project and developing it without what Adam Smith called the 'frenzy of the desperate'? As he noted, this frenzy took the form of an anxiety that hobbles and finally blocks innumerable attempts to make the most of our abilities and to turn them into material and immaterial goods we could truly feel as our own, and that we could offer to our communities. Can basic income then break the bonds of dependence, and guarantee the peace of mind we need to be able to set out on a chosen project and thus avoid these huge losses of talent and creativity that are the toll of capitalist dispossession?

And more: the power to negotiate exactly what? In a world marked by racial and sexual divisions of labour, in a world, too, where remunerated work is increasingly less of a guarantee of sufficient income to cover life's basic needs, in a world where employment is simply scarce as a result of automation of labour processes, in a world where the political sphere (in which it is true that people also work) is presented to us as a distant space that is difficult to reach, in a world like this, basic income, by unconditionally guaranteeing our existence, can help us when it comes to proposing and, if necessary, forcing other divisions of labour, remunerated or otherwise. This would allow the flourishing of the multi-active lives that André Gorz called for, lives with room for different games in changing proportions that we can establish ourselves according to our wishes and needs. For example, what uses of time can we propose and, if necessary, force in order to share out work, all work, and open ourselves without frenzy or coercion to the care of life and sociopolitical participation?

Another of the values that needs to be rescued Trojan horse-style, (re)signified and (re)dignified, is that of flexibility. Central to the analysis of self-fulfilment that we find in the young Marx, or in famous passages of *The German Ideology* in which the right to choose games and shape them at any time or in any corner of our lives is upheld, flexibility is once again a value that is being discussed. Recently, social movements in the wake of the financial crash of 2008 put forth the need for organising 'liveable lives', which are such because, among other reasons, by living them we show we're capable of harmoniously accommodating and managing for ourselves a very wide range of true conglomerates of work, and doing so flexibly. How to interpret this?

It's well known that the value of flexibility has all too often been embraced by employers that only aspire to cut costs by eroding the legal and institutional mechanisms protecting the lives and employment conditions of working populations. As a result, flexibility has been viewed on many occasions as a strategy that is, at first sight, suspicious. Nevertheless, there can be no doubt that humans need flexible lives where we can autonomously carry out a variety of tasks in keeping with our needs, and that will change during our life cycle. When and how can we carry out productive work, and when and how can we do care work? When and how can we enter (or leave) the sphere of waged work, and when and how can we engage in our own productive projects? When and how can we open the doors to artistic work? And political work? And what amounts of these kinds of work do we want to do at each stage of our lives? And still more, shall we leave some space for spontaneity in relation with all these questions? The old Fordist story of just one job for your whole life must be questioned and is, in fact, questioned by present-day social movements that see a (not very probable) return to Fordist lives, secure but monolithically centred on *one* single activity, as an unambiguous sign of a major absence of economic sovereignty. We want to start a game, and we want to (be able to) open ourselves to different kinds of games and to define them.

So, far from Fordist telegraph pole rigidity – with lives ultra-structured around *one* occupation – on the one hand, and coerced flexibility – with its thousand scraps of lives ground down by the millstone of precariousness – on the other hand, how can we think and bring about ductile, multi-active and ultimately flexible lives which, like reeds in the wind, bend and adapt to different and changing needs without ever snapping or ceasing to be what they are? In other words, how can we govern, individually and collectively, our (re)productive lives? How can we co-determine them and be self-determining as we live them? Once again, the unconditional nature of economic and social rights, like the right to a basic income, makes it easier for individuals and groups to take control of their own flexibility effectively and securely. Is *our* flexibility a condition for the possibility of our freedom?

LIFE

The basic income proposal is here to stay. But why now? A couple of years after the onset of the financial crisis, the historian and sociologist Marco Revelli spotted on a wall of the Polytechnic University of Turin a slogan that would travel the world: '*Ci avete tolto troppo, adesso rivogliamo tutto*'

('You took too much from us and now we want everything back again'). Faced with the neoliberal turn of capitalism, this 'first enraged generation' Revelli speaks of said that it felt part of a class that, sometime earlier, stopped wanting *something*. It actually wanted nothing less than *everything* and now recovering that was the political objective. 'We want everything back again.' But what *everything* are we talking about?

The constellation of powers left by the Allied victory in the Second World War allowed the consolidation of a social pact, first forged in the automobile industry of Detroit and then exported to Europe, and this deal stipulated the following conditions. First, working populations were to be guaranteed a certain degree of socioeconomic security in the form of a job with a minimally decent salary – at first, only for men – and certain *ex post* public welfare policies that came into effect after some kind of misfortune. Second, the revolutionary impulse of that 'spirit of '45' achieved other feats that should be emphasised: the institutionalisation of collective bargaining, the armour-plating of certain social rights and the inclusion of working classes and their organisations into the institutions and their legal systems. The victorious dimension of the pact did achieve this much for the working classes.

But every pact requires concessions. As is clear, the plan couldn't be more *employment-centric*. The game was to be played exclusively in the field of wage labour, paid work that allowed not the slightest possibility of divorce. And more than that: the *employment-centrism* which generated a whole new imaginary that is still present today, especially among the older population, was a manifestation of an explicit abandonment by working populations, represented by trade unions and left-wing political parties, of the key objective of the workers' movement from its very beginnings and until then – control of production and the taking over of the mechanisms through which we decide, in the productive sphere, what to play and with what rules. The question of the constitution of the productive unit and its democratisation was wiped off the agenda of the organised left.

But today the pact is broken or, better said, smashed to smithereens. The neoliberal turn of capitalism, which has been in ferocious operation since the mid-1970s and openly and starkly displayed in its austerity-minded management of the latest crisis, has meant destruction of the basic elements of the small but relevant safety net held out by reformed capitalism to the working population, at least in the North because, in the South, the pact was generally limited to a vague gesture pointing to a hazy horizon of hope.

'You took too much from us and now we want everything back again.' How can we interpret that? Evidently, this 'first enraged generation' has dared to re-examine the conditions of the pact and to get indignant. And it's had the courage to try to move into action. What happens when a pact is broken? Any pact entails a victory and concession. And if the breaking of the pact is one-sided, the betrayed party can feel not only rightly enraged but also legitimised in organising sociopolitically to recover what was conceded as a result of the pact in question; in this case, control of production, and effective and determinant participation in decision-making about what to produce and how; that is, what to play and by what rules.

But how can this question of control of production – or, in somewhat more classical terms, collective control of the means with which we produce material and immaterial goods and reproduce life – be raised today? How can this *everything* be recovered, even if only as a political objective? Needless to say, it would be pointless to present basic income as a single, univocal answer to this question. But, yes, it is possible to identify the senses in which a basic income can help us to 'want everything back' at a point in history when they 'took too much from us'. As we've seen, this is a flow of income that unconditionally guarantees our existence, endowing us with bargaining power, which is necessary to aspire to other kinds of work, other kinds of organisation of production, other uses of time and other social relations, and to another world that could be, perhaps, one we'd truly have in common.

'Wanting everything', 'wanting everything back', means aspiring, in Polanyi's sense, to *(re)embed* the economy into politics. However much liberal mythology argues the opposite, the economy has always been embedded into politics. All economic decisions of any import have responded, and still respond, to somebody's political choices. For example, there is no market that is not the result of a political decision about how to exchange certain goods and services. But, as Polanyi says, it is also evident that, with the spread of capitalist social relations, mass participation in political processes of decision-making about the kind of economic life we wish to have has been fatally shrunken. 'Wanting everything', 'wanting everything back', means aspiring to recover spaces where these decisions are made and democratically filling them, placing them within the reach of the people's power.

For example, a Polanyi-style project of (re)embedding the economy into politics must allow us to recover the right to decide whether we want or don't want to resort to markets when we're organising economic life. Do we want to sell labour, land and money, the three 'fictitious commodities' that Polanyi said should not be marketable? Do we want to sell human organs? Our right to vote? The pears on the pear tree? The services I can offer as a physiotherapist or tattoo artist? The veggie burgers at the organic food place on the corner? Here, I suggest that, even if it's necessary to establish a certain 'prohibited area' with regard to goods and services whose commodification should be unthinkable – the right to vote, for example – individuals and groups situated at historical-contingent junctures are the ones who should be able to take on the task of deciding when, and in what measure, we might sell goods, services and skills in the markets, if we eventually want to do so. The market is another of those institutions that shouldn't be anathematised. Doing this would mean (and quite often it does mean) once again presenting the (neo)liberal world with a gift that is too costly for the emancipatory projects we might conceive for the contemporary world. But this isn't to say that we should live in market societies. The idea is not to renounce the market as a possible mechanism of coordination so, instead of thinking about the kinds of market societies we'd like to live in, we should ponder societies *with* markets. 'Wanting everything', 'wanting everything back', also means taking for ourselves the capacity for deciding when, where and how markets should be present. 'Wanting everything', 'wanting everything back', therefore means taking for ourselves the ability to decide once again what game we're playing and what rules should bring order to the game. The same goes for markets.

Accordingly, basic income, an unconditional guarantee of our existence, equips us to participate effectively in the decision-making processes pertaining to the social institutions we want to establish and to which we want to bring goods, resources and activities. Nevertheless, we should proceed with extreme caution with regard to the possible emancipatory potential of the proposal since not too many things can be taken for granted. It's therefore necessary to ponder the broad outlines of the *popular political economy* (to use the expression employed by the left wing of the French Revolution) of which basic income would be a part. This popular political economy would include but would also transcend the proposal but, without it, a good part of its transformative potential would be lost. Let's see why.

This 'popular political economy of basic income', to use this expression, has to be open to three big questions or sets of questions. First, a basic income must help to nourish true political cultures for the collective organisation of free labour, and of freely associated labour. A society with a basic income can't be an atomised society in which people try to set out on their individual(ised) ways in the heart of socially disjointed spaces. This isn't about making a moral judgement on the individual option but, rather, a matter of taking into account, from a position of the most clear-cut pragmatism, the fact that only the sociopolitical structuring of very diverse struggles and projects can make effective our collective and individual efforts to give dignity to our lives. Second, there is no possible social emancipation if a basic income does not come with equally universal and unconditional in-kind benefits. This is simply a question of accounting logic: the freedom to choose the game and set its rules evaporates when, instead of a real package of economic and social rights, we only have a basic income in our pockets and the obligation to go, frenzied and anguished, to the markets to supply ourselves with other resources that are equally necessary for a decent life, among them healthcare, education, housing, care and energy. In other words, far from becoming the Trojan horse to bring down this neoliberalism that is bent on stripping the state of its mechanisms of social protection, a basic income must act as an organising mainstay of these sets of mechanisms, endowing them with the universal and unconditional logic they have so often lacked. Third and finally, thinking about basic income must go hand in hand with calling for anti-accumulation limits on private economic power. However much a base is guaranteed, the possibilities of setting out from it vanish when the paths are blocked or ravaged by the rentier voracity of just a few.

'You took too much from us and now we want everything back again.' When the popular political economy is present, basic income can show that it's able to unfold its emancipatory potential. And this situates us at the frontiers of capitalism. While being perfectly compatible with private property and markets, basic income helps us to rethink property and markets beyond the forms of strictly capitalist logic. Or perhaps we have already seen some kind of capitalism in which the decommodification of labour power was thinkable, a decommodification of labour power that would, moreover, open the doors to, among other things, forms of property that are common and not exclusive?

The project of basic income is, then, one that is aimed at (re)appropriating our lives and, in doing so, it takes up a position at the intersection between the world of public policy and that of self-management. On the one hand, it is part of, and organises, sets of economic and social rights that must act as leverage in activating all the lives we can imagine. On the other hand, it helps us to get around state directives, which are so often controlling, disciplinary and stigmatising, and it aids us when we aspire to give form to what is imagined in practices and spaces that are as self-managed as we are capable of or want.

But can considering the unconditional presence of resources raise a problem which, as in Mandeville's beehive, would put an end to collective prosperity? Recall that Mandeville's dissolute bees brought affluence to the hive precisely because, deprived of resources, they were compelled to work hard in order to satisfy the desires of their own self-interested psychology. And recall, too, that the abundance of their hive vanished when the bees asked the gods to fill them with virtue, which made them happier and more detached, but also cast them into an uncivilised, idle world where only scarcity reigned. Could basic income constitute a tragic project that would inevitably self-cancel by destroying the motivational bases of human action?

In the eighteenth century, Adam Smith contested Mandeville's fable, speaking of systems he called 'licentious' because they ignored the richness of the human motivational apparatus. Indeed, since classical antiquity, a host of studies have shown that the reasons that move humans to act include self-interest, of course, but they also go beyond that and incorporate mechanisms such as observance of social norms, the need to empathise and feel part of an inclusive setting and, above all, a pleasure in autotelic activities, which is to say tasks that we feel are close to our own nature and that, therefore, are an end – *telos* – in themselves, rather than being aimed at any material benefit we might instrumentally extract from them. In fact, studies in the fields of experimental economics and psychology, as well as basic income trials and experiments carried out around the world, point in exactly the same direction.

Erik Olin Wright called for a shift from 'static justifications' of basic income, which refer to the kind of world basic income constitutes (one with less poverty and precariousness, etc.) to its 'dynamic justifications', which are concerned with the world that basic income 'sets in motion'. Needless to say, a setting with less poverty and less precariousness is highly desirable, but we are now at a historic juncture when the need to hope for new worlds goes beyond the mere desire to resist. The epic of resistance is exhausting, hence the interest in dynamic justifications of basic income. First, basic income frees us from the need to plead for, or uncritically accept, the activities 'offered' – imposed on us – today and that we instrumentally engage in order to survive. Second, basic income allows us to occupy ourselves with autotelic activities, which is to say with work, remunerated or not, that really fulfils us. Can we conceive of the possibility of contented bees whose well-being comes from the fact that they are diligently active in the world of chosen occupations? Now is the time for us to feel hopeful about the field of open possibilities basic income brings with it.

As I said at the beginning, basic income hasn't come along so that we can live cap *in* hand. Basic income *is* one more cap, one of the many caps *with* which we can imagine and practise forms of life that are far from any blackmailing fear of poverty. Can we conceive of this possibility, or must we keep feeling that we are lucky and even grateful because we've been able to keep working for someone else in the regime of 'part-time slavery' that Aristotle associated with wage labour when this is our only option? Can we contemplate ways of deproletarianising ourselves – and this doesn't necessarily mean leaving remunerated work altogether – not in order to languish in tedium and idleness but to become free workers who, as such, can decide how to live?

At present, there is an open debate about what to do with zoos and their captive animals. Traditional zoos are no longer acceptable. Non-human zoo animals can't be kept in the conditions in which they now live. What would be the best destiny for them? Experts in ethology have meticulously explored several options. In the public presentations of their reports one idea is clear: freeing the animals into nature isn't an option. Those born in captivity don't have the necessary skills to fend for themselves in environments they don't belong to, and those that were captured have lost those skills. Both groups need another space: another zoo, but a twenty-first-century one. Are we humans in an analogous situation, or do we still have the skills to live in our own environments, which are none other than those that we can and are willing to invent?

PART I

Cartographies of Social (Dis)order: Why Something Like a Basic Income?

On 15 May 1891, Pope Leo XIII promulgated the encyclical *Rerum novarum* (On New Things – Rights and Duties of Capital and Labour) which has undoubtedly been one of the most influential documents in shaping the modern world. In this encyclical letter, subtitled 'On the Conditions of Labour', and written with the caution of those who fear 'the spirit of revolutionary change, which has long been disturbing the nations of the world', those who fear that this desire for change 'should have passed beyond the sphere of politics and made its influence felt in the cognate sphere of practical economics',[1] the Holy See had the following to say:

> The great mistake made in regard to the matter now under consideration is to take up with the notion that class is naturally hostile to class, and that the wealthy and the working men are intended by nature to live in mutual conflict. So irrational and so false is this view that the direct contrary is the truth. Just as the symmetry of the human frame is the result of the suitable arrangement of the different parts of the body, so in a State is it ordained by nature that these two classes should dwell in harmony and agreement, so as to maintain the balance of the body politic. Each needs the other: capital cannot do without labor, nor labor without capital. Mutual agreement results in the beauty of good order, while perpetual conflict necessarily produces confusion and savage barbarity.[2]

These words may seem strange or old-fashioned, but they contain a description of the world and an associated political precept, both of them of an organicist nature, that have inspired, and still inspire, political projects and institutional designs of many different kinds and in many different social spheres but always with a single aim: to maintain the 'balance' and 'harmony' of social 'bodies' which, though they may fall ill, can also be healed. Human societies are then bodies; organic structures that house power relations and real divisions in distinct social classes. Yet these are bodies that are able to channel conflict and find the 'beauty' that derives from 'agreement', which is none other than the ability, mediated by coercion if necessary, to place each social group in the niche it naturally belongs to. Organicist political action, then, aspires to preserve or re-establish a vertical, stratified order where everyone knows what is right and what to abide by, an order of enduring legitimacy from which it is not wise to stray, ever.

By contrast with such concepts – although we'll later see some interesting intersections between the two worlds – the liberal universe denies the core of this vision. Here, there is no split whatsoever. The world has no defined social structure. Individuals are simply limited to circulating their particular, non-transferable value judgements or preferences, which must be material-ised in agreements – in contracts – that are devoid of conflict. The nature of the world, therefore, is strictly psychological. There is nothing written about tastes and, moreover, tastes tend to flow together in social spaces, which is to say markets, which are especially suited to their merging and aggregation. In 1949, Ludwig von Mises, the father of the Austrian school of economics, put it like this in his *Human Action*:

> The market is not a place, a thing, or a collective entity. The market is a process, actuated by the interplay of the actions of the various individu-als cooperating under the division of labor. The forces determining the – continually changing – state of the market are the value judgments of these individuals and their actions as directed by these value judgments. The state of the market at any instant is the price structure, i.e., the totality of the exchange ratios as established by the interaction of those eager to buy and those eager to sell. [...] Every market phenomenon can be traced back to definite choices of the members of the market society (2007: 257–8).

Mises' explanation of the workings of the world, unlike that offered by Pope Leo XIII, is openly *a-institutional*. There are no social institutions that must be politically managed on the basis of a recognition and understand-ing of the underlying conflict of adversarial, belligerent social relations and scenarios. Such discord simply doesn't exist. And there is no need to prob-lematise what isn't problematic. Individual preferences govern social life, and markets in particular, and if these choices aren't constrained, nobody gets upset. Everyone's happy.

Almost a century before Mises, Karl Marx, as an heir to the republican understanding of the world (Domènech, 2004), offered a picture of social life that is antithetical to that depicted in liberal doctrine. Of course there is conflict, he said. Of course there are power relations. Of course there are social institutions. And of course, he concludes, these aren't the products of choices and preferences exogenous to social life but of social-relational features that are wholly endogenous to this social life and related to interactions between agents and groups of agents with more or less bargaining power:

> Society does not consist of individuals, but expresses the sum of interrelations, the relations within which these individuals stand. As if someone were to say: Seen from the perspective of society, there are no slaves and no citizens: both are human beings. Rather, they are that outside society. To be a slave, to be a citizen, are social characteristics, relations between human beings (Marx, 1973: 193).

Hence, the social construction of institutions, occurring in places that are necessarily conflictive as they are marked by scarce resources and competing interests, is what makes us more or less free.

In any case, we have here an odd and interesting triangle. I have presented these three revealing quotes in order to understand their vertices. With each one, we have a social ontology and an associated normative standpoint. By *social ontology*, I understand a certain vision of the relations and mechanisms by means of which we humans constitute societies. When we speak of social ontologies, we're simply referring to the image of social life we're dealing with. What do we observe in the world? What are its basic components and what devices drive it? What is out there?

Undoubtedly, the answers that Leo XIII, Mises and Marx give to these questions sketch three universes, not exempt of intersections, that reveal three conceptions of the world which, to a great extent, will determine the game board on which, in theory and practice and through to the present day, sociopolitical conflict and the political-normative options of the contemporary world will be played out.[3] First, to start with Mises, we have the isolated atoms typical of liberalism. The liberal tradition presents, on a descriptive, ontological plane, a gaseous universe in which the different elemental particles erratically circulate without being guided through or obstructed by unnecessary channels, and without tracing recognisable trajectories that might structure them with other particles (though, for the moment, I'm not trying to ascertain whether such descriptions bear any resemblance to reality). The world has no structure, or has it to a minimum degree, in a vaporous state. By and large, it's supposed that this is the case: the *laissez-faire* doctrine which, as we shall see later, rests on a true ontological impossibility points, on the normative and political planes, to the need to let these atoms, these veritable undirected monads, roam around and bump into each other so that, when there are complementary 'value judgements' or preferences, agreements – contracts – can emerge from the willingness and concurrence of the parties that are concerned.[4]

Second, Catholic social ontology, that of Leo XIII, presents a world where atoms form cells, and cells form tissues and organs, and organs form whole bodies and these bodies can be healthy or afflicted by ailments and diseases, from the slightest and most bearable to the most serious and threatening. Thus far, we have the establishmentarian description of the world – the social ontology – according to which social life is a body housing organs with different tasks, whose proper functioning depends on a harmonious arrangement of these parts within the whole. It follows from this that, on the normative political level, the establishmentarian universe appeals to calm within the overall edifice. In fact, there is a vertical equilibrium that must be achieved and maintained by any means necessary.

It should be noted that this structure is overtly pyramidal. In establishmentarian societies, there is a backbone consisting of a *few* leaders – the *oligarchy* – and many who are led, most of them poor. Hence, the pyramid. And it's true that the lower you are in the pyramid, the more pressure you have to bear. Yet the fabulous thing about this organicist proposal resides in trust in the capacity of *all* humans, those at the top and those at the bottom, to shun the 'savage barbarity' of those who aspire to bring down the house, and to participate in the serene joy and peace of mind that derives from knowing that one is a co-author of this '[m]utual agreement [that] results in the beauty of good order', of which Leo XIII spoke: the pyramid can attain an awesome splendour. And if this capacity is scarce, there will always be punitive mechanisms to correct erring conduct and put the structure to rights.

At the third vertex of the triangle, we find the social ontology and political precepts of democratic republicanism upheld, among many others, by Marx. The republican social ontology shares with the organicist ontology of Leo XIII an awareness that the world is split into classes and social groups whose distinctions have to do with unequal access to (and enjoyment of) resources and opportunities. But where the establishmentarian organicism prescribes mechanisms to sustain the vertical arrangement of the world, democratic republicanism pursues ways of horizontalising social relations. Republican fraternity therefore contests both the liberal notion of a gaseous 'non-order' disintegrating social bonds and the organicist proposal that we must bear the weight of the great pyramid on our shoulders. On closer inspection, republican fraternity would aspire to erode that pyramid in favour of free circulation of flexibly self-managed multi-active lives that are open to a wide range of relationships along paths that can be adapted to the contours of who we are and what we dare to be and do.

But what institutional relations follow from the analysis of social life that we owe to these three important traditions? In particular, what kind of income policies can we associate, if we can associate any, with each one of them, and also with the intersections that often appear among them? In brief, how do the ethical-political backdrops of these perspectives come together so that they come to shape specific ways of approaching and resolving the famous 'social question'? The following chapters are devoted to my attempt to answer these questions.

1

The Psychosociology and Politics of Elitist Verticalism

'The increased self reliance and closer mutual combination of the working classes; as also, finally, [...] the prevailing moral degeneracy' have determined the 'momentous gravity of the state of things now', said Leo XIII. There is, then, an open conflict which, as could not be otherwise, revolves around the conception and delimitation of property rights. This is a clearly political battle between 'a small number of very rich men' and 'the teeming masses of the laboring poor' upon whom the former have laid 'a yoke little better than that of slavery itself'.[1] Far from the asepsis of the liberal ontology, which declares an absence of hostilities in the world, Catholic social ontology not only recognises that social life is fraught with power relations but it also draws attention to the suffering this means for the great majority. Nonetheless, there is no way that the solution might mean distributing property. This would be 'unjust, for they would rob the lawful possessor'.[2] Like John Locke, church social doctrine establishes that, 'God [...] hath given the world to men in common' but, unlike Locke, who introduced important prescriptive clauses to prevent private appropriation of external resources that would plunge the vast majority into dispossession,[3] the former, at least in Pope Leo XIII's encyclical, asserts that 'God has granted the earth to mankind in general, not in the sense that all without distinction can deal with it as they like, but rather that no part of it was assigned to any one in particular, and that the limits of private possession have been left to be fixed by man's own industry, and by the laws of individual races'.[4] Everyone's pushing and shoving but the early bird gets the worm.

The solution to the social question – the 'opportune remedy', as Leo XIII puts it – is, then, not to be found in violating the inviolable, the principle of exclusive, excluding private property, but in smoothing over the rough patches that may appear in a world divided into owners and their hirelings to make it more bearable. The solution to the social question lies in keeping 'the populace within the line of duty', ensuring that state power and the 'authority of the law should intervene' in order to 'protect lawful owners from spoliation'[5] and, where necessary, banning trade unions and other workers' associations that don't respect these property rights. And this must be done in the knowledge that the propertied class is also responsible for the crucial task of easing the hardship suffered by those who, struck low by the vagaries of chance, are beholden to the former for a roof over their heads. The 'roof' here means capitalist companies, but also schools, hospitals, leisure and even labour organisations, neighbourhoods, cities and even whole territories when they are ruled by the great organicist smoke and mirrors of the paternity-docility binomial. Sound familiar?

So, fathers worthy of the name are needed. Fathers who are kind to their children are needed, fathers who are willing to provide them with all the care that rectitude requires, but at the same time able to instruct them, strictly and uncompromisingly, until domesticating them and turning them into submissive beings that pose no threat to the stability of the social body. Children must never stop being children. There is no coming of age to be reached. Ortega y Gasset says that sustaining (vertically, of course) a modern society, (i.e. avoiding or attenuating the much-feared 'rebellion of the masses') requires emulating these exemplary – for there can be no docility without exemplariness (Domènech, 2006) – paternal figures in every single aspect of social life.

In their zeal to order the world vertically, these *fathers* frequently express themselves bluntly, resorting to harsh tongue-lashings when the progeny runs amok and starts being disruptive. 'They're not citizens. They're just hippy hobos', said the former president of the Community of Madrid, Esperanza Aguirre, when referring to the *indignados* who were occupying *her* squares. 'They're not citizens. They're just *racaille* [rabble, trash]', said Nicolas Sarkozy, then France's minister of the interior, internal security and local freedoms, and future president of the Republic, when commenting on the explosion of rage by citizens of the *banlieues* who, anyway, weren't very convinced that they were actually fully fledged citizens. Other times, the progeny gets the idea that their parents are stealing and taking for themselves what belongs to everyone – think of what some see as corruption. This is a gross error of perception. Should parents give explanations to their children when they're managing, with sacrifices and magnanimity, the resources of a home which, moreover, is theirs? 'There's class warfare, all right, but it's my class, the rich class, that's making war, and we're winning', asserted the mega-rich Warren Buffett in November 2006. And that's how things are. His description of the situation, free from the slightest whiff of ambiguity, couldn't be more accurate, for which we must be grateful. That's all very well, but organicist doctrine dictates that we should try to manage that victory prudently and compassionately.

We've often heard the famous order that parents issue to naughty kids: 'Go and stand in the corner and think about what you did!' It would appear that the organicist political precept tries to create as many small havens as necessary so that docile citizen-children can be deposited in a safe place – safe for the pyramid, of course. But these aren't really 'thinking corners' but veritable '*non*-thinking corners', where we withdraw, and from which we delegate to some 'parent' our power to think and decide for ourselves. These parents can take several forms: company masters and owners of all sorts of establishments, as well as supposed experts, politicians and mandarins who 'don't represent us' – as the Spanish *indignados* movement used to proclaim – because it never even occurs to them that they are accountable to anyone.

And it's really like that. According to the organicist social ontology, which various kinds of fascism also came to embrace, individuals are fragments that are somehow assigned to some parts, organs or strata of the pyramidal body that constitutes society. And this assignation isn't questioned. Questioning it is what causes the disorders, ailments and deformities the social body might suffer. This, then, is an organism whose vital signs need to be stabilised by finding a formula, a cure, that will make it possible to lock into their niches, of greater or lesser pre-eminence, all individuals: rich and proletarian, capitalist and labourer. Paul of Tarsus put it like this: 'Let every soul be subject unto the higher powers. For there is no power but of God: the powers that be are ordained of God.'[6] Pope Leo XIII would add, it's true that this suffering must be tempered by the stern, yet protective and affable hand of *paternal* authorities who are willing and able to tame the plebs by the most compassionate means possible. Only thus can the 'perpetual conflict' be ended. Only thus will 'these two classes [...] dwell in harmony and agreement, so as to maintain the balance of the body politic'. Only thus will the different wills of classes be bridged and will 'rich and poor join hands in friendly concord'.[7]

In Germany, at the beginning of the twentieth century, the Catholic social philosopher Max Scheler was thinking along the same lines. It was essential, he said, that the working class should 'become an established stratum'. He was aware that '[t]he working class made itself as much as it was made', as E. P. Thompson (2012 [1963]) was to say several decades later. And letting the working class 'make itself' was tantamount to permitting the presence of powerful dynamic forces that were capable of eventually dissolving the class itself as a social body and constructing a horizontal world without classes, but consisting of fraternally united human groups, where everyone establishes reciprocally free social relations and everyone is self-determining. An established stratum, on the other hand, 'is something static, something that man adapts to, something man does not freely choose as a "profession" but rather something in which he has been installed. [...] The idea of stratum and a certain hierarchy of strata – of the goods and tasks corresponding to each stratum – is inseparable from the Christian idea of community.'[8]

In short, the established strata of Leo XIII, Ortega and Scheler – like today's neo-establishmentarian versions of it that also want to send us to the many 'non-thinking corners' they have established – aimed (and in large part succeeded) to interlock the world and thus consolidate the capitalist socioeconomic order, because without this underpinning, without these supports, society collapses. Hence, the crucial contribution of the modern forms of establishmentarianism at the end of the nineteenth and during the twentieth and twenty-first centuries resides in the idea that this assemblage, which places everyone in his or her right place, is provided by capitalist market relations, aided by the state's repressive apparatus, which is responsible for protecting property rights, and the soothing balm of an organicist discourse portraying social harmony and taking the form of all sorts of contracts, starting with job contracts, as the way to salvation. As such the capitalist enterprise is seen as a true organ for the family management of conflict where owners punish and reward, just as any parents worthy of the name do with their children.

Leo XIII claims that, by means of such action, the capitalist enterprise prepares the poor man – now free of pride and the yearning for sedition, and conscious of the burden of suffering and pain he must bear – for peace. Hints of all this are strewn throughout the encyclical *Rerum novarum*, which expounds on the relief that masters must provide for their workers, thus encouraging rich men and employers to fulfil their paternal duties to their servants, to those who depend materially on them in order to live. What duties? Basically, enabling them to work, and helping to make sure that these abilities remain intact. It's worth looking at this in some detail.

If the working class must abstain from damaging capital and offending the person of the proprietor, as well as renouncing all forms of violence and conspiracy against legitimate (property) rights, Leo XIII also establishes that the employer class must undertake to provide workers with decent jobs, not to use violence against them, to establish a working day that doesn't exceed the worker's strength, to provide time for rest so workers can recover the energy they've spent and thus assure that they can get back to work, to pay a salary that will cover the basic needs of a frugal worker with good habits, not to bring children into the labour market until their bodies, their intelligence and their souls are satisfactorily developed, to offer women suitable and seemly employment, and to encourage the spread of mutual aid and employers' and workers' societies as long as they do not aim to harm justice and public health or, in other words, property rights. Above all, one dictum summed up what the pope was really concerned about: there should be 'a continuous supply of work at all times and seasons'.[9]

A 'continuous supply of work at all times and seasons': how could the pope's stipulation be put into practice then and today? It's a commonplace that what an employer requires and appreciates is the security of hiring a disciplined and willing worker. And we know that the main disciplinary mechanism of capitalism is material and symbolic dispossession, which obliges all those who are trapped in it – the majority – to beg for work. This isn't a bad beginning. The pieces are in place to ensure that there is no lack of discipline. Yet, if the aim is to erect establishmentarian orders in which everyone accepts without resistance the tasks and functions assigned to each level, it might make sense to demand a bit more effort. One example would be the nineteenth-century English workhouses which offered lodging and work to those who couldn't support themselves. And then there is the New Poor Law of 1834, ruling that poor relief wouldn't be given to those who refused to enter a workhouse, which is to say those who contemplated the possibility of declining to work for others, those who contested the allocation of roles determined by the capitalist order.[10] The rules of the game, therefore, were and are very clear. The dispossessed majorities have to hasten to join the labour markets in order to get a job. If they don't succeed, the dispossessed majorities have to swear obedience to employment agencies that might be able to offer them an alternative – another job, of course. As is clear when looking at the game as a whole, the freedom to choose and engage in an activity that one feels is one's own is conspicuous by its absence from start to finish.[11]

This strategy has recently come to be called *workfare* or *welfare-to-work*. With this system, states introduce conditional subsidies and other public policy schemes but only allow access to people who show they are willing to look for a job in present labour markets – the nature of which they can in no case question – and to participate in apprenticeship and job training projects that reinforce their status as instruments of labour serving the interests of others. Pure obedience to paternal authority, as Guy Standing puts it (2002,

2009). Conditionality in public policy then tends to take on openly organ-icist overtones: only those people who are willing to accept the 'hierarchy of the establishment', the pecking order expressed by 'the goods and tasks corresponding to each stratum of the establishment', as the Catholic thinker Max Scheler put it, can receive relief and assistance.

It's therefore surprising to find public policy proposals which, despite coming from emancipatory traditions, continue to give wage labour the role of an *inevitable* mainstay of the processes of social structuring. Interest-ing examples of this would be proposals of job guarantee described by such authors as Garzón and Guamán (2015), Philip Harvey (1989), Murray and Forstater (2013) and Randall Wray (1998). The notion of guaranteed work is based on the idea of seeing the state as employer of last resort. But why *last*? Because, in the *first* instance, the capitalist labour market still exists. Hence, the onus is on the dispossessed classes, which perhaps should once again be called *established strata*, to enter labour markets whose nature can't be disputed. It would seem that this is their lot, a fate for which they are marked out by the dynamics of capitalist dispossession. If they find work, which is supposedly available because of 'a continuous supply of work at all times and seasons', according to Leo XIII, everyone can be happy. If not, then the dispossessed classes, the established strata of instruments of labour serving the interests of others, are supposed to line up at a counter and ask for a job. Once again, this is a game, which could be called organicist, in which the freedom to choose and engage in an activity one feels as one's own doesn't exist. Apparently, there is a link between the social-Catholic hierar-chical structure and conditionality that can never be broken, regardless of the fact that those authors and actors who conceive this conditionality are clearly situated on the left of the ideological spectrum.

It's worth drawing attention to the fact that job guarantee proposals keep emphasising the importance of the fact that these job-seeking 'counters' don't necessarily operate at the whim of state discretion (the state isn't arbi-trary, by definition), but they can be democratically swamped by citizens so that they themselves can decide, from below, what kinds of jobs the state offers. Moreover, advocates of guaranteed work consider the possibility that workers could turn directly to the state without having to go through the prior obligation of looking for jobs, most of which are openly exploita-tive, that are 'offered' on the capitalist labour markets. At this point, I won't enter into the technical viability of this possibility. What needs to be said here is that, evidently, such refinements would mean that the job guaran-tee proposal is much more horizontalising, much less establishmentarian, than what I have described, but it's also true to say that these provisions are always on the theoretical or prescriptive plane. In effect, practical proposals for introducing job guarantee schemes end up sending us back to square one of Leo XIII's establishmentarian game: you poor people of the Earth, go first to the capitalist labour market where we know you'll be exploited, and if you can't find an exploiter, come docilely to see us and, *in the last instance*, we'll try to find 'something' for you.

To conclude, are these establishmentarian schemes necessarily a problem? They're undoubtedly not if, on the level of descriptive analysis and keeping moral values out of it, we embrace and understand as being true a certain social ontology – an organicist description of the world – and conclude that social life is a body, a mechanism consisting of instances and components, each and every one of which performs precise functions under specific conditions, just as the interrelationship between the nervous system, the immunological system and the respiratory apparatus have done, are still doing and will do in a healthy organism of a sleek vertical structure. It happens, nevertheless, that on the descriptive level, too, we observe that things are actually a bit different; that there are many possibilities for human relationality, which aren't restricted to an establishmentarian order made up of predictable, unchanging layers and strata. And it also happens that there are reasons for thinking, still on the descriptive level, that these many relationalities include the possibility of questioning the edifice and finding mechanisms of social coordination that could establish horizontal, fraternal ties. This is not a historical or ontological impossibility. To put it simply, it can be done. And, finally, it happens, and perhaps even more importantly than on the political-normative level of analysis, that there are countless reasons for assuming that the possibilities for a dignified life for everyone are to be found right here, in horizontal social orders, as I'll attempt to show further on.

2

The Fallacy of Autogenous
Social Orders

As we've seen, Buffett says there is class warfare, and that it is his class, 'the rich class, that's making war, and we're winning'. But why does this idea of class struggle makes its appearance here? The liberal universe couldn't be more uncomfortable with a social ontology that points to the presence of social institutions structuring our relations beyond what our sets of preferences, or what our particular, non-transferable psychology, dictates. The world, Mises informed us, is the result of a long process of accumulating 'value judgements', desires and aspirations anchored in our particular structure of beliefs and inclinations. Liberal social ontology, then, is about the emergence of autogenous social orders whose presence has nothing to do with ties of dependence and power relations. Warren Buffett's institutionalist slip would have been appreciated by the bulk of the republican tradition, from Aristotle to Marx, as it would be concurred with today by anyone who understands that the world is home to rival social groups, and it's precisely this rivalry that structures life in society. For liberalism, however, Buffett's institutionalist clanger is simply that: a slip of the tongue, a gaffe made by someone who didn't understand or forgot that there are no victories or defeats in the world, no conquest and dispossession, no combat and resistance, no attack and defence, no strategy and response. There is only straightforward concordance between the aspirations and appetites of those who dwell in it (Mises, 2007).

At this point, it might be a good idea to give an account of exactly what I mean when I talk about 'liberalism'. What is it in the historical and political senses? And what is it not? One useful attempt at answering these questions would inevitably involve looking at the history of the term and the intellectual and political tradition associated with it. In brief, historically speaking, liberalism is the doctrinal body which, having appeared at the beginning of the nineteenth century,[1] tends to strip freedom of any consideration of the material – and symbolic – conditions of existence of subjects who are deemed to be 'free'. In other words, classical liberal 'doctrinaire' thinkers and their twentieth-century heirs (Mises, Hayek, etc.) tend to equate freedom with 'equality before the law', or *isonomy*: we are free to the extent that the legal-political system does not determine that we are lawfully dependent on third parties. Thus, we are free to the extent that slavery and feudal serfdom have been abolished, or free if we all theoretically receive the same treatment from the institutional bodies that govern the modern world (so, a liberal person typically wonders if it's written somewhere that people *must* sell their labour power under conditions that might not be satisfactory). Clearly, liberalism ignores the material and symbolic conditions that shape the world governed by this law that is (supposedly) equal for everyone, while arguing that state intervention must be limited to ensuring that the law is effectively equal for all citizens with no exceptions, making certain that the job contracts and commercial agreements that are being signed see the light of day in conditions of absolutely solid legal security. So, although declaring that *legal* mishaps for the parties concerned must be avoided, nineteenth- and twentieth-century liberalism isn't bothered by the fact that these parties are on a patently uneven playing field in *material* (and also symbolic) terms. To sum up, the bulk of historical liberalism rests on a great big legal fiction, which establishes, by means of the notion of 'equality before the law' or *isonomy*, the supposition that signatories of contracts (including those who live in conditions of dispossession and material, and thus legal, dependence vis-à-vis other parties) freely and voluntarily enter into a relationship through the contract.[2]

I should also add that part of the confusion over the matter of the bounds of liberalism arises from the fact that there are authors commonly labelled as 'liberals' (in some cases they even call themselves 'liberals') who, obviously coming from outside the field of this liberalism that is blind to the material and symbolic conditions of freedom, take a critical stance regarding modernity which, one way or another, leads them to decry the basic mechanisms of capitalist social structuring. John Stuart Mill and John Rawls are two examples. The former, aware of the dangers for individual and collective freedom posed by the presence of power relations among social classes, affirms that, yes, there are social clusters in the world that are often moved by factional interests. He then advocates intervention by the public powers aiming at the social extension of small property owners, both agrarian and industrial. The latter, thoroughly aware of the liberticidal nature of capitalism as it really exists, asserts that the social justice he calls for is not possible in this system, not even in welfare state capitalism, which leads him to affirm the moral and political superiority of what he calls a 'property owning democracy' and also forms of 'market socialism'. In fact, some analysts have presented Rawls (and especially referring to his late works) as a republican, albeit dressed up in the language and analytical uses of Anglo-Saxon academia of the last third of the twentieth century (Francisco, 2006), or going so far as to describe him as a 'reticent socialist' (Edmundson, 2017).[3]

Finally, some scholars equate 'liberalism' with an absence of 'comprehensive doctrines' or, in other words, the act of banning closed views as to what a 'good life' is; views that some people try to impose on other conceptions of 'good', different ideas about what a decent, meaningful life might consist of. Once again, John Rawls' work would clearly fit with this type of 'liberal secularism'. Yet it should be added immediately that, while it is true that the various forms of liberalism – the Rawlsian variety among them – are openly 'secular' in this sense, so too is well-understood republicanism, and maybe even more profoundly so. Far from romantic reconstructions of the republican tradition in which it would be a passionate ode to civic-political life turned into an ultimate aim, an end in itself, the republican tradition offers especially useful tools for, first, grasping the fact of power relations that manage to impose certain life projects, certain notions of the good life, on others and, second, structuring institutional bodies (and hence the importance of civic-political life, but only on this basis) that are able to abolish these bonds of dependence in order to make sure that *all* life projects have real possibilities of being carried out. As Bertomeu and Domènech (2005) state, the possibility of (non-arbitrary) interference by public powers is what should allow truly high degrees of tolerance and neutrality to be attained, since this *non-arbitrary* interference by the institutions must prevent the presence and consolidation of *arbitrary* interference by private actors that might thwart the development of the life projects of large social majorities. There is nothing more 'neutral' and 'tolerant', then, than republican sociopolitical precepts and action.

I end this digression about the conceptual and historical scope of liberalism as a tradition to return to my earlier point, namely that liberal social ontology declares the non-existence of bonds of dependence and power relations while also hinting at an idea of order that is understood as a random coming together of individuals with complementary aspirations and preferences.

We frequently see how this liberal social ontology is traced back to the approaches offered by Mandeville in his famous work, *The Fable of the Bees: or, Private Vices, Publick Benefits* (1997 [1714]) to which I referred above.

Published in England over the first 30 years of the eighteenth century, it tells the story of an orderly, prosperous hive, which is so because the bees that reside in it limit themselves to satisfying their most immediate desires and inclinations, with total indifference to anything else that might be happening around them. It is precisely this selfish, industrious spirit[4] – this mindless nurturing of 'private vices' or, in microeconomic terms, private preferences or desires – that brings innumerable 'public benefits'. The industrious activity of these prodigious bees, operating in spontaneous, distributed, *(un)structured* and, of course, totally unintentional ways, ends up bringing into being a prosperous world full of goods that bring satisfaction to all of them.

But the bees commit the sin of hubris, essentially by daring to aspire to virtue. They beg the gods, and Jupiter in particular, to give them the strength of will they need to renounce their licentiousness and excess in order to cultivate a sober way of life in harmony with their social environment. This is a fatal error. Jupiter grants their wish and, in time, the hive becomes a dreary, despondent space where scarcity reigns.

The analogy is served, and the liberal world wastes no time in pouncing on it and turning it into the catchphrase of its political-scientific creed. Among other things, Bernard Mandeville must have been offering nothing less than an overt apology for *laissez-faire*. But the liberal world moved too fast. The liberal world, like the bulk of contemporary hermeneutics, ties up the loose ends too hastily and thus errs. The liberal world forgets that Mandeville, together with Jonathan Swift, was one of the best English satirical writers; that the cynical, provocative Mandeville was constructing a show to ridicule those who, legion in his day, believed that abstract reason or revelation can guide us in an earthly world to ultimate truths; that Mandeville was embracing unto himself a 'radical philosophical anarchism' that was a commonplace in Renaissance thought (recall the daring of Giordano Bruno) that strove to question the capacity of abstract ideals for constructing life in society. We grope, Mandeville is saying. And it can't be otherwise. An heir to Montaigne and Spinoza, Mandeville was intimately acquainted with the French philosophical and literary tradition and also the philosophical and political thought of the Low Countries of the day, and this Anglo-Dutch writer was recovering the heterodox thinking, of Epicurean and Averroist roots, which held that the soul is mortal, and the finitude of this soul means that humans are incapable of discovering immutable general rules. If, moreover, he takes from seventeenth-century Epicureanism the conviction that humans have no choice but to live for what we find profitable and pleasurable, then Mandeville is equipped with the necessary ingredients for plotting a great send-up of those who entrust everything to hyper-rationalism.[5] Between this and extolling the psychopathic egoism of *laissez-faire* – psychopathic because it underpins an idea of indifference to the fate of others – there lies a great abyss. Marx himself noted this in his *Theories of Surplus Value*: 'Mandeville was of course infinitely bolder and more honest than the philistine apologists of bourgeois society' (1863).

But, as I noted above, the liberal tradition took the joke seriously. It finds in Mandeville's fable the perfect excuse to proclaim to the four winds that there is no order in the world, that the world is purely and simply guided by the changing but always legitimately sovereign appetites that each individual harbours. The nature of the world is strictly psychological. There are no power relations in the world.

The Spanish artist El Roto makes this abundantly clear in one of his cartoons, satirically of course. The text says: 'According to the laws of the market, if the castaway is hungrier than the shark, he will eat the shark.' It's a matter of preferences or, better perhaps, the intensity of these preferences. The efforts that have exhausted the castaway and the destructive capacity of shark's rows of teeth and muscles of its jaw are of little matter because, well yes, if the castaway's hungry enough, he'll eat the shark.

In fact, these 'laws of the market' that El Roto refers to are the laws enunciated by the psychologising neoclassical economic theory, which appeared with the Marginalist Revolution in economics dating back to the last third of the nineteenth century when it unquestionably came hand in hand with liberal social ontology and political precepts. The old 'political economy', which was how the human and social sciences were studied and taught from Aristotle through to 1870, and which many people continue to practise and uphold today, had an 'institutionalist' methodology. Indeed, it was *political* economy because it was alert to the bonds of dependence and power relations, both material and symbolic, that permeate all social institutions, among them markets, households, workplaces, political and legal regulations, and laws, etc. And this interest in power relations at the heart of social institutions required non-compartmentalisation and the interrelationship of phenomena and explanatory strategies, which is why we find a mixture of philosophers, jurists, economists, sociologists, historians and anthropologists in figures such as Aristotle, Adam Smith and Karl Marx. The disintegration of the social sciences was yet to come.

But after the final third of the nineteenth century, the group of 'marginalist' or 'neoclassical' *economists* – a term which, by the way, was still a neologism that had only previously been used by a few French physiocrats – set out on a path that would, like a sharp blow against a thin pane glass, smash to pieces what was once a coherent set of social sciences. This marginalist (now become orthodox) economics abandons any study of power relations that breed in social institutions – and invites nascent exotic disciplines such as sociology and anthropology to specialise in exotic questions – and moves on to understand the world as a set of individuals who bring with them certain tastes and preferences. The social ontology of marginalist or neoclassical economics couldn't be more psychological. If two people sign a labour contract, it means that the one who becomes an entrepreneur *prefers* the adrenalin rush that comes with running a business, and that the one who becomes a wage labourer *prefers* a lower income in exchange for the peace of mind that comes with working for others a certain number of hours per day and being spared the headaches that come with the work of management.[6] The conduct of both subjects supposedly reveals their preferences. In brief, we have two complementary sets of what Mises calls 'value judgements', two groupings that have bumped into each other and – wonder of wonders – have fitted nicely together. Everyone's happy.

Everyone? Of course, institutional economists, from Veblen to Elinor Ostrom and still more recent ones, have rebelled and continue to rebel against this kind of analysis of social reality and have come to suggest that, however many preferences and psychological relations there are, and they certainly do exist, the labour contract is also the result of the power relations inherent to the social institutions in which they are embedded: class, gender and perhaps ethnic relations, distinctions associated with geographic origins, symbolic capital that has a lot to do with our place of birth, where we have grown up and where we have formed expectations about the kind of life we think we should have, and so on. Might it be the case that someone has been forced to sign this labour contract? This isn't a question we can be indifferent about.[7]

Hence Abba Lerner (1972: 259), a theorist of market socialism among other things, says that '[a]n economic transaction is a solved political problem. Economics has gained the title of queen of the social sciences by choosing [as its object of study] solved political problems as its domain.' This is pure denialism. In fact, it deals with 'solved' political problems because they are denied, ignored and neglected political problems that are treated as if they don't exist. Out there in the world there are only tastes – or so says neoclassical social ontology – and it's a good idea to let tastes flow for there is nothing written about tastes, as the famous axiom of neoclassical economic theory, *de gustibus non est disputandum*, asserts.[8] Moreover, tastes tend to be harmoniously matched.

The Austrian school of economics, that of Hayek and Mises, also took Mandeville's tease seriously and explicitly denies any hint of a power relation. Here, again, we have Mises on the matter:

> Perhaps the eulogists of slavery were not entirely wrong when they asserted that many slaves *were satisfied* with their station and did not aim at changing it. There are perhaps individuals, groups of individuals, and even whole peoples and races who *enjoy* the safety and security provided by bondage; who, *insensible* of humiliation and mortification, are *glad* to pay with a moderate amount of labor for the privilege of sharing in the amenities of a well-to-do household; and in whose eyes subjection to the whims and bad tempers of a master is only a minor evil or no evil at all. (Mises, 2007 [1949]: 629)[9]

Accordingly, there are slaves because this is what they *prefer*, because it is what their particular *psychology* advises. In the passage from the *Grundrisse* (1973) cited above, Marx is clear that, '[t]o be a slave, to be a citizen, are social characteristics', the result of phenomena endogenous to social life. Mises, by contrast, would have it that the condition of slavery or citizenship is prior to social life, is exogenous and comes from *outside*, namely from our psyche. And with these particular tastes and inclinations, we shape the world and occupy our allotted place therein.

Contract, Mises asserts, means symmetry. If the republican tradition, whose analysis of social life always presents unmistakeably institutionalist overtones, tends to cast suspicion on equality before the law or the *isonomy* that governs liberal societies – and according to republicanism, this *isonomy* is perfectly compatible with myriad power relations extending into all the interstices of social life – the liberal Mises views the world with different eyes: 'Where and as far as cooperation is based on contract, the logical relation between the cooperating individuals is symmetrical. They are all parties to interpersonal exchange contracts. John has the same relation to Tom as Tom has to John' (Mises, 2007 [1949]: 195). Indeed, 'no physical violence and compulsion can possibly force a man against his will to remain in the status of the ward of a hegemonic order' (Mises, 2007 [1949]: 196). If inequalities exist, they are purely and simply the result of differences in the innate qualities of individuals and, finally, the ups and downs of their lives.

THE FALLACY OF AUTOGENOUS SOCIAL ORDERS • 49

The world lacks forces that might structure it in any particular way and thus constrain the action of individuals. Light years from Marx, but also from the establishmentarianism of Leo XIII and Max Scheler too, Mises conjures up modern market societies as something like a festival of unrestricted individual choice held in an open field without any fences:

> The selection of the market does not establish social orders, castes, or classes in the Marxian sense. Nor do the entrepreneurs and promoters form an integrated social class. Each individual is free to become a promoter if he relies upon his own ability to anticipate future market conditions better than his fellow citizens and if his attempts to act at his own peril and on his own responsibility are approved by the consumers. (Mises, 2007 [1949]: 312–13)

He has no doubts: if you want to, you can.

We also find echoes of Mandeville's prank in the pluralist social and political science that appeared after the Second World War and has remained influential to the present day. Consider the notion of *polyarchy*, which we owe to Robert Dahl (1971). According to him, a polyarchy is a political-juridical regime based on freedom of association permitting the coexistence of many centres of political action. Dahl's social ontology is born, then, in open opposition to the description of the world offered by the classical theorists of elite autocracy, such as Pareto, Mosca and Michels. Instead of asymmetries of power managed from above by certain oligarchies, Dahl suggests that what we find in social life is a whole plurality of interest and affinity groups occupying positions of equal power that enable them to construct civilly isomorphic relations. 'John has the same relation to Tom as Tom has to John', Mises said, at the level of individual analysis. With regard to the interaction of social groups, Dahl suggests that the social group or organisation X has the same relation with the social group or organisation Y as the group or organisation Y has with the group or organisation X. It matters little whether X and Y are Microsoft, the Brazilian Landless Workers Movement, the Catholic Church, Barcelona Football Club, the Blackwater Protection mercenary group, the Spanish Platform for People Affected by Mortgages, Monsanto or the Happy Hoppy Hare Huggers Club. There are simply groups of individuals with their own particular desires, interests and projects – Mises' famous 'value judgements' – that interact together in a space free of power relations that would establish a well-defined social structure. The bees of the pluralist polyarchy buzz around in a hive that accepts everyone and, like the markets of perfect competition, offers everyone the same opportunities to externalise their own *preferences*. The pluralist social ontology, then, could not be more neoclassical.[10]

Evidently, the shadow of Mandeville's jest is long – very long. There is no shortage of people who, with greater or lesser degrees of cynicism, take up the old piece of mischief and point to the presence of automatisms in the circulation of social life, automatisms that rather than being socially regimented, rest, purely and simply, on clusters of intentional psychologies.[11] So, what kind of public policy and, in particular, what kind of income policy would it make sense to foster on the basis of (neo)liberal postulates?

The actually existing (neo)liberalism, which is much more interventionist and regulatory than what the theory asserts and the mythology repeats (Harvey, 2007), turns out to be inclined to introduce conditional subsidies and to strengthen these conditions so that the working class really 'works' (and recall how workfare, to which I referred earlier, functions). Both Europe and Latin America – but this is also true for other latitudes – have witnessed over the last few decades the extension of these public policy schemes, on many occasions under the auspices of such international institutions as the World Bank and the International Monetary Fund (Lo Vuolo, 2013; Standing, 2009, 2017).

Nonetheless, this is a betrayal of orthodox liberal creed. If the world lacks structure, if social life can be reduced to a monumental collection of handshakes between agents with equal abilities to realise the projects their psychology nurtures, if in the last instance it's true that where there's a will there's a way, what's the point of public policy schemes which, however discreet and selective they may be, can end up distorting the automatic process of social harmonisation of these projects harboured by individuals? In this regard, perhaps the idea of the (then) British prime-minister-to-be, David Cameron, of constructing a true 'big society' (Cameron, 2009) would be more faithful to Mandeville's tease than the efforts of his predecessors, including Labour Party politicians, to introduce workfare schemes.

But what does this *big society* consist of? Cameron's version of it, which had been theorised from since the early 1990s (Willetts, 1994), is that space in which a voluntarist and entrepreneurial climate is created, permitting local communities and the ordinary people who inhabit them to take over the power that was once concentrated in the hands of politicians and state agents, so they can get on with their own life projects, ranging from 'lifelong' capitalist companies through to 'socially innovative' self-managed spaces.[12] All things considered, Cameron asserts, the mere possibility that such projects can get off the ground depends very particularly on politicians and state agencies (the famous 'daddy state') beating a retreat and taking with them the public policy devices that had, with excessive care, narcotised into indolence the British and European populations since the end of the Second World War. Cameron's 'big society' is, then, Mandeville's hive, where the bees unintentionally manufacture the world by means of their devotion, industrious but also indifferent with regard to others, to private desires and projects. It's better, therefore, if the state does nothing. A society becomes a *big society* when it is the people who 'get things done', people whose interests never clash but unfold in parallel. And in those cases where complementarity exists, they intertwine.

Those of us who support the basic income proposal can't just exclaim that this whole thing is bluff and bluster and has nothing to do with us because this kind of bragging, which is undoubtedly more than bragging, could well splatter us too. Indeed, more than a few people see basic income precisely as a way of levering a *big society*. Ultraliberal authors such as the American Charles Murray (2006) have suggested that this retreating state that would make way for a truly liberal 'big society' could incorporate – within the 'minimum' set of tasks it would still perform, once the welfare state is dismantled – the universal and unconditional provision of basic monetary resources understood as a last instance safety net. I devote Chapter 14 to demonstrating that such a possibility constitutes a true dystopia because basic income only has an emancipatory sense if it belongs and contributes to the structuring of a real *popular political economy* consisting of many far-reaching mechanisms.

3

The Liberal-Organicist Synthesis

The orthodox liberal credo is frequently betrayed, which isn't surprising because it's difficult to keep order in a world that supposedly lacks order. Perhaps it should be assumed that some (dis)order does exist and that something must therefore be done about it. If it turns out to be true that the story of the hive is pure mythology – or, still more, a huge, enduring piece of mischief – it will be necessary to get into it and tidy it up a bit. Indeed, faced with the threat posed by the horizontalising political projects the contemporary world is coming to know, more than a few jumpy liberal thinkers and political actors have not hesitated, and do not hesitate, to slide towards establishmentarian positions in order to sustain, using force if necessary, the 'natural order' of things. If we are to assume a social ontology that doesn't accept the existence of autogenous social orders like that of Mandeville's hive, it's better to intervene in order to construct or sustain a vertical order. 'A fascist is nothing other than a frightened liberal', or so goes the famous pronouncement attributed to Lenin, Gramsci and Churchill, depending on who you're listening to. There is no better way to sum things up.

If you think otherwise, just ask the British trade unions that were smashed by the clearly visible iron hand of the liberal Margaret Thatcher. Or those who suffered from the consequences of the revelation of the liberal Spanish minister of justice, Alberto Ruiz-Gallardón, who said that 'governing means, at times, distributing pain'. Historically scrutinised, liberalism has shown very little interest in democracy, when not showing open hostility towards it, and it's well known that it's the labour movement that is really responsible for the democratic elements the modern world possesses (Domènech, 2004). At best, the liberal tradition has had to incorporate democracy as an uncomfortable fait accompli. Well, what sense is there in giving voice and the vote to a mob that can't see beyond its own nose?

In all likelihood, we find the first expression of this curious liberal-organicist synthesis in the political precepts of the conservative wing of French physiocracy, which prevailed in France's economic policy at the end of the *Ancien Régime* and which, after the revolution, tried to contain the 'democratising excesses' of the *sans culottes* social movements. Take, for example, the figure of Le Mercier de la Rivière who, after some years as a colonial administrator in the slave colony of Martinique, published his main work, *The Natural and Essential Order of Political Societies*, in 1767. Here, he affirms that any discussion about inequalities in access to property must be stopped. As Florence Gauthier (2002) says, Le Mercier de la Rivière postulates that inequality of social conditions is something that belongs to the divine order, something resulting from an unequal distribution of property that should also be understood as the consequence of a divine law. In Gauthier's words (2002: 53): 'He had the revelation that certain natural laws determine political societies and that the political belongs in the realm of the divine.' Hence, these laws of creation are divine, natural or physical laws.

Using a prophetic, almost theological tone, this French physiocrat is talking about nothing less than a natural order that is the work of God and only God, while affirming the existence of a 'social physics' with a very specific aim, namely to establish and maintain the natural order of social life. To achieve this, it would be necessary to terminate all attempts to submit to debate or discussion any aspect pertaining to the distribution of property and allocation of external resources. In the end, we're talking about physical laws and, once demonstrated, these are not to be disputed (Gauthier, 2002: 53). But who demonstrates these laws?

Here, the political project of physiocracy shows its most anti-democratic and organicist face. There are some 'experts' who are truly capable of shedding light on the laws in which natural physics takes shape, a ruling group that is indisputably capable of making the nature of these laws visible to the eyes of decision-makers. The masses, however, don't understand and can't understand anything. This then justifies the presence of a 'legal despotism' that is by no means arbitrary. Only those few men who, touched by the grace of God, have evidence of this natural order with which God has endowed us can rule. In effect, this 'legal despotism is necessarily inscribed in this conception that gives physical laws a character of indisputable evidence: a political society is not found in the essential natural order unless it submits or is submitted to physical laws. Hence, the function of political power is to ensure that society conforms to these laws' (Gauthier, 2002: 59). And it's worth noting, once again with Gauthier (2002: 69), that the political precepts of Le Mercier de la Rivière in *The Natural and Essential Order of Political Societies* come 'not from abstract ideas but from the most specific kind of practices of the colonial slave-owning and segregationist society in which he had lived'.

Later on, French nineteenth-century doctrinaire liberals, and twenti-eth-century theorists of liberalism and neoliberalism, would resuscitate the old Pauline apology for domination – 'there is no authority except from God, and those which exist are established by God' (Romans 13:1–7) – by way of a providentialism which, like the social theology of physiocracy, points to a supposed intrinsic ability of markets, so long as they are assisted by the enlightened mind of the expert oligarchy, to assign to all social agents a role, a certain niche within the existing economic order, which is what it is – it's better not to touch it lest we ruin everything.[1] Recently, after the neolib-eral turn of capitalism, which started in the early 1970s, this discourse has become omnipresent among a technocracy or, let's say, a neophysiocracy that is constantly warning us about the dangers lurking in the introduction of 'distortions' into the natural order of markets or, as Leo XIII put it in 1891, 'confusion and disorder into the commonweal'. Take, for example, this technocracy's insistence on freezing monetary policy along Friedman's lines and removing it from the public agenda which, in good measure, is what happened with the Maastricht Treaty that was signed in February 1992.

To sum up, it's a matter of ensuring that any operation that individuals want or might want to carry out in the social body, in the establishmentarian pyramid, occurs in the security provided by a framework of clearly defined property rights and an unambiguous process of assigning tasks and func-tions, starting with labour contracts. For example, François Guizot, one of the fathers of nineteenth-century doctrinaire liberalism, anticipates Leo XIII when he states in his *General History of Civilisation in Europe* (1828) that, 'when the world submits to its natural course, the natural inequality among men freely unfolds and each occupies the place he is capable of occupying'.[2] This is nothing more nor less than what Domènech (1989: 239) called 'the political-theological embassy of liberal apology for capitalism: that the city of God should come to Earth shaping a *natural order* in which the supreme judges would be men themselves and their pillars, property rights, the market, and rule of law'.[3]

Let's pause for a moment in the domain of labour contracting. In a passage of *Human Action*, the liberal Mises also drifts into positions typical of the liberal-organicist synthesis. He says:

> The joy of labor [...] depends to some extent on ideological factors. The worker rejoices in his *place* in society and his active cooperation in its pro-ductive effort. If one disparages this ideology and replaces it by another which represents the wage earner as the distressed victim of ruthless

exploiter, one turns the joy of labor into a feeling of disgust and tedium. (2007 [1949]: 590–1)[4]

In the framework of the capitalist economy, then, there exists a 'common venture' that situates us beyond the simple antagonism that would be defined by the 'hostile clash' of supposed 'incompatible interests'. The job of capitalist competition is to assign to each member of the 'social system' the tasks and 'places' from which he or she can render better service to this 'totality' we call 'society'. 'Social order' means 'harmony' among the projects of the members of the pyramid: indeed, the 'ward' prefers 'obedience' and integrates himself into the 'hegemonic bond', into the 'hegemonic societal body' (Mises, 2007 [1949]). The echoes of organicist thought and terminology couldn't be more evident.

Moreover, the providentialist distortion of Smith's metaphor of the 'invisible hand' constitutes a palpable manifestation of the liberal-organicist synthesis. The confluence in the nineteenth century of the doctrinaire liberal credo and Christian establishmentarian organicism enabled many people to suggest, repeatedly, that the invisible hand was the modern instrument employed by divine providence to *confine* humans in their appropriate niches. Adam Smith couldn't have been more distant from such an approach as he always insisted on the need to constitute politically – which is to say from *within* social life or endogenously – a world free of privileges, both late feudal and proto-industrial, so that the bulk of the ordinary people in that social life – artisans, peasant farmers, producers and free traders – could develop their life plans unimpeded by obstacles and hindrance, without being constrained by the dictates of a supposed planner external to social life who would establish fixed laws and 'natural and essential orders' (Casassas, 2010, 2013).

However, Adam Smith was hijacked by the attempt at the liberal-organicist synthesis. It doesn't matter that Smith stressed the importance of the social genesis and making of human freedoms and destinies. Freedoms, he said, are constructed in an earthly world and thanks to the efforts of broad collectivites that are committed to the task. It doesn't matter that Smith's moral philosophy had imbibed from the best of the materialist tradition which, in the last instance, goes back to Lucretius and Democritus. Who cares? As Argemí (2006) argues, the formulations of the social scientists and Christian theologians of the second half of the nineteenth century – all of whom were openly inclined to an apologetics of a capitalism that was in full bloom and development – determine that the supposed action of the 'invisible hand' must be understood in terms of intervention by a capricious and divine providence that arranges the order of the world in such a way that the devotion of individuals to the activity entrusted to them, in the social niche allotted to them, appears as the necessary and sufficient condition for enjoyment of 'moral sentiments' that have been devalued to the status of catechetical 'good practices and habits'. Social calm and the peace of mind of everyone depend on this.

So what, then, is the role of political institutions? In particular, what kind of income policies follow from all these approaches? Once again, the liberal-organicist synthesis leads us to the disciplinary regime typical of capitalist labour markets and also to the logic of conditional subsidies. We've already seen that the liberal-organicist system is the response to a big fright. What fright? The fear of those who control the worlds of production and labour that those of us who produce and work for them will stop doing so. In fact, this, and this alone, is at the heart of the ambitions of contemporary emancipatory traditions: providing ourselves with tools so that we can all reject impositions and gain access to those activities (in plural) that we truly feel are ours. This is why liberal-organicist political precepts are geared, first of all, to making us work in capitalist labour markets and, in the case of women, to do whatever is necessary to get them to reproduce the workforce. No wonder property rights and labour-contracting arrangements – temping agencies, for example – have been set up to hurry along up the business of setting the dispossessed majority to work. Second, liberal-organicist political precepts also aim at introducing public policy schemes that 'activate' the working population, reinforce their 'employability' – recall again the famous 'workfare' – and enable them to return to the labour market in cases where they have dropped out of it. Capitalist social structuring crucially depends on the proper functioning of all these mechanisms.

Needless to say, the devices used by liberal-organicist politics acquire, in the past and in the present, overtones of a demophobia which we've already seen in the governing practices of the physiocratic elite in France. In fact, all of these 'labour training and activation' policies are highly discretionary for those governing bodies which, like the 'legal despotism' advocated by Le Mercier de la Rivière in eighteenth-century France, and without asking too many questions to anyone, vertically determine the division of labour – of *all kinds of work* – for our world. Anyway, what would the lazy, ignorant masses know about what's good for them and what's in everyone's interests? Heavy doses of paternalism are called for in order to restore and maintain order and calm the troubled waters.

4

Resisting Tutelage: Fraternity for the Civilising of a Conflictive World

Leo XIII said that, in human society, the class of owners and that of workers, true 'brother' classes, 'should dwell in harmony and agreement, so as to maintain the balance of the body politic'. They need each other: 'capital cannot do without labor, nor labor without capital'. And that is no small thing, for '[m]utual agreement results in the beauty of good order'.[1] It happens, however, that more than a century earlier, Adam Smith, who was much more resolved to study the wage setting and labour contracting that really existed, had stated that: 'In the long-run the workman may be as necessary to his master as his master is to him; but *the necessity is not so immediate.*' Indeed, when there are disputes between the 'two parties, *whose interests are by no means the same* [...] the masters can hold out much longer. A landlord, a farmer, a master manufacturer, or merchant, though they did not employ a single workman, could generally live a year or two upon the stocks which they have already acquired. Many workmen could not subsist a week, few could subsist a month, and scarce any a year without employment'. The fact is that workers are faced with 'the *necessity* [...] *of submitting* for the sake of present subsistence'.[2] This is precisely the state of affairs where the subalternity of the working class is to be found. Hence, as opposed to an organicist social ontology that doesn't question the existence of social classes but denies that there is conflict among them, and a liberal social ontology that contests the very idea that there is any kind of social structuring or compartmentalisation of the world into classes, Adam Smith, together with the bulk of the republican tradition, from Aristotle to Marx, affirmed that there is a social structure that violently divides us. For Smith, social life is split into classes in conflict, into classes or ranks that are rooted in deeply unequal processes – 'bloody' ones too, as Marx noted somewhat later – of private appropriation of external material and symbolic resources (Casassas, 2010, 2013).

According to this institutional social ontology, embraced by the republican tradition and inherited by socialist traditions, conflict thus appears as something inherent to social life. This is always the case, unless institutional mechanisms (e.g. in the sphere of work) are introduced to ensure that social interaction can take place on a basis of civil equality, which is to say in conditions of mutual recognition by social actors as independent subjects in their own right. Seriously speaking, this is the only way the word *contract* can be used in any minimally robust sense. In effect, if a contract is to be a contract, it must be a real *(con)tract* (like a digestive tract, which goes back to the Latin *contractus*, to draw several objects together, to shorten, lessen, abridge (distances), with a reduction of differences). And a real *(con)tract* is an agreement or *treaty* between two genuine peers or civilly similar social actors, with the aim of instituting something in *common*, for example a working relationship.[3] However, when dispossession obliges the lower, expropriated classes to act 'with the folly and extravagance of desperate men'[4] and, finally, to sign contracts blindly, these contracts are not *(con)tracts* (or any kind of being drawn closer together) but outright impositions by privileged groups.

Yet these contracts that aren't *(con)tracts* are signed – masses of them! Their social expansion in the contemporary world has gone unchecked, turning labour markets into massive carceral institutions. But why carceral? Basically, because human beings don't seek them out (*en masse*) because we want to – because that's what we *would prefer* – but because capitalist dispossession forces us to enter them, frequently in a 'desperate' state of 'folly', and to sign *non-contracts* so as to obtain the means of subsistence that Adam Smith wrote about. And, once we're in them, we're like prisoners clinging to the bars of their windows looking with dread, not inwards, but outside at a harsh desert, the desolate wasteland left behind by large-scale dispossession which we don't want to go back to under any circumstances. Here, I stress that it's not in vain that the labour market, under capitalism, constitutes the only space reserved for the vast social majorities whereby they can find some sustenance by means of a salary or daily wage. This is a real prison without jailers because no one in their right mind wants to escape, so the capitalist labour markets take advantage of our fear of the outside world, our anxious eagerness to remain locked in these markets, and to apply whatever disciplinary mechanisms are deemed necessary (now including guards and foremen (Jayadev and Bowles, 2006)) to get the labour force to work (Roberts, 2017).

It's true that labour markets sometimes spit us out. It's not easy to employ so many people and, moreover, it's not a bad idea to have a large pool of unemployed workers who, begging for a job at any price, put downward pressure on the working conditions in the market (Kalecki, 1943; Manjarín and Szlinder, 2016). And desperate problems call for desperate remedies.

Nobody is unaware of the fact that it's advisable to find bars we can cling to, in the form of a job or something like a job, at any cost, including 'folly' if need be or, failing that, a conditional benefit, or something like it, that will guide us towards a future job. As Guy Standing puts it (2011, 2014), capitalist precarisation turns us into true and skilled 'supplicants' of both things.

As early as the fourth century BCE, Aristotle had noticed that the subaltern condition of the wage labourer was not much different from that of the slave. The manual worker, he said, is faced with a kind of 'limited' slavery.[5] Why? Might it have something to do with the fact that we're speaking of 'manual' workers, people who work with their hands? No, not at all. Aristotle's thesis is based on the empirical evidence that, in Athens of the fourth century BCE, too, wage workers tended to be dependent on the will of others. This was a dispossessed population with scarce resources who, as a result of this – when they signed a labour contract for 'services' whereby they sold their labour power for a wage – were at the complete disposal of those who bought such labour power (Domènech, 2004). Like the slave, the wage-earning worker delegates to the proprietor of the means of production the power to decide what is produced, how, why, at what pace, with whom, in what environment, and so on. But he does so for a certain number of hours per day, which makes him a 'limited' or 'part-time' slave.[6] Engels (1845) described the situation of the mid-nineteenth century as follows:

> The only difference as compared with the old, outspoken slavery is this, that the worker of today seems to be free because he is not sold once for all, but piecemeal by the day, the week, the year, and because no one owner sells him to another, but he is forced to sell himself in this way instead, being the slave of no particular person, but of the whole property-holding class.

The approach to basic income presented in these pages aims to offer suggestions for overturning the capitalist disciplinary machinery. In the 'outside' world of this carceral labour market, there is something more than a 'desolate wasteland'. All things considered, no sane person should abstain from seeking mechanisms to counteract large-scale dispossession and explore the open territories that are not wastelands at all, which spread out before one when social orders are horizontalised and resources are made available so that everyone without exception can freely choose a life. That's all very well, but what resources and procedures, which make them available to agents, are we talking about? I'll discuss this briefly and conclude.

The republican tradition – from Aristotle to twentieth-century constitutionalism, passing through the Dutch, English, American and French revolutions and, finally, Marx and the various kinds of socialism – couldn't be clearer. It is impossible to choose a life freely, impossible to decide freely whether to do some jobs but not others, unless we previously have sets of resources that make us socially invulnerable actors. Freedom requires property. But this property shouldn't be understood purely and simply as having a duly registered title deed in one's pocket, although this shouldn't be overlooked either, but as a guarantee of access to, and control of, material and immaterial goods that are decisive, in every space and society, for living dignified and meaningful lives. Just as the distribution of wealth through sweeping agrarian reforms had a key role in the political agenda of modern republican revolutions, it's up to today's republicanism to find ways (in plural) to assign resources to citizens as a whole so that each and every one of us can reject lives that are imposed on us (Widerquist, 2013) and claim, individually and collectively, the lives we really yearn to live. Freedom requires property, then, because property confers bargaining power (Casassas, 2016a, 2016b; Casassas and Raventós, 2007).[7]

This old republican insight was to be taken up by the bulk of the socialist tradition, which sought to find mechanisms for distributing resources pertaining to industrial society in order to improve everyone's ability to (co-)determine the world around us, starting with work and production. Indeed, socialist movements inherited the aspirations of the left wing of the French Revolution (Domènech, 2005) and also, to go back a little further, of the German revolutionaries of 1520 and the English revolutionaries of 1640, who tried to bring the poor peasantry as a whole, as well as the class of small artisans, into civil society or, in other words, into a world made for and by free men or *freemen* and not by serfs or *bondsmen* (Harrington, 1992). Thus, at the International Working Man's Association congress, held in Geneva in 1866, Marx (1866) had the following to say about the cooperativist movement: 'Its great merit is to practically show, that the present pauperising, and despotic system of the subordination of labour to capital can be superseded by the republican and beneficent system of the association of free and equal producers.'[8]

Freedom requires property because property confers bargaining power and Marx and most socialist traditions assure us that the most effective and feasible way of obtaining resources that give us this power of negotiation, enabling us to reject what we don't want and achieve what we do, entails putting into practice whatever possible forms of 'republican association of free and equal producers' we can imagine today.

And imagining forms of this possible 'republican association of free and equal producers' nowadays, which should definitely extend to and include reproductive work, is nothing other than putting together new kinds of the 'moral economy of the crowd' which, by means of sets of material practices and symbolic representations rooted in an everyday life chosen by ourselves, would allow us to establish horizontal social orders where everyone has a voice and a vote. Thinking about freedom at work – in *all domains of work* – from the standpoint of emancipatory traditions means, then, resisting the paternalistic tutelage of establishmentarian and liberal-organicist orders, (dis)ordering the blocks of the pyramid and rearranging the resulting pieces so that we are the ones who, from each and every one of the spaces and interstices of social life, shape the world.

So, why something like a basic income? What role might this measure play in favour of a fraternal horizontalisation of social life? As I've said, republican freedom requires property, this being understood as access to (and control of) sets of resources that give us the bargaining power necessary to (co-)organise an interdependence that is satisfactory for everybody. Such resources must therefore be subject to the minimum possible conditions, if indeed there must be any at all. Accordingly, the unconditional nature of basic income, a monetary grant at least equivalent to the poverty line, given to all citizens individually, universally and unconditionally, can only strengthen the emancipatory character of income policies, just as unconditionality does, when it exists, in health policy, to give just one more example. Unconditional resources are resources we possess *ex ante*, from square one of the social interaction. In brief, they are resources that empower us to move through social life as a whole – job centres, domestic spaces, the counters of public administration, spheres of sociopolitical participation, and so on – without exposing our wishes and freedom to the rapacity of certain social actors who might want to impose on us forms of life we simply don't want.

Hence, unlike the conditional subsidies of traditional welfare systems or the *workfare* world, and also unlike the jobs allotted to us by those who advocate so-called *job guarantee*, subsidies and jobs that make us interact with an inevitable status quo and which, in case of accident, go into action to help us *ex post*, paternalistically and establishmentarian style, in keeping with our status as castaways – poor, sick, incapacitated and victims of all possible kinds of misfortune – basic income is part of an unconditional package of measures which, saving us from disaster every inch of the way, allows us to bypass the status quo, starting with the capitalist labour markets, and equips us to make our way amid fraternal or, in other words, democratic and democratising social relations. The possibilities for individual and collective self-determination crucially depend on things being like this.

PART II

Holding the Gaze:
Republicanism and Democracy

'A guy from some foundation came to sell us a project that they want to do with the poor. And they're asking where they are.' This is a true story. So true that it happened in the offices of the public administration of some place in the south of Europe whose name I prefer not to remember. The person telling me about it couldn't get over his astonishment. 'The deal was a joint venture between a fitness centre chain and a takeaway food chain and it's all about runners-in-solidarity who get together in teams to get food rations for the poor by doing jogging. And they wanted us to give them information about where these poor people are.'

This book isn't against jogging or running or joint ventures or takeaway food. I'd even say that it's not unconditionally against trading with poverty – in the end, 'the poor', whoever they are, and given the particular forms of their poverty and also the absence of viable alternatives for getting out of the mire, should be asked about how they want to deal with the situation they're in. And what can I say? There are many forms of survival. And watching a bunch of 'food runners' arrive every morning with their little glowing backpacks and pious smiles might even be a little bit funny. We can keep something of the right to joke because the poor person doesn't necessarily lose the ability to unmask grotesqueness because of being poor. Anyway, the lentil salad might taste good. Who knows?

But this book is unconditionally against poverty. So is the person who told me the story about the runners, who is still astounded by what he'd experienced. There is a moral intuition, of deep Kantian echoes, according to which benevolence towards the dispossessed rides on the back of earlier injustices, which is to say all the acquisitions and confiscatory appropriations of people's freedom that are transferred intergenerationally. In fact, the former couldn't exist without the latter. So, setting up teams of food runners isn't only cringe making because it's such a mawkish idea, but it's also shocking because of what it tells us about the consolidation of birth-right privileges rooted in a profoundly unequal distribution of property rights. There is no philanthropy without prior spoliation and dispossession of common goods, which is why Kant insisted, before Marx, that it's essential to 'expropriate the expropriators' by means of income tax systems and public policies that would unconditionally guarantee the presence of resources to ensure a dignified existence for everyone. Taxation can't be a discretionary, voluntary, philanthropic handout of the type that Mises, Hayek and other members and supporters of the Austrian school find acceptable. In the best of cases, philanthropy has the property of all the forms of love: however deep and rapturous they are, they can cease to be so and can fade away, for they are at the mercy of fate. A life worth living isn't guaranteed by love but, as Kant said, it's guaranteed politically, through institutional devices that guarantee genuine positions of social invulnerability so that we can all go about our lives without imposed hindrance or constraints.[1]

We've come thus far, then, to point out that if proposals such as that of a basic income make sense, it is because they free us from the obligation to beg for a lentil salad, or to celebrate and be grateful for the runners' capricious decision to turn up nimbly and joyfully with the little bag full of benevolence, runners we don't even know, and perhaps don't want to know. Proposals such as basic income equip us with resources *before* we have to face the situation of managing a conflict and not *after* the conflict has ended up with an unequal, expropriating and openly confiscatory distribution of resources that could have been for everyone but have now become private property, the result of privation, and hence excluding property. These are proposals born of an awareness that poverty – exclusion from access to existing resources – is not only privation but also dependence on the arbitrariness of others, a fatal threat to effective freedom (Raventós, 2007; Szreter, 2022). Because of all of this, they are proposals that meet the demand posed by democratic republicanism that the public powers, which we should understand and nourish as a true common good, should unconditionally make available to everyone all those resources – material and symbolic – that are deemed necessary so that all of us can be self-determining in all the spheres of social life. I now look at this in more detail.

5

Socioeconomic Independence
and Worlds in Common

So far, I've been talking about rejecting lives that have been imposed on us and conquering, individually and collectively, the lives we really yearn to have. This, in a nutshell, expresses the republican ethical-political precepts that inspire all the pages of this book. And this requires property or control of sets of (im)material resources that make us socioeconomically independent. Marx said it in a famous passage of his *Critique of the Gotha Programme*, and he couldn't have been clearer:

> [T]he man who possesses no other property than his labor power must, in all conditions of society and culture, be the slave of other men who have made themselves the owners of the material conditions of labor. He can only work with their permission, hence live only with their permission. (1875: 6)

But you have to be daring to live 'without permission'. Audacity is an indispensable immaterial resource for anyone who ventures to live without the tutelage of others. But it's difficult to be bold when we're materially and/or symbolically dependent on those whose tutelage we want to shake off: there is too much obedience and too much servility, and probably for too long. If we are to live without having to ask permission, every day, of 'those who have made themselves the owners of the material conditions of labor', our daring needs, more than anything else, to go hand in hand with a whole renewed rebelliousness aimed at challenging the property rights that emanate from these confiscatory, usurpatory appropriations of external resources, which Kant and Marx spoke of (and, before them, John Locke (Mundó, 2015, 2017) and Adam Smith (Casassas, 2010, 2013)), a revitalised rebelliousness that is determined to find and clear the way for assaulting, and for submitting to, communal control of the spaces in which we engage in all kinds of work. Only when we have managed to take effective control of adequate sets of resources can we become fully bold and live the lives we have truly chosen. Can public policies of a universal and unconditional nature, such as basic income, come to constitute real levers for popular reappropriation of these many and varied spaces of work and life? As we shall see, there are abundant and powerful reasons for thinking they can.

More recently, Philip Pettit (2012, 2014) has suggested a metaphor that we can use when trying to ascertain whether individuals or groups enjoy this ability to get on with freely chosen lives: the 'eyeball test', or test of the gaze. Are we in a position to hold the gaze of those with whom we interact? When we are about to engage in any kind of social relationship, are we able to look others in the eye without fear of reprimand or reprisal? Or are we obliged to lower our gaze because we are materially and/or symbolically dependent on them? According to Pettit, a free life in the republican sense, in demo-cratically established social relations – in the domain of work, for example – requires the ability to hold one's head high and be prepared to (co-)deter-mine, free of threats and coercion, the world around us.

Within the theoretical distillate of the republican tradition that we owe to philosophers who, in the wake of the historiographic work of Skinner, Pocock and other members of the Cambridge school, have worked out the basic conceptual lines of republicanism, the notion of freedom as non-dom-ination stands out as aspiring to provide the backbone for the whole republican theoretical construct. Let's see what this definition of republican freedom has to offer. Pettit (1997, 2001) says that we are free when we are not subject to arbitrary interference and, *moreover*, when we live in a social and institutional milieu which guarantees that there isn't the slightest possi-bility that we would be submitted to such interference. That the slave should feel well treated by the master, either because he is a kind person or because the slave is skilled in flattery, is not enough. Neither is it enough if the wage worker, a true 'part-time slave', is listened to when those who control the productive unit decide how to classify and direct his or her activities. It's not enough when the desires and aspirations of a woman are met by the partner on whom she depends. In short, not being subjected to (arbitrary) *interfer-ence* isn't enough because this is very much about not being *interferable*. The slave, the wage worker and the woman of my examples are in situations of socioeconomic and, hence, civil dependence, which makes them profoundly vulnerable as it means that they can be forced to act and live to suit inter-ests, values and procedures that they in no way experience as their own. They simply adapt their conduct to what's expected of them, even when the dictum hasn't been explicitly formulated. There are automatic and inertial forms of behaviour and also of self-censorship that are closely linked with what (we believe) those who dominate us want from us.

However, the tradition of classical or doctrinaire liberalism that was codified at the beginning of the nineteenth century (Domènech, 2004) is committed to the notion of freedom as equality before the law, or *isonomy*, which, as we've seen, is limited to demanding that there should be no interference in the private sphere of the individual's existence. Hence, one is 'liberally' free when not declared as a slave or serf – as we all have to be 'equal before the law' – and *lucky* enough to live without too much meddling by others. What counts is non-interference. It matters little, then, that wage workers or dependent women – and even slaves, if we take the argument through to the end – are wage workers, dependent women or slaves, which is to say, social actors situated in a social and institutional milieu that makes them prone to interference, submitted to another's arbitrary will. For liberalism, the material conditions of freedom are nothing more than a pipedream, a superfluous intellectual artifice without the slightest political-normative interest. The republican tradition, by contrast, understands that no freedom is possible without materially based personal independence.

Here, I need to introduce two nuances without which the sense of the republican approach to freedom vanishes. First, presenting socioeconomic independence as a necessary condition for republican freedom doesn't mean understanding it as a sufficient condition as well. Indeed, there are significant cultural and symbolic factors that can undermine all efforts to materially consolidate the positions of those who are socially vulnerable. For example, however many material resources are made available to women, they will have scant room for manoeuvre while the cultural representations of the patriarchy remain firmly entrenched in the world. The battle, then, must also be a battle for the cultural and symbolic hegemony that is equally as necessary as the material base.

The second point, which is more than a nuance, leads us to the very heart of the republican political project: the socioeconomic independence I speak of must never lead us into a world consisting of a whole jumble of isolated, unnoticed atoms. The republican project is one that is aimed at the construction of society, a shared social life. Hence, the socioeconomic independence I'm talking about is the tool that should make possible the emergence of an interdependence that is truly desired by all parties. Indeed, the world is *already* interdependent. The tale of a Robinson Crusoe secluded in some remote corner of the world is simply that: a story. The question, then, is to find out who participates in the process of shaping this consubstantial inter-dependence, and how.

This brings us to the importance of being able to distinguish analytically and empirically between 'arbitrary' interferences and 'non-arbitrary' inter-ferences. In Pettit's (1997: 55) words:

> When we say that an act of interference is perpetrated on an *arbitrary* basis, then, we imply that like any arbitrary act it is chosen or not chosen at the agent's pleasure ... that it is chosen or rejected without reference to the interests, or the opinions, of those affected. The choice is not forced to track what the interests of those others require according to their own judgements.[1]

The problem, then, is *arbitrary* interference. In fact, the act of interfering in a non-arbitrary way – of intertwining our life stories and instituting social relations that are respectful of the interests and desires of those involved – isn't only non-problematic, it also constitutes the starting point for a meaningful life in society. In other words, the materially and symbolically grounded independence promoted by republicanism leaves the way open for being able to administer all the ways of saying 'no' that are necessary to be able to pronounce the many kinds of 'yes' to the multitude of social relations we probably desire but which, since we are dispossessed, we must renounce because we're obliged to clutch at the straws we are 'offered', for example, in the labour markets. It's not, then, a matter of again 'saving our lives' – in the labour markets once again – and forgetting about living, because it turns out that we are tied hand and feet by the arbitrary will of others. It's about being able to look up and equip ourselves with the necessary resources to get moving and to (non-arbitrarily) interfere with others as much as is necessary to keep living in and reproducing a world that is effectively common. Are we capable of cultivating, as Marina Garcés (2013) suggests, a singular and collective voice that will let us say 'this life is mine'? Or, what amounts to the same thing, can we recover Harrington's revolutionary gesture, which, in the middle of England's convulsive seventeenth century, incited us not to go through life as *bondsmen* but as *freemen* – and free women too, we would add today – who unite to take for themselves a life of their own (Harrington, 1992)?

But the *neo-republican* analysis of Pettit and Skinner can and must be taken beyond Pettit and Skinner themselves because, despite the brilliant sophistication of their proposal, neither Pettit nor Skinner have proven able to give due emphasis to the significance of the central social institution in the normative republican scheme: property and the rights associated with it. The importance of the task of studying the formation of the sociohistoric contexts in which concepts are analysed and managed is beyond dispute. But this means placing the text being studied in the context, not only of other texts of the day – and Skinner (1969) refers to this when he insists that we should try to put the 'text in context' – but also, and especially, in the context of the social and economic structure and that of the historical struggles in which individuals, situated in openly confrontational social classes, fight for control of the material bases of existence. This is something that the academic neo-republicanism of the Cambridge school, from which Pettit imbibes, has rather neglected. It would be difficult to find a more perspicacious summary of this than that offered by the Marxist feminist historian and philosopher Ellen Meiksins Wood (2008):

> Historical contexts, for them [the founding fathers of the historiographical Cambridge school], are languages, utterances, words. It appears that only some words are worth listening to; but, more fundamentally, the social and material conditions in which words are deployed are deliberately excluded. In Skinner's magisterial two-volume history of political ideas from 1300 to 1600, The Foundations of Modern Political Thought, which deals with a period marked by major social and economic developments that loomed very large in political theory and practice, we learn little, if anything, about – for instance – relations between aristocracy and peasantry, about agriculture, land distribution and tenure, about urbanisation, trade, commerce and the burgher class, or about social protest and conflict.

It turns out that when one pays attention to this socio-historical context surrounding the shaping of republican political discourse, one realises that 'this theory and this political practice' that are at stake are closely linked with property rights over external resources. In other words, when one places texts in the contexts not only of other texts but also in the bulk of social relations structuring a historically given society, the question of property or of control over a significant set of resources that would confer sufficient bargaining power to pass Pettit's eyeball test takes on a central role, and it is precisely this that Pettit neglects.[2] According to the sociology of republican freedom, therefore, this social and institutional scenario that must guarantee not only that we do not suffer (arbitrary) *interference* but also that we aren't *interferable* – for such is the condition of the free man – must result from property and this property, as we have seen, shouldn't be understood as having a duly registered title deed in one's pocket (although this shouldn't be ruled out either) but should be understood in broader terms, which is to say as access to (and control of) sets of resources that can guarantee the socioeconomic independence of everyone.[3] Hence, the insistence on emphasising the inherently *property-focused* nature of the republican approach to freedom (Bertomeu, 2005; Casassas and Raventós, 2007; Domènech, 2004; Raventós, 2007).

Freedom, then, requires that we're guaranteed resources without which we'd be at great risk of being subjected to the arbitrary rule of others. But wait a minute! Some theorists of what's been called 'radical republicanism' or even 'republican socialism' have made a point of asking whether we're really sure that these 'other agents' interfere or try to arbitrarily interfere in our lives in a fully *intentional* way. Recently, more than a few voices have been raised to suggest that this domination, which should concern us, has something 'structural' about it.[4] Basically, there are two reasons for this. First, in capitalism, the way property rights are organised to exclude the working population from access to (and control of) productive resources is what makes capitalist exploitation and class domination inevitable. Second, all of this means that, in the end, workers don't toil for Mr or Ms A, B or C (as did slaves, who knew all too well who their master was) but do so for *some* of them, namely A, B, C or any other member of the entire alphabet, of the capitalist *class*. So, the workers of today's world are obliged to work for others, for at least *some* member(s) of the property-owning class, but, unlike the slave or the feudal serf, they can't identify their *own* particular overlord. In this sense, we'd have forms of 'structural' or 'class' domination. This is why, as we've already seen, Engels suggested in his *Condition of the Working Class in England* (1845) that 'the only difference as compared with the old, outspoken slavery is [...] that the worker of today [is] the slave of no particular person, but of the whole property-holding class'.[5]

So much for 'structural' domination. But there is more to it than that. Other analysts have suggested that, in this capitalist domination, there is an 'impersonal' element that would also call into question the supposed intentionality of the owners of the means of production in their role of dominators. Why? Because what rules, at the end of the day, are *impersonal* 'market forces' that oblige workers *and entrepreneurs* to comply with the social roles assigned to them. Both are slaves to 'market' imperatives, to a vast array of accumulated decisions that have been accruing over time.

Hence, domination would be 'impersonal' because it's not connected with the action of identifiable specific agents. In brief, workers are limited to their tasks as workers, and entrepreneurs, if they want to survive as such, are limited to their own particular functions: managing, exploiting, competing, etc.

Theories about the 'impersonal' and 'structural' components of capitalist social domination have certainly made it easier to understand the limits of freedom in this social formation. Yet are we sure that the intentionality of social domination tends to be diluted under capitalism? Might this not actually be an exercise of *structuralism* with all the possible ontological and methodological problems entailed by structuralist leanings? On closer inspection, I believe it's perfectly compatible to assume that the main structuring mechanisms of contemporary capitalism have been intentionally engineered by certain actors while stating at the same time that (1) domination is *perceived* to a greater extent than in the premodern world as something that's linked to a certain social 'structure' and even something 'impersonal'; and (2) that the fact that there is intentional action by the dominating minority doesn't exclude unintended and even undesirable or perverse effects of this action, for example when the dominating minority is 'obliged' to perform its roles as such.

In other words, in complex social formations such as capitalism it may be more difficult to work out who dominates whom and how, but we should try to ensure that an account based on the supposed 'market forces' or on attributeless 'rules of the game' doesn't end up containing more metaphysics than explanatory potential vis-à-vis the reality that surrounds us. In still other words, of course it's difficult to achieve an exhaustive reconstruction of the whole causal chain underpinning the ways in which the population is dominated – or how it's stripped of its freedoms – but it's important not to forget that there have been efforts to explain at least part of it, not least by Marx who, in chapter 24 of *Capital* (1976 [1867–94]), volume 1, set out to identify the original driving forces that gave rise to this very long sequence of events. In the same vein, it's also important to bear in mind the problems of mechanistic circularity arising from certain twentieth-century brands of structuralist Marxism.[6]

To take a common example, the home-delivery driver who, in order to make ends meet, must combine this work with other contracts or mini-contracts, may not be sure about exactly who the dominator is, who placed him or her in this position, and against whom he or she must fight, assuming it were possible, but this doesn't mean we can forget about trying to understand and explain, for example, the reforms of labour markets and legislation that have allowed the emergence of labour scenarios and contractual relationships such as those the delivery driver is well acquainted with (and it should be made clear right away that no theorist of 'radical republicanism' has suggested that we should stop inquiring into these reforms or any other mechanism that would explain the emergence of structures that shape our world). In fact, these reforms are linked with certain concrete authorships, interests and *intentions*. As Raymond Boudon aptly suggested, if we open up 'black boxes' (and so we should), we might come across real surprises in the form of causal mechanisms of an intentional nature that don't, not even partially, escape our wish to identify and explain them. As Cicerchia (2019) rightly suggests, we mustn't give up on explaining the social processes that reproduce the 'structural domination'. In effect, certain frequently identifiable agents occupy certain social positions that prompt them to *intentionally* produce structures which, as we know, even if they harbour high doses of unforeseen effects, still tend to create relations of domination.

It's a good idea, then, to find out whether 'structural' domination is an ontologically objective reality or, on the contrary, a problem of, let's say, 'perception'. Affirming the inevitable nature of labour domination in the also inevitable capitalist labour markets is perfectly compatible with stating, too, that this 'structural inevitability of the market' – of markets in plural, starting with labour markets – is the result of the intentional action of certain actors, of certain social minorities or oligarchies who (1) have had and do have the ability to consolidate, legally and institutionally, processes of dispossession; and (2) who have held and do hold in their hands the tools and the *will* to constitute markets in a way that turns them into self-serving oligarchic spaces by means of a 'tyrannical political economy', as Robespierre put it – needless to say, far from being metaphysical entities that dropped out of the sky, markets should be understood as social institutions that were constituted and are reproduced in keeping with a certain intention or set of intentions. None other than Adam Smith (1981) insisted that the fixing of terms and conditions of commercial exchanges is not infrequently the result of 'concerted' and thus highly intentional sets of actions by members of the capital-owning class in conditions of the utmost secrecy for, without such concealment, he said, public opinion would put a stop to it. Likewise, Søren Mau (2023) has recently offered a notion of 'economic power' as one held by capitalists which, while not operating *directly* through material or ideological coercion, is based on the ability, peculiar to them, to (*intention-*

ally, I would add) reshape the material and symbolic conditions of social reproduction.[7]

As for 'impersonal' domination, it must be asked to what extent it is true that the capitalist class or, better said, its members are *forced* to dominate the dispossessed, and also the extent to which the working class or, better said, its members are *obliged* to meekly accept this domination, as if they were inescapably doomed to it. It's evident that there is and always has been (even in precapitalist social formations, however much the theorists of 'impersonal domination' associate this struggle to stay in the group of dominators with the strictly capitalist world) a battle among elites to survive as elites, for example through the most ferocious competition and also the most brutal exploitation. However, this doesn't mean that there hasn't been a *decision* by the dominators to remain in that group, just as it doesn't mean that there can't be a *decision* by the dominated to cast off the yoke of class domination.[8] Hence, the elites dominate, but not because 'they have no choice but to do so' if they are to perform their allocated roles. Elites dominate because, once the pressures they're submitted to in their particular social setting are understood, they *decide* to dominate, because they *decide* to take on the roles they've been given in this social context, and they believe and bring into operation – or take for granted, naturalise and reproduce over time – a whole repertoire of practices aimed at consolidating these roles and positions of privilege.[9]

As usual, a strictly structuralist view of the functioning of human societies ends up eroding the space which, from the realm of theory, we give, on the one hand, to individual and collective choice, that is, to the capacity of 'agency', and, on the other hand, to moral responsibility. And this is something that should be avoided. To keep dominating or to stop dominating, to rebel against oppression or to bow our heads in surrender, are possibilities for action that are, of course, conditioned by the social structure we're in but, ultimately, such courses of action are an expression of the responsibility we choose to take when faced by structural injustices, which we erroneously tend to believe aren't ours. And, after all, the world's made up of layer upon layer, not of guilt and reproaches, but of shared moral and political responsibilities which, thus understood, could lever myriad forms of emancipatory collective action (Young, 2011).[10]

To sum up, the socialist-republican approach to freedom must be able to detect (1) the social forces that turn institutions such as markets into inevitable realities, with all that entails in terms of loss of individual and collective freedom, which is what 'structural' domination is all about; and (2) the social dynamics that make all of us, dominated and also dominators, feel pressured to accept certain social roles, which is what 'impersonal' domination is all about. And all this would need to include taking into account, as far as it's epistemologically possible, all those real mechanisms, which harbour enormous doses of intentionality, moulding the scenarios and structures in which we find ourselves inserted. Not doing this could lead us into the dead end of structuralist imagery, which would have disastrous consequences in terms of the explanatory potential of our theories and, in the end, the chances of conceiving of collective action and putting into practice a wide range of forms of social transformation of the world. Needless to say, the authors I've just cited – Gädeke, Gourevitch and Roberts, though the list could be much longer – are aware of the risks of both socially disembodied atomism and the most speculative structuralism, and offer promising avenues for understanding the human production of this domination which so often takes on structural dimensions.[11]

Be this as it may, it is convenient to close the digression on the question of structural domination, pick up the thread and stress the need to be aware that the world is conflictive. It's conflictive because it's split into social classes that are entrenched in profoundly unequal processes of appropriation of external resources. The food runners aren't food runners, and the poor who receive their lentils aren't assisted poor because they have extra-social preferences, constructed in a vacuum which encourages them to do what they do and, moreover, are complementary. Rather, these possible preferences are endogenous to social life and are based on vast processes of social structuring that are continually defining positions of subalternity and privilege. This is the social ontology on which the bulk of the republican tradition rests. As such, it is up to each space and each historical moment – or, better, up to those who are living in them – to respond to the big question that the republican approximation to freedom places on the table: property of what?

In the ancient world and the early modern period, including that of American independence, the response to this question was very simple: male landowners – and sometimes owners of slaves and livestock – were free. Yet in the modern world, real estate property, landed property, is being displaced by the ownership or collective control of productive facilities and equipment, or the means of production (Casassas, 2010, 2013; Domènech, 2004) and, well into the twentieth century and in those societies where it was politically possible, by public ownership of resources conferred within the framework of social policy schemes. So, an approach to basic income that rescues from oblivion the link between republican freedom and *property*

– and we could also say socioeconomic independence – requires a thoroughgoing critique of the many conditionalities that welfare regimes have brought with them (since guaranteeing freedom can't be subject to conditions of any kind) and prompts us to think of the principles of universality and unconditionality in public policy as contemporary mechanisms for interpreting this idea of property, of socioeconomic independence, which the republican tradition has always presented as a necessary condition of effective freedom (Casassas and Raventós, 2007; Domènech and Raventós, 2007). This is the republican sense of basic income.[12]

But could the introduction of a basic income constitute, in itself, a terribly arbitrary act of interference? It should be mentioned here that, unlike the liberal tradition, republicanism envisages the possibility of the public powers interfering non-arbitrarily in the sphere of social existence of individuals and groups. To quote Pettit (1997, 2001) again, the crux of the matter lies in the factional or non-factional nature of this state intervention. Is it seeking to promote the interests of a certain sector of society? To the extent that the public authorities can be held accountable for political action aimed at guaranteeing freedom as non-domination for the population as a whole, it will be understood that their acts of interference, however much they resort to the coercive power of the law – for example, with a tax law aimed at collecting taxes to finance a basic income – will be acts of non-arbitrary interference.

Of course, this doesn't mean that the republican tradition is unaware of the possibility of the despotic degeneration of government institutions. In fact, republicanism offers an especially helpful analytical perspective for detecting: (1) when forms of domination, or *dominium*, appear or, in other words, when arbitrary power among private, individual or collective agents arise (the first threat to republican freedom); and (2) when the public powers that have been designed and instituted to combat *dominium* nourish the second great threat to republican freedom, namely *imperium*, which is to say, cronyistic, clientelistic and/or disciplinary practices by state bodies that give rise to new forms of arbitrary interference in people's lives.

To sum up, we have here an interesting triangle that needs to be recognised and filled with content. Let's take its three vertices. First, each human life, which includes a physical body with its particular needs, as diverse as they may be, and a horizon of desires and aspirations (e.g. in the domain of work, remunerated or non-remunerated) constitutes a singularity that must be accepted and respected as not only legitimate but also as *already* present, *already* tangible, *already* here. Second, a democratic approach to the question of shaping political communities requires affirmation of the right of *all* these lives to be lived, individually and/or collectively, in an equally free manner. At this point, it's worth mentioning that the republican tradition, as well as the socialist, understands equality, not as a strictly uniform distribution of resources, but as reciprocity in freedom (Domènech, 2004; Roberts, 2017), or, if one prefers, 'equality in freedom', which might involve different resources endowments, all of them adapted to the needs of each person). And third, these lives that are to be liveable in conditions of freedom need to be protected and sustained by public-common authorities that are aware of the liberticidal nature of both *dominium* (bonds of dependence and power relations among private agents) and *imperium*, which is fuel to the fire when the institutions are not only unwilling to combat *dominium* but also extend the reach of arbitrariness by consolidating oligarchic and despotic attitudes with regard to people's lives.[13]

In short, we want to be left to our own devices. Please, spare us all that lentil salad, food running and the other thousand joint ventures for *ex post* aid. And please don't come to us with that trite tale about fish and fishing rods. We all know the story: what we need isn't fish but someone to give us a fishing rod and teach us how to fish. Cut it out, right now – please. Maybe we don't want to go fishing with a rod. There are many ways to go fishing. Maybe we don't even want to fish. There are many ways to live your life. Let us do that ourselves – please. We only want to be allowed to do that. Have we turned into *laissez-faire* fans? No way. As I've said and shall repeat in detail, the *laissez-faire* of the liberal doctrine – as we know, deregulated markets where, allegedly, agents operate without hindrance or restraint – doesn't, even in the best of cases, exceed the status of mere mythological construction. Leave us alone, then, so we can stand up and dare to allocate politically, among all of us, the resources – and why not a basic income, among others – that would allow us to be personally independent so that, from then on, we can continue weaving an interdependence that we can recognise as something that's ours, something for our lives. Leave us alone so we can do it – please. We're fed up, all of us. We want to do what we like – all of us, without exception, and of course in common.

6

Bargaining Power: Exit Options for Entry Doors and the Emancipatory Potential of Basic Income

I'll continue with triangles. In 1970, the economist Albert O. Hirschman presented an interpretive framework for social relationships in situations of conflict and deterioration that could be useful at this point. When the social milieus in which we move go into 'decline', meaning that at least one of the parts involved feels that the relationship causes more distress and dissatisfaction than anything else, one of the three following responses, or some combination of them, tends to result: *exit* from this relationship, recourse to raising one's *voice* to challenge its functioning and trying to modify it and, finally, rationales of *loyalty* to the relationship in question, one with which we sometimes nurture emotional ties that prevent us from considering leaving it or altering it (Hirschman, 1970). Hirschman applied his analytical scheme to 'firms, organizations, and states', but reading his triangle from the standpoint of the vision of social life and freedom offered by the republican tradition allows us to apply it to any kind of social relationship. We'll now see how and why.

Imagine any wage worker. Or, to be a little more specific, imagine one of the many home-delivery workers, plying our streets and bringing food on bicycles equipped with one of those large cubic containers. As we know, these are people who frequently don't get paid for the hours they spend working but for the number of deliveries they make, which can have seriously harmful consequences for their mental health and physical integrity. Imagine, too, a woman who, besides carrying out a certain amount of paid work, has to take on most of the reproductive work necessary to keep the home fires burning, and does so in conditions that are openly abusive. What will the worker on the bicycle or the woman of 'double presence' – in the labour market and in the household – do if they become aware that their situation is preventing them from living a dignified and reasonably free existence?

First of all, they'll try to make their voice heard. When the social relationship in which we're immersed doesn't satisfy us, the most immediate response might be expressing discontent. As Liza Herzog (2016) puts it, we speak of 'epistemic equality' in the domain of labour – but this analysis can easily be shifted to the household – when the necessary regulatory frameworks are introduced so that all those involved in a workplace will be able to state how they would like this space to be organised. However, the fact is that this epistemic equality is a rare occurrence, basically because those who should raise their voices go into these workplaces devoid of (im)material resources, which is why they have no bargaining power and must accept the rules of the game and the practices they find there, which turns labour relations in a true 'employer dictatorship' (Anderson, 2015). In these circumstances, the voice, if there is one, becomes a mere whisper, and the whisper is lost in the racket of many orders and regulations that are heteronymously imposed or, in other words, at the blast of a whistle. On other occasions, the voice is listened to, but the listener does so as a good businessman, a condescending husband, a benevolent slave owner, who listens and understands the situation of those who depend on him. These actors listen in the same way as they might stop listening, because they operate in an extremely asymmetrical social and institutional framework that equips them to ignore, if they so wish, what their subordinates might wish and express.

Voice alone will probably not be enough. So, we'll now look at the second vertex of Hirschman's triangle: exit. Another response to a deteriorated social situation is to leave it – to 'leave', for example, paid work, or at least the especially perverse forms it can take – which is the same as refusing to nourish social ties we don't like and, perhaps, daring to establish another kind of sociability or, in this case, another type of work culture. But in order to leave, you have *to be able* to leave, and to credibly threaten that there is a possibility that we're going to leave. And *to be able* to leave, you need to have relevant sets of (im)material resources – a basic income among them – that will open up genuine escape routes for imagining and practising other forms of life. Take divorce, for example. The right to divorce was never formulated with the idea that people *have to* divorce. It was designed and formulated so that people *can* divorce when cohabitation becomes impossible. Similarly, devices such as a basic income, providing for us from cradle to grave, must allow us to conceive and, if necessary, take the 'exit' option much more easily.

As we've just seen, this has a liberating potential that is manifested in two ways. First, the 'exit' option enables us to *effectively* leave behind harmful and unwanted scenarios. Second, the mere threat of a possible 'exit', whether it comes to pass or not, and as long as the threat is convincing, tends to give more strength to our voices (Casassas, 2016a; Haagh, 2019; Taylor, 2017). If people whose lives are damaged by arbitrariness show that they are able to stand up and leave, their voices will be heard, or at least they won't be as muted as they were. It's not surprising that this is the case. If we can show that we have the power to put an end to the social relations that are the mainstay of our shared life, these previously arbitrary external bodies, now fearing a possible rupture that will cause them problems, and maybe even ending up with their being ignored, would be more interested to know about our interests and procedures, which means that our ability to (co-)determine a shared life would extend and prosper.

The equation, then is simple: there is no republican freedom without bargaining power. No bargaining power is possible without the ability to undo and recreate social ties, without an 'exit' option that would open the way to other 'entries'. And there is no 'exit' option without unconditionally guaranteed (im)material resources. Hence, a basic income, but also benefits in kind equally understood as constitutive rights of citizenship and, finally, skills and abilities in paid or unpaid work that aren't taken from our control, would all form part of a set of certainties that give us a secure place in a world that we experience as our own.

Is this the end of the story? Does all this mean that having an 'exit' option is the necessary and sufficient condition for republican freedom? The answer is 'no'. It's still necessary to examine the third vertex of the triangle, which concerns the question of 'loyalty'. Are there situations in which, even if we can escape – 'leave' – a liberticidal scenario, we don't decide to do so? This would be due to strong emotional or symbolic ties, which are frequently connected to veritable swarms of social norms or customarily sedimented behavioural patterns that perpetuate certain forms of social existence. Take the wage-earning worker who can't so much as think about terminating a contract that binds him to a person for whose parents and grandparents his parents and grandparents worked. Or the woman who understands that breaking off her marriage means destroying the moral and psychological infrastructure of a whole life. It might be objected, and not without reason, that these fearful ways of staying in a relationship have nothing to do with 'loyalty' since this requires an act of conscious and duly considered consent; that 'forced loyalty' isn't loyalty at all but submission to several forms of symbolic power and, even more, that such acts of 'obligatory loyalty' constitute a violation of the rights that all humans should have to establish genuine bonds of 'effective loyalty', which can only appear in a social setting that isn't too asymmetrical. Be that as it may, what is hardly objectionable is that these forms of 'symbolically induced loyalty' exist, and this can undermine any freedom that is gained when the 'voice' is strengthened by the real possibility of 'leaving'. In fact, this is why I have argued that the enjoyment of material resources (e.g. a basic income) constitutes a necessary but not sufficient condition of republican freedom.

But to be able to leave is a great help. Being able to bargain and (co-) determine forms of life is something that requires the ability to imagine and practise *other* forms of life that are closer to what we are or want to be. So, *any old exit* won't do. Recently, *libertarian* schemes, such as that proposed by Karl Widerquist (2013), have emphasised, perhaps too acritically, the liberating potential of the 'exit'. It is necessary to ask where it leads, how, with whom and why. Along these lines, Simon Birnbaum and Jurgen De Wispelaere (2016, 2020) and Stuart White (2020) have perceptively pointed out that, without a basic income of a sufficient amount, and without a whole framework of public policies that will also contribute towards consolidating true positions of invulnerability for everyone, leaving a job could mean a 'desperate exit'. We could certainly argue that being able to desperately leave a building in flames is preferable to staying inside and suffering the burning and eventual collapse. Nevertheless, it's true that a frenzied and quixotic exit, which is almost doomed to failure, isn't the same as a thoroughgoing rethinking of our forms of life in an institutional setting of social relations that offer real opportunities for another kind of existence.

This is why Birnbaum and De Wispelaere (2020) insist that the potential of basic income to allow us to 'exit' hostile work environments must be analysed with realism and caution. To start with, workers need a feasible alternative to be able to resort to the exit option, and also an institutional context that allows them to move effectively from the job that is abandoned to the new workspace, to the new activity – within or out of the labour market. Clearly, basic income can help a lot in this sense, but other policies and devices are also important, even decisive: targeted income policies (e.g. unemployment benefits) of an amount that is higher than that of basic income, in kind public policies of many sorts (e.g. healthcare, education or housing) and/or community-based self-managed resources. Indeed, all of them can help to bridge the gap between leaving one job and moving on to another activity. Otherwise, the 'exit' may not be practicable, and therefore it may also happen that our threat that we are going to leave will not be credible, such that the bargaining power of workers vis-à-vis employers is eroded.

In addition, Birnbaum and De Wispelaere (2020) also point out that it is necessary not to nurture a culture according to which what is necessary is always to 'exit': according to them, one can choose to remain in the workplace and try to dignify it by negotiating better conditions. This can be obtained through a basic income, but workers can also use other means, such as the fight for legal frameworks that better protect them from certain labour abuses or the promotion of worker representation in the governing bodies of companies (Anderson, 2015; Gourevitch, 2013; Hsieh, 2008).

Let's push the line of reasoning a little bit further. We also know that being able to 'exit' does not necessarily have a positive impact on the (democratic) quality of employment: under capitalism, there are legal frameworks and a structure of property rights – for example, regarding the control over the means of production – that make the employment contract something that is inherently dominating (White, 2020). That is quite true, but it is precisely for this reason that unconditional measures such as a robust basic income are needed, which should always be within broad packages of measures that are also unconditional. It is necessary to affirm at all times a certain principle of 'institutional pluralism' when it comes to analysing the role of basic income within the broad institutional framework, in order to effectively combat the labour domination that takes place under capitalism (Breen, 2017). Indeed, the hypothesis at this point is that basic income and the accompanying measures must allow (1) abandoning these liberticidal environments, that is, decommodifying the labour force, as feminist authors such as Silvia Federici (2013) and Kathi Weeks (2011) claim; and (2) help nurture other cultures and economic practices that are compatible with an elementary principle of economic democracy.

In other words: we must proceed with great caution in the face of the possibility that the necessary awareness of the limits of basic income when it comes to 'exiting' capitalist domination and eradicating it leads us to abandon a strongly needed critical culture regarding wage labour under capitalism. Under capitalism, performing wage-earning work for others may provide certain rewards – to start with, wages themselves – but it tends to erode our freedom and sovereignty. We can never lose sight of that. It is about thinking and fighting – if necessary, using basic income – to open paths and introduce mechanisms that allow the creation of environments for work – both paid and unpaid – that operate according to post-capitalist logics.

Instead, we find examples of a certain 'submissive' attitude towards work within capitalist environments, of a certain tendency to take work within capitalist environments as a fait accompli that, at most, we can try to regulate to make it less hostile, in the affirmation, which is undoubtedly partially reasonable, that 'exiting' may cause possible future employers to perceive in us a lack of ambition or loyalty, or that 'exiting' may lead to us losing the rights that we now enjoy because we stay in the labour market, such as decent pensions or other conditional income policies (Birnbaum and De Wispelaere, 2020). In the same vein, analysts such as Iñigo González-Ricoy (2014) and Keith Breen (2017) insightfully alert us that a basic income 'only offers a real exit option for those wanting to escape a bad job by moving to a better one when such better jobs are available. If better jobs are not available, many workers exercising their right of exit will face the prospect of replacing one bad job with another or of potentially falling into long-term unemployment' (Breen, 2017: 429–30). All of this is of crucial importance, but so is, and much more so, the affirmation of the need to use basic income, among other measures, as a tool to build working trajectories, inside and outside labour markets, that truly confer meaning and lead to effective 'goods of work', as Anca Gheaus and Lisa Herzog (2016) name it, that therefore place us far from the whims of potential exploitative employers. In other words, the alternative to current jobs should not consist in limiting ourselves to 'moving to another job' – maybe a better one? – but in transforming the whole mode of organising work and work environments. In order to achieve this, basic income alone is not enough (especially if it is a low basic income), but we cannot settle for living locked up in prison labour markets in which, lacking a basic income and accompanying measures, the best we can achieve is that the inevitable subservience is regulated and oppression becomes less harsh.[1] Undoubtedly, the sociopolitical ambition with which we can and must think and present the basic income proposal under today's circumstances must be much broader and more motivating. We will dwell on this question in a moment.

For this reason, as Birnbaum and De Wispelaere (2020: 922–3) themselves suggestively state in the wake of Erik Olin Wright (2010), who raised the need to understand basic income as (part of) a 'socialist alternative' (Wright, 2006a, 2006b), there is need for 'a culturally defined respectable standard of living, [...] combined with access to an infrastructure of social participation enabling opportunities for recognition and esteem beyond the employment contract', that is, taking away from the kind of contracts that are being signed within capitalist labour markets the centrality they occupy in today's world. And, for this, a robust basic income that is surrounded by other equally unconditional measures, thanks to the bargaining power or 'social power' that it confers, can play a decisive role.

In the same vein, according to Gourevitch (2016), who is explicitly sceptical about basic income because of its potentially individualising nature, the crucial element is our ability to keep constructing what might be called a 'popular culture of free work', which would hold out clues for thinking about alternative workspaces where we can meet fraternally and cooperatively. Indeed, all sociopolitical organisations that could be useful in this regard – unions, social movements, self-managed spaces, and so on – are essential for ensuring that a basic income is a tool for being able to 'exit' in a common project for spaces that are free in the republican sense (White, 2020). What is probably at stake is to think of the 'exit' not as a disorderly, atomised stampede, which is what the aforementioned libertarian frameworks might end up suggesting, but as an attempt of the bulk of the working classes to move ahead with other practices, other tools and other horizons (Birnbaum and De Wispelaere, 2020). As Gourevitch (2013) himself points out, social justice within the realm of work – both paid and unpaid – requires the ability not to 'escape' from it, although some circumstances might recommend it, but to democratically 'transform' it. As it will be seen in Part III, this book is committed to the task of exploring those social scenarios and mechanisms through which basic income could help to promote this kind of democratic transformation of work.

Lisa Herzog has expressed concerns that are similar to those of Birnbaum and De Wispelaere and Gourevitch when she warned of the possibility of 'people coming and going in unpredictable ways' (Herzog, 2016: 33). However, it's worth noting that this 'coming and going in unpredictable ways' is a privilege that few people enjoy today. Why not universalise this ability? Why not, therefore, make it a right? Once again, universalising it doesn't mean forcing this 'coming and going' of people, just as having the right to divorce doesn't oblige anyone to divorce. In fact, neoliberal precariousness *forces* this 'coming and going' in ways we don't choose at all. But it's necessary to be able to divorce and sometimes unpredictably, as is required by the enjoyment of republican freedom as non-domination. In a nutshell, if the republican project presented here aims at shaping free, and as a result stable, social relations that invite us to stay – in the workplace, at home, in spaces for community life, etc. – we need to introduce mechanisms that equip us, in the event that this harmonious and non-dominating coexistence deteriorates, for a non-atomising exit.

Being able to leave is a great help. After all, an elementary idea of economic democracy depends on it. In effect, democratising economic and social life means instituting environments and devices that allow the fourfold ability to (1) decide what kind of social relations we want to 'enter' to engage in some kind of work; (2) determine the (im)material nature of the space where we decide to be and to work, which requires the ability to use a 'voice' that will be effectively listened to; (3) opt for 'leaving' this space if its nature and conditions of functioning go against what we want for our lives; and (4) if we do opt to leave, to turn to a social milieu outside the prior workplace that, far from constituting a quagmire in which we can't put into practice projects that are truly ours, offers tools for second or even subsequent opportunities so that we can effectively restart our (re)productive lives in other terms and conditions, those of Harrington's free men and women who show that they are genuinely able to live lives of their own (Casassas, 2016a).

All of this leads us to a debate that not only is inescapable, but that I would not at all like to escape from: can universal basic income be seen as part of an openly democratising project, as part of a broad political project that brings together some of the most significant core elements of contemporary emancipatory traditions?

To start with, it should be said that it is normal for an abstract political measure with no history of real application to give rise to different intuitions, to hypotheses that do not coincide at all and to concerns of a very different nature about its possible consequences in terms of promoting republican freedom and socialist values and practices (Calnitsky, 2017).

But this book aims to shed light on the role that basic income can play in the redefinition of socialisms, here understood as heirs to the democratic wing of the republican tradition. As already seen, according to this tradition there is no freedom without property or, in other words, without unconditional access to control and enjoyment of (im)material resources of many kinds that confer bargaining power or 'social power'. As in the ancient world – and until the eighteenth century – that republican freedom was achieved, fundamentally, through landed property; and just as nineteenth-century socialisms suggested that collective ownership or control of the means of production could act as a guarantee of that freedom, today we can suggest that the principle of unconditionality in the making of public policy, together with common-based forms of predistribution, may become ways of updating for the contemporary world the old republican-socialist link between freedom and property or control of resources (Casassas, 2007; Casassas, Raventós and Szlinder, 2019).[2]

Let's see in what sense all this can be so. To begin with, as we have just observed, basic income can promote both the exit from freedom- and dignity-limiting work relations and the possibility of raising one's voice and thus defending and promoting the interests of historically minorised individuals and groups within the spaces where both paid and unpaid work is carried out. For this reason, it can be asserted that basic income has a true affinity with the socialist project (Calnitsky, 2017; Van Parijs, 2018).

This is so, above all, when we realise that 'leaving' does not necessarily mean leaving a place individually, but it can also be a way of laying the foundations for processes of institutionalisation of solidarity (Calnitsky, 2017). On this point, the perspective that was developed by Erik Olin Wright (2016) is highly enlightening. As we will see later, according to the 'real utopias' theorist, basic income should not be of interest only for 'static' reasons to do with calculating the number of people who could be freed from poverty and social exclusion; basic income should be of interest, above all, when we understand its 'dynamic justifications': by eliminating situations of poverty and social exclusion, basic income frees up time, energy and the capacity for social and political imagination that will allow us to put into circulation freer, more liveable lives, which normally implies that we do it hand in hand with other people and large social groups. This is the reason why Erik Olin Wright (2019: 74) ensures that basic income is valuable for 'enabling people to opt for a life centered around creative activity [and this must be interpreted in a broad sense, not in the strict sense of "artistic" activities] rather than market-generated income'.

But, of course, the fight for basic income cannot be left in the hands of 'experts' who can limit themselves to claiming that they have had 'a very good idea': the danger of idealism is well known, especially when we are faced with a clearly conflictive proposal, which leads to the assumption that oligarchies will not passively accept emancipatory forms of basic income that expropriate them from the resources and social power that they currently hoard (Gourevitch and Stanczyk, 2018). The struggle for basic income, then, must be established in the context of diverse social struggles, all of which are strongly intertwined and oriented to guarantee unconditional access to many kinds of resources – health, education, housing, water, energy, transportation, culture, etc. – and, from there, access to lives that have been freed from capitalist submission and that we can truly control. In this direction, Gourevitch and Stanczyk (2018) rightly point out, strongly organised working classes are needed to achieve ambitious objectives in democratising terms such as those proposed here. I do not object to this statement – quite the contrary. But my hypothesis is that only ambitious objectives such as those proposed here – basic income and other unconditionally guaranteed public-common resources, namely ambitious objectives that form the backbone of true 'non-reformist reforms' (Calnitsky, 2018) – can stimulate and build a powerful organisation of the working classes such as is needed. Perhaps the future of socialism – or, in other words, the future of projects aimed at democratising the entire social and economic life – depends on there being enough audacity, in terms of truly transformative proposals and societal horizons, so that the bulk of the working population finds reasons and incentives to engage in mass movements with large-scale efficacy and for some decades to come.

Having said this, we cannot rule out, as if it were an act of faith, that the 'exit' of the popular classes from the work environments that currently oppress them is an atomising exit. Again, the warning in this regard from authors such as Alex Gourevitch (2016) must be taken into account. For example, the fear, which is widespread among certain union environments, that the basic income individualises the negotiation between capital and labour, is far from constituting a case of paranoia. However, neither can we forget that social atomisation is *already* a clear reality in the daily life of the bulk of the working population, in the same way that we cannot magically assume that widespread precariousness and dispossession (e.g. due to the lack of unconditional resources such as basic income) have to ineluctably lead us to an effective collective struggle of a transformative nature: the pure surrender, the lack of consciousness about the situation in which one finds oneself, the acceptance and even joyful assumption of the (supposedly) meritocratic discourse that accompanies the dispossessing dynamics of the neoliberal turn of capitalism constitute realities that are present in the daily lives of huge numbers of workers. Besides, the fear that individual policies such as basic income could atomise social relations and disrupt collective struggle could also assail us with devices such as unemployment benefits, and it would not occur to us to fight these policies; rather, we tend to organise collectively to defend their presence and enlargement.

This is why Calnitsky (2017) suggests that emancipatory collective action must be nurtured by promoting its conditions of possibility – for example, through a basic income – in a *positive* sense, not leaving collective action as the only way for survival under conditions of despair of individuals that have been terribly beaten by capitalist dispossession – it seems obvious that this second strategy does not agree with the socialist objective of expanding, in the degrees that are possible, the domain of human autonomy. As always with political action, the levels of success of the effort to turn basic income into a fully emancipatory tool will depend, to a large extent, on the work of political organisation and the generation of new emancipatory imaginaries that can be achieved around such a measure. Let's go back to unionism: can unionism stop fearing basic income for its possible individualising effect and get to work to turn it into a huge (universal!) resistance fund? For example, with a basic income in their pockets, workers might be less inclined to 'defect' in case of long strikes and become scabs, since the fact of having a guaranteed material existence and, with it, a temporary – or definitive – alternative to employment, could reinforce the power of attraction of trade unionism towards collective action (Calnitsky, 2017). In short, trade unionism must be able to see basic income not as a threat but as a tool to imagine and articulate new forms of work organisation (Haagh, 2018).

Another of the reasons that have led certain left-wing critics to point out the 'dangerous' nature of the basic income is found in the possibility, which in no case can we rule out, that this measure is used by neoliberal forces such as the Trojan horse to destroy the welfare mechanisms that currently exist or that can be conceived. The neoliberal argument is sometimes as follows: we dismantle the welfare state, and, in return, we offer some peanuts in the form of a basic income. This possibility, regarding which we cannot fall into any type of denialism, is discussed later, and I stress the need for the basic income proposal to be part of and even constitute the backbone of a whole package of measures that updates the fraternal and collectivist spirit that inspired the 'popular political economy' that the left wing of the French Revolution, the very antecedent of nineteenth-century socialism, promoted at all times.[3]

Perhaps fearful of this possibility, authors such as Barbara Bergman (2004) have proposed introducing or strengthening universal services instead of a universal basic income. But putting things this way is tantamount to falling into totally unnecessary dichotomies, unless we assume, as Gourevitch and Stanczyk (2018) seem to do, that the fiscal limits set by austerity-based right-wing political forces are real – indeed, Gourevitch and Stanczyk seem to suspect that a basic income inevitably leads to the removal of vital public programmes. The financial viability of a universal basic income that is *coupled with* universal services is a matter of political will, so it will depend on the ability of those social and political movements aimed at achieving the entire 'package of measures' to accomplish their objectives. The problem, then, is not technical but entirely political. In addition, it is worth stressing the need for this 'broad package of universal and unconditional resources' to contain a portion 'in cash', since this helps to promote the effective freedom of people when it comes to making free decisions in their daily lives. Indeed, people's preferences and needs are profoundly heterogeneous, which is why having resources that can be used with the meanings and objectives that each individual and group may want to give them constitutes a political goal of great importance in emancipatory terms. Finally, left-wing analysts such as Barbara Bergman should realise that a broad package of measures that also includes basic income ensures that not only certain goods and services – health, education, housing, transport, energy, etc. – be decommodified, but that the labour force itself has the possibility of being decommodified too, which has always been one of the most ambitious political objectives of certain Scandinavian welfare models (Esping-Andersen, 1990).

Be that as it may, and as Calnitsky (2018) suggests, it seems evident that all policies – health, education, housing, care, unionism-driven strategies, the promotion of public employment and income policies – can be intentionally perverted and/or can be the object of unintended effects (of course, socialist ideas can also be applied in a frightening way) (Calnitsky, 2017). An example of the 'potentially dangerous' nature of measures that no one would say could be harmful are educational policies. Indeed, public education can be put at the service of expanding the capacity for critical judgement of the population as a whole, but it can also become a neoliberal mechanism for the instrumental preparation of 'human capital' for its immediate and ephemeral use by voracious and myopic contemporary labour markets. But are we going to stop defending and fighting for quality public education because there is a risk that it will be captured by sociopolitical groups that want to give it a non-emancipatory sign? It seems reasonable that we won't.

Another argument that is mobilised by certain left-wing critics of basic income is that this policy can be used by the elites as a pragmatic means to avoid the anti-capitalist radicalisation of precarious population. The idea is quite straightforward: given the rise of socioeconomic insecurity, the granting of a certain amount of monetary resources can prevent popular classes from questioning the status quo and imagining and fighting for transformative social scenarios. In this text, instead, we propose to analyse reality in reverse: basic income can become a means, pragmatic or quite the opposite – oriented towards the creation of an emancipatory collective culture – so that the working population can become radicalised in a democratising sense; remember that, in etymological terms from the Latin *radix*, 'radicalising' means addressing the 'root' of the problems that are being faced. Indeed, only measures such as basic income – which put desire, freedom and the possibility of asserting the importance of a life that is lived together at the centre of the political agenda, within breathing and unfractured communities – can curb political apathy, at best, and at worst the most rabid forms of the far right. Mental space and a reduction in the financial stress that grips many lives are needed to open up the possibility of emancipatory political movements being articulated – with no time to breathe, mired in financial stress, it is even understandable that people cling to dedemocratising projects such as those that make a ghostly promise to make your own country 'something great again', even though this constitutes a motto that is empty of substantive content in terms of real protection of the working population.

Finally, perhaps the most ambitious criticism that basic income can receive from the left is the one that establishes that, instead of conferring unconditional income, it is about the working classes taking collective control of the means of production or simply looking for ways to disconnect from the capitalist system (Gourevitch and Stanczyk, 2018; Roberts, M., 2016). But at this point we cannot abandon a realistic analysis of the correlation of forces that we find in our societies: are there signs that this can be achieved in the short or medium run? Could this claim constitute a tremendous act of voluntarism, as Calnitsky (2018) seems to suggest? In any case, I would go even further: basic income and collective control of the means of production are not only compatible goals, but the former can become a useful mechanism to achieve the latter. As we will see in Part III, thanks to the bargaining power one has when one's material existence is guaranteed, basic income is not just 'money', but rather constitutes a tool that is easily translatable in terms of (1) time to conceive and negotiate other forms of work and life; (2) the ability to assume the risks associated with the act of exploring alternative paths; and (3) a cushion, a fallback position or some initial endowment capable of granting us security from the start and the right to second, third and subsequent opportunities to deploy, as Harrington would say, 'lives of one's own' in which we tend to effectively take 'collective control of the means of (re)production'.

Besides, who said that in post-capitalist societies – socialist, communist or, simply, more just and democratic – the conflict that originates in the scarcity of available resources and in the plurality of conceptions of the good life is going to disappear? Even more: is it truly desirable that the entirety of social life be subjected to (democratically driven) centralised planning? Who said that we cannot wish to place certain aspects of our lives in commercial environments and, perhaps, with non-exclusive forms of private property? If this were the case, the ability to negotiate, in a decentralised way, the allocation of resources, assets and activities of many sorts may be not only necessary, but even desirable, which is why the presence of unconditionally guaranteed pools of resources – among them, a basic income – can still play a crucial role.

In short, it is possible that, at present, the debate does not consist of saying if we are in favour of basic income or if we are against it. Most likely, the great debate will be around what kind of basic income, and with what political objectives, we want for our societies. In this sense, the left would do well to equip itself for this political contest and undertake the task (1) of not presenting basic income as a panacea that cures all ills; (2) of not limiting itself to pointing out which social problems basic income does not solve (it is evident that neither basic income nor any other measure can solve all our problems); and (3) of using basic income, among other paths and devices, to unite the oil drops that we have scattered on the table and nourish the mesh that we need in order to build, inhabit and reproduce the common world that we urgently need.

7

Universalisation of Citizenship and Universalisation of Property

Will the home-delivery riders be able to get off their bikes? Will the women of 'double presence', always available, always self-sacrificing, succeed in proposing and, if necessary, forcing true co-responsibility of all the members of the household in caring tasks? And to take another case, this time beyond the bounds of Europe, will the adolescent girls who are subjected to *suman-gali* in Indian spinning mills be able to free themselves from the contractual practices that bind them to work that not only isolates and exploits them as teenagers but also prepares them for marriages in which they will also lack both voice and vote?[1] To take one more case, can applicants for support for the poor free themselves of the role of mere 'supplicants' (Standing, 2011, 2014) of monetary and in-kind benefits with all that this entails in terms of social stigmatisation, infantilised behaviour and subjection to (the possibility of) arbitrary conduct by bureaucratic bodies?[2]

All these questions can be answered by asking whether we enjoy these social positions of invulnerability that should make us not only people who aren't subjected to (arbitrary) interference but also non-interferable or, in other words, people who are free in the republican sense, people who are equipped to take and keep taking truly autonomous decisions. At this point, it's helpful to return to Philip Pettit in order to rescue a conceptual distinction of enormous analytical and political interest. In his view (Pettit, 2001, 2006), the republican tradition understands that freedom doesn't revolve around 'choices', understood in the abstract – so, accordingly, freedom isn't *choice-based* – but points to individuals and groups that are situated along the way to seeing their choices through. Hence, from this viewpoint, freedom is *chooser-based*. In fact, the entity that may or may not merit being called *free* isn't the 'decision in itself' but the 'subject who makes it'. Pettit (2006) asks whether these choosing subjects are free to the extent that their choices are freely made. Or are the choices free inasmuch as they're made by free choosing subjects? Pettit doesn't hesitate to state, along with the greater part of the republican tradition, that social freedom can't be understood without considering the socioeconomic and institutional conditions that make it possible to guarantee, or not, that the subject who chooses is in a situation of freedom as absence of domination. The affirmation of social freedom thus requires the presence of politically outlined and instituted frameworks and signs indicating that individuals are protected from the very possibility of arbitrary external interference. A slave, like the home-delivery rider, the woman of 'double presence', the *sumangali*-bound adolescent and the 'supplicant' of public benefits, can freely make decisions if those on whom they depend are kind enough to concede this possibility, but neither the slave, nor any of the other figures I have mentioned, can be considered as enjoying republican freedom since they are tied, hand and foot, to those, to cite Marx again, thanks to whom they 'live only with their permission'.

Accordingly, Pettit says:

> On the chooser-based view, choosers will be free so far as they have resources that give them a shielded standing among others and their choices will be free so far as that standing ensures that they are not obstructed in making those choices; we can say that in making those choices they exercise or manifest their social freedom as choosers. (2006, 134)

To sum up, only in politically guaranteed conditions of socioeconomic independence can individuals attain the social position of Harrington's *freeman* who, unlike the *bondsman*, can live by his own lights and make decisions based on judgements that are also free (Casassas and Raventós, 2007). This is the sociological awareness with which the republican tradition goes about its portrayal of social life, a portrayal that shows a world seething with asymmetries of power and with which it demands the presence of institutional mechanisms that aim to politically shape a regime of free chooser subjects (Casassas, 2005).

But what 'institutional mechanisms', what 'socioeconomic conditions', are we talking about? At this point, the question that is central to the republican tradition, namely property, reappears. A person isn't free unless he or she has the means to define and manage property rights that are designed to do the opposite of excluding people from leading a dignified existence; in other words, means that aim, rather, to sustain a civil(ised) society consisting of men and women who are always able to pass the eyeball test.

But let's return again to the old question: ownership of what? Just as, until the eighteenth century, this 'property' was essentially related with access to (and control of) land, and just as the various forms of socialism, aware that after the demographic explosion that resulted from the Industrial Revolution it was no longer possible to link republican freedom with the distribution of land, reinterpreted republican *proprietarianism* in terms of collective control of the means of production (Domènech, 2004, 2005), today we need to think about new public-common tools that in no way exclude agrarian reform or control of production – and reproduction – which would guarantee this condition of socioeconomic and civil inviolability presented by the republican tradition as the condition for the possibility of effective freedom.

Needless to say, this is no easy task, least of all in a world such as the modern one in which, on paper at least, it is stipulated that nobody should be deprived of the status of full citizen. But if democratic republicanism is to be consistent with the core of its ethos, it can't ignore the task at hand today, however conflictive it may be in social and political terms. 'Universalisation of citizenship' demands 'universalisation of property', which is to say universalisation of socioeconomic independence, universalisation of control of the (im)material bases of our existence and universalisation of the ability of individuals and groups to live 'upon their own'. Given that, in today's world, we work with an idea of political community that, far from being limited to a small group of people (males who are *born* as property owners), includes almost all the inhabitants of our communities with the criminal and criminalised exception of the migrant population, which is denied the most basic civil and political rights, it's necessary to universalise this principle of 'social-republican property' (Simon, 1991), defined and defended by republican theorists and revolutionaries as the first step towards the exercise of citizenship by individuals and groups (Casassas, 2007; Casassas and Raventós, 2007; Raventós and Casassas, 2004). Indeed, without a well-founded idea of independence that gives all individuals the real possibility of deciding their own life plans and autonomously going ahead with them, the notion of *citizenship* is impoverished to the point of becoming a mere mirage. But is it possible *today* to think about and introduce public policy schemes that would contribute to this universalisation of the conditions of life of 'property owners'? Of course, the kinds of property rights and relations that shape capitalism as a social formation constitute a true privilege, thus being incompatible with the goal of achieving relevant levels of freedom as the absence of (arbitrary) interference for all (Widerquist, 2023). Instead, one may wonder, could a basic income, together with other institutional mechanisms, be the materialisation of this old 'proprietarist' yearning of democratic republicanism? In what follows, I give a clearly affirmative answer to this question.[3]

To sum up, a moment ago I raised the question of managing property rights aimed at sustaining a civil(ised) society in which everyone would be equally free. What would these property rights consist of? And what role might a basic income play in this republican understanding of property? One thing needs to be made clear at the outset. The understanding of property as the exclusive and excluding dominium over external resources is a product of liberalism, and it has never had any place in the republican tradition. Take, for example, the famous description of property popularised in the second half of the eighteenth century by the Tory judge, jurist and politician William Blackstone, which has come down to our own times as one of the core elements of the (neo)liberal doctrinal corpus:

There is nothing which so generally strikes the imagination, and engages the affections of mankind, as the right of property; or that *sole and despotic dominion* which one man claims and exercises over the external things of the world, in total *exclusion* of the right of any other individual in the universe.[4]

By clear contrast, the republican tradition, from the times of Aristotle and, later on, with Roman civil law and public law, which were to find an echo in the 'radical wings' of the natural law tradition (Tierney, 1997; Tuck, 1979), always understands property, including private property, as something that plays an important social role: satisfying the basic needs of the community and guaranteeing an autonomous existence for everyone.[5] This is why the institution of property appears in republicanism as a strictly fiduciary relationship. Jordi Mundó (2017: 451), for example, reconstructs Locke's approximation to the matter of property, precisely as a principal-agent relationship, as trusteeship:

Humans only have the natural (ownership) right over that which guarantees their survival but in no way must they possess in any absolute sense what goes beyond that because this comes to be seen as inherently public property. Private ownership of all that is necessary for (inalienable) life and liberty would thus be seen as a trusteeship which, as such, is not absolute, exclusive, and excluding, but is revocable because it must ultimately serve the common good.

The idea is simple enough. The public authorities are an instrument established by the sovereign people, who act as a 'principal' so that external resources will be distributed in such a way that everyone can satisfy his or her basic needs and live a dignified life. The principal therefore entrusts those who govern, who are nothing more than 'agents' in the principal's service, with the task of defining and implementing property rights which, even if they are compatible with the private gain of those individuals who have acquired them, have the primary function of preserving the lives and freedom of the inhabitants of a world that should belong to everyone in common. The trusteeship, this *commission* based on relations of trust – *fiducia* in Latin – has then a multilayered nature: first, the sovereign people, as the 'principal', commissions the rulers, that is, its 'agents', to grant property rights according to criteria that will make them compatible with a dignified social existence for everyone; and second, the public powers, which now act as the 'principal', delegate to property owners, who operate as their 'agents', the task of using resources in such a way that not only do they not deteri- orate but that also maintains them over time – and still more if they are to be passed down – as a source of benefits for the community as a whole. The public powers, then, are at once 'agents' of the sovereign people (their 'prin- cipal') and the 'principal' of the 'owners' (their 'agents') to whom they entrust the mission of making productive and careful use of resources they possess.

At the end of the eighteenth century, Founding Father Benjamin Franklin took up once again the terms of the intellectual and political battle that John Locke had so well synthesised a century earlier in a letter addressed to another Founding Father, Robert Norris, on Christmas Day 1783 in which he stated:

All the Property that is necessary to a Man for the Conservation of the Individual & the Propagation of the Species, is his natural Right which none can justly deprive him of: But all Property superfluous to such purposes is the Property of the Publick, who by their Laws have created it, and who may therefore by other Laws dispose of it, whenever the Welfare of the Publick shall demand such Disposition. He that does not like civil Society on these Terms, let him retire & live among Savages. – He can have no right to the Benefits of Society who will not pay his Club towards the Support of it. (Franklin, 1839, II, 171)

Almost a century and a half later, in 1917, the revolutionary Constitution of Mexico was to revive this notion of property as a fiduciary relationship when its famous Article 27 declared that all property has a social function, and it is the republic's task to rein in owners so that they will be responsible for the property. This article was a benchmark as it marked the beginning of contemporary social constitutionalism which, as expressed in the Weimar, the Austrian, and the Second Spanish republics, was to inform the most advanced social and economic developments of European constitutions after the Second World War (Domènech, 2004; Pisarello, 2011, 2014). Take, for example, the 1978 Spanish Constitution which in Article 128 (1), without going as far as the 1948 Italian and the 1976 Portuguese constitutions in shielding economic and social rights (Pisarello, 2011), did offer an unequivocal echo in the following limited fiduciary view of property: 'The entire wealth of the country in its different forms, irrespective of its ownership, is subordinate to the general interest.'

But what does basic income have to do with all this? The answer's simple enough. Contemporary republicanism has a fourfold task: first, recognising and legally and politically registering all the material and immaterial resources that are part of a world that should belong to everybody in common; second, instituting property rights – in all their modalities from private to public-common, with hybrid solutions where necessary – over these resources; third, checking whether owners' use of resources is appropriate for satisfying the needs of society as a whole, or not; and fourth, introducing corrective measures to ensure that the 'entire wealth of the country' is truly distributed in such a way that inhabitants can proceed with their life plans with equivalent degrees of freedom. The ultimate aim of national wealth can be none other than the achievement of such reciprocity in freedom. Hence, when faced with private, openly confiscatory and exclusionary appropriation of resources, the republic must then take on the Kantian and Marxist task of 'expropriating the expropriators', for example by means of tax systems that are able to guarantee the right of existence of the entire population by means of a basic income.[6]

8

Unconditional Freedom: Basic Income as Predistribution

What is at stake here, in accordance with the ethical-political precepts of democratic republicanism, is the need to guarantee unconditionally and *ex ante* the material and symbolic conditions of freedom. As we've seen, freedom has definite conditions, so we're not free, for example, if we're socio-economically vulnerable, but this freedom 'with conditions' must apply to the population as a whole. In this second regard, it must be freedom 'without conditions' that is *unconditional*, as its presence must not depend on any external judgement and must be guaranteed from the very start, *ex ante*. But why *ex ante*? And *before what*, exactly?

The debate on predistribution has recently appeared quite forcefully in Anglo-Saxon political philosophy as part of an effort to give shape to an attractive radical political agenda that has been updated for present times (Barragué, 2017; O'Neill and Williamson, 2012a). And even if it conceals problems and conceptual ambiguities that need to be sorted out, the predistributive agenda includes some truly promising elements.

The general analytical framework of predistributive theory was already present in Hacker's (2011) seminal text. Instead of making the bulk of economic and social policy revolve around burdensome tax and transfer systems, it would be better to come up with a legal framework for regulating wealth and wage formation that would make it possible to protect people 'from the very start', 'before the fact', *ex ante*. Needless to say, it's difficult to conceive regulatory frameworks for social and economic life that aspire to distribute private economic power in a way that is less damaging for individual and collective freedoms without resorting to important degrees of tax burden. Yet let's accept the predistributive endeavour of empowering groups and individuals 'from the very start'.[1]

When I said 'before the fact', exactly what 'fact' was I referring to? At this point, it's worth making a distinction between a 'moderate' approach to predistribution and an 'emancipatory' approach (Casassas and Guerrero, 2022, forthcoming). The 'moderate' view of predistribution raises the need to introduce regulatory frameworks that make it possible to tame the capitalist beast by trying to make everyone easily 'employable' and transforming the world of work into a less hostile environment. It's clear that the 'moderate' approach takes capitalist labour relations as a fait accompli. Hence, the 'fact before which' we are supposed to be protected is the point at which we prepare to engage in an activity governed by wage labour contracts that are deemed to be inevitable. By contrast, the 'emancipatory' approach to predistribution, the one we are more interested in here, establishes that it is necessary to situate 'the fact' one step further back so that the 'fact before which' we need to be equipped is the prior decision about what we want to do with our (re)productive lives, about what we want to do in the domain of work or, rather, domains of many kinds of work, remunerated or not. For example, to what extent do we want to become established and inhabit the labour markets?

As can be seen, the emancipatory approach to predistribution ties in with Polanyi's (1944) idea that we root basic decisions about our social and economic life in broad sociopolitical processes that enable us to be conscious of existing alternatives that equip us to continuously shape a (re)productive sphere we really feel as our own. Similarly, the emancipatory approach to predistribution imbibes from republican reflections on societies of the 'free chooser subjects' (Pettit, 2001, 2006) I mentioned above and the republican-ising ideal of Jeffersonian origins, recovered by Rawls (2001) in his late and also republicanising works,[2] of a *property-owning democracy*. This is worth looking into in more detail.

Let's go back, then, to the society of 'free chooser' subjects for, after all, my analysis is concerned with the moral value of equal access to (republican) freedom for everyone.[3] As I said, no republican freedom is possible unless the public authorities guarantee positions of social invulnerability for everyone. There can be no guarantee of 'free decisions' without having previously constituted spaces for non-arbitrary social interaction among 'free chooser' subjects. In late Rawlsian terms the idea consists in empowering individuals and groups 'from the very start' or 'before the fact' in order to make aid 'after the fact', also called 'redistribution', unnecessary or at least less imperative (Rawls, 2001). The backdrop doesn't change. What Rawls has to say, together with the greater part of the republican tradition, is that when we're living in the morass of dispossession, we're obliged to 'accept' any form of discipline and subordination that others wish to impose on us, and this undermines our freedom.[4] This is why *ex ante* measures that empower social actors 'from the very start' are preferable to any *ex post* mechanism that is designed to heal wounds. We shouldn't wait for people to fall into poverty – which is to say a lack of freedom – to hold out the 'remedy' that will, conditionally, alleviate poverty (a lack of freedom, once again). As the old saying goes, prevention is better than cure.

To go back to predistribution in the strict sense, some theorists, Hacker (2011) and Heckman (2012) among them, explicitly state that the kind of regulatory frameworks they suggest would improve the salaries of wage workers, their working conditions, their forms of political organisation, and so on. There can be no doubt that such goals are most desirable, but it's also worth stressing that Hacker and Heckman take wage labour as an inevitable fate. On the contrary, the emancipatory approach to predistribution demands, as we have seen, that institutional mechanisms designed to favour effective freedom of agents must be introduced 'before' the point at which they become wage workers or housewives with very little power to oppose unwanted arrangements, or 'supplicants' of conditional welfare programmes with zero possibilities for (co)determining the nature and functioning of this so-called assistance. The institutions of a political community of predistributive orientation must confer on everybody the ability to decide whether we wish or don't wish to become wage labourers, housewives or users of public benefits.

This is where basic income enters the scene. The fact that this income flow goes into action unconditionally, *ex ante*, 'from the very start', helps individuals and groups to build an interdependence based on the autonomous decisions of everyone. In fact, and as we'll see in Part III, basic income plays a crucial role as an emancipatory tool because it enables everyone to decide what to do and what not to do in the (re)productive sphere, with whom, at what pace, with what time use and what kind of social environments to construct. In particular, the analysis of how all this is manifested in terms of individual and collective ability to decommodify resources and activities, starting with labour power, is offered.

In this precise sense, basic income, like related measures such as unconditional healthcare, high-quality universal education, housing policy and care measures for everyone, shows an interesting parallel with the proposal of a property-owning democracy.[5] As Rawls puts it in his later work:

> The background institutions of property-owning democracy work to disperse the ownership of wealth and capital, and thus to prevent a small part of society from controlling the economy, and indirectly, political life

as well. By contrast, welfare-state capitalism permits a small class to have a near monopoly of the means of production. Property-owning democracy avoids this, not by redistribution of income to those with less at the end of each period, so to speak, but rather by ensuring [...] widespread ownership [...] at the beginning of each period, all this against a background of fair equality and opportunity. The intent is not to simply assist those who lose out through accident or misfortune (although that must be done), but rather to put all citizens in a position to manage their own affairs on a footing of a suitable degree of social and economic equality. (2001: 139)

With these words, John Rawls, who in no way saw himself as a supporter of basic income (Rawls, 1988), reinterpreted for the contemporary world the old Jeffersonian ideal of endowing all citizens with a level of resources that would make them personally independent – 'proprietors' – and thus to lay the material foundations of a truly civil(ised) and truly democratic society. And if Rawls was clearly sceptical about the idea of a basic income, the British economist James Meade, who inspired Rawls' recovery of the idea of a 'property-owning democracy', wasn't remotely so. In fact, he proposed a 'social dividend' that would provide all citizens with a constant flow of income equivalent to an equal share of the profits of capital (Birnbaum and Casassas, 2008). Meade's idea won't seem foreign to us:

The essential feature of this society would be that work had become rather more a matter of personal choice. The unpleasant work that had to be done would have to be very highly paid to attract to it those whose tastes led them to wish to supplement considerably their incomes from property. At the other extreme those who wished to devote themselves to quite uncommercial activities would be able to do so with a reduced standard of living, but without starving in a garret. (Meade, 1964: 40)

Recently, authors such as O'Neill and Williamson (2012b), Alan Thomas (2016) and Stuart White (2011, 2012) have studied in depth this idea of a 'property-owning democracy' and have related it to a broad range of packages of measures conceived in such a way that they wouldn't in any way exclude the presence of unconditional income flows. If the aim is to strengthen social positions of invulnerability for individuals and groups in the sense of Meade and Rawls' later work – which is what O'Neill, Williamson, Thomas, White and others aspire to – predistributive mechanisms operating *ex ante* are needed in order to prevent massive 'initial' resource inequalities. A strategy based on subsidies that come into operation *ex post* or when the situation of poverty – or lack of freedom – is already inevitable is radically insufficient from a republican perspective. First, it obliges us to live at the mercy of other individuals, and we've already seen how this constitutes the first great threat to republican freedom, namely *dominium*. Second, the paternalist, pervasive nature of the conditional programmes of traditional welfare regimes introduces the second great threat to republican freedom: *imperium*. The need for means testing, administrative monitoring of the conduct of users and the forms of oversight of the processes of an (alleged) social reintegration of assisted persons constitute the seed of highly stigmatising arbitrary interference by public institutions. As Van Parijs (2006: 14) puts it: 'A work-unconditional basic income endows the weakest with bargaining power in a way a work-conditional guaranteed income does not.' In brief, in a republican community, socioeconomic security must be understood as a basic right and there is a strong case to be made that a fully universal and unconditional basic income can be part of a package of measures to guarantee that right in today's world (Birnbaum and Casassas, 2008).

As just stated, what is at stake are the conditions for the possibility of a truly civil(ised) and truly democratic society. By contrast with the Thatcherite neoliberal insistence that there is no such thing as society – a resoundingly cynical assertion given Margaret Thatcher's attempts to dismantle, piece by piece, the civil society that the British working classes had been constructing for decades – the republican project of predistributing resources to offer a universal guarantee of 'freedom without conditions', of '*unconditional* freedom', aims at consolidating the individual and collective right to nothing more nor less than society. There can be no civil(ised) society or effective democracy without the possibility of meeting up with others in settings where we can all look each other in the eye and recognise ourselves as singular entities equally called to live our own lives without coercion, and to do so in common. The alternative to civil(ised) society isn't the asocial haze that Thatcher invented but what was to be proposed two decades later by her epigone David Cameron, who aspired to construct a supposed *big society* – yes, 'society' – through the survival instinct of the dispossessed, on the one hand, and the creativity (and power of discipline, naturally) of their dispossessors, on the other.

Freedom that is unconditionally guaranteed to everyone – in this precise sense, *unconditional* freedom – therefore requires the presence of (im)material resources that are properly distributed among all citizens. When these resources aren't the result of capricious handouts but are unconditionally obtained, they can consolidate our positions of invulnerability as citizens who are free in the republican sense. In other words, citizens must be capable not only of *enjoying* these resources but also of *controlling* their receipt, management and reproduction over time. Without this capacity of 'democratic control' over a resource (Casassas and De Wispelaere, 2012), of being able to do with it what we individually decide and/or agree upon with others, humans can be offered *welfare*, understood as a 'provision' for satisfying our needs, but we can only gain *freedom* when the resource in question is obtained and governed from public-common instances led from below. Just as the well-treated slave showered with gifts and attentions remains a slave because he or she has no control over his or her life, citizens who benefit from welfare support or income transfer policies that are beyond their control – either because they're administered by bureaucratic bodies that are accountable to no one, or by ruling castes or vanguards that paternalistically end up fossilising truly constituent processes of mass-based democratic origins – may attain higher levels of *welfare* but we can hardly conclude that they become *freer* citizens. Freedom requires not only the resource but also control over its use. Indeed, incidental access to the resource based on the changing whims of external agents bears little relation with the extension of republican freedom. Hence, *freedom* and *welfare* shouldn't be confused. For all these reasons, unconditional measures that come into play *ex ante*, independently of any circumstance pertaining to our existence, equip us with tools that are not only able to satisfy our needs but also to do so in keeping with our wishes, aspirations and ways of life, which is to say, respecting freedom. This is what a basic income does.

It's all about freedom. As mentioned above, this book is about the need to guarantee 'unconditionally' the material and symbolic conditions of freedom. And this isn't just playing with words, as I shall show before concluding. The question of freedom presents two closely intertwined dimensions. First, freedom is a longing, an impulse to create the social spaces and relations we might desire, an aspiration to produce life. In this sense, freedom takes on its affirmative dimension and becomes *freedom to*. Second, freedom means protection against arbitrary interference by outside influences that might put an end to the creative acts I've just mentioned. In this second sense, freedom becomes preventive and is *freedom from*, *freedom against*. But freedom is both things: the creative act (or positive) and the preventive act (or negative).[6] This is not unlike riding around the city on a motorbike, putting on a helmet and obeying the traffic lights. The act of getting around involves the (active, creative) wish to imagine and cover an itinerary and, at the same time, the (protective, negative) awareness that we'll only manage to do this in regulated contexts with safety mechanisms for avoiding collisions where those using the flimsiest vehicles always have the most to lose.

Hence, by contrast with the famous distinction between 'positive freedom' and 'negative freedom' which (as the heir to that made by Benjamin Constant (2010 [1819]) at the beginning of the nineteenth century in his essay 'The Liberty of Ancients Compared with that of Moderns') we owe to Isaiah Berlin (1969), the republican approximation to freedom brings the two dimensions together. First, republican freedom indicates a whole multiplicity of positive creative gestures for imagining and putting into practice one's own life, alone or sharing it, which is what the classics of republicanism, from Pericles and Aristotle to Marx have always upheld. Second, the republican approach to freedom is underpinned by a meticulous sociology of domination that constantly warns us of the restrictions that this creative action can come up against in social life. And these restrictions are related to the presence of ties of dependence that must be undone politically so that we can be 'negatively' *free from* the mere possibility of arbitrary interference by other agents, a situation that, once again, was pondered by the greater part of the republican tradition, from Pericles and Aristotle to Marx. Both aspects are necessary and inseparable. Indeed, negative protection is absurd if we don't decide to start moving around in the world. Why would we have traffic lights if nobody wanted to get around in any kind of vehicle?[7] We mustn't underrate the creative, *doing*, positive dimension as if this was simply not our thing. Likewise, the attempt to imagine and live, radically and positively, one's own life in one's own world without giving due attention to the 'sociological-political' task of identifying, managing and (negatively) demolishing the power relations that permeate social life as a whole,[8] would be a fruitless and, it would seem, romantically tinged endeavour that would only lead us to the abyss of personal and sociopolitical deactivation. Would it be possible to move around the world without a minimal map of the reality outside, which can't be ignored, where accidents can end our lives, and against which we therefore need political and institutional protection?

The basic income proposal responds, then, to a twofold aspiration, one that is *at once* positive and negative. First, basic income works as a lever for activating, in the republican sense, the free forms of work and life that we (unconditionally) want to assert loud and clear. Second, basic income contributes (also unconditionally) towards providing us with the material and symbolic conditions we need to protect the possibility that these kinds of work and ways of life could become a reality.

PART III

Flexible, Multi-Active Lives:
The Dimensions of Social Power

There was this time, a few years ago, when a close friend of mine was waiting for his turn at a temping agency. He had an early afternoon appointment. These were already the days of scrappy little jobs, discontinuity and CVs, dozens and dozens of CVs. He was sitting there listening to flamenco with his earbuds. My friend has always liked flamenco. He's a man of flamenco clubs and other musical adventures. He was waiting there patiently. He knew all about job centres. There were lots of people and, for some reason, things were moving very slowly. The minutes and hours went by. The most recent arrivals were told, sorry, but they had to come back another day. Darkness fell. People who'd been summoned filed past him, entering a little office and coming out a few minutes later. Too many people, too many hours. My friend was getting more and more testy. Finally, when his tolerance levels had almost hit zero, his name was called and he entered an office. A scrawny, sweaty man picked up some papers and, half crouching, filed them away in a cupboard. Still not looking at my friend, he told him to sit down. 'Sit down. Now let's see'. He kept fiddling with the papers. Suddenly, he stood up straight, looked at him, sat in his chair and asked, 'Let's see. Alright you then, what can you do?' My friend is very patient. He knows how to listen and understand. This is probably why he also knows how to get indignant. I don't know whether it was indignation, his ability to listen or the remarkable sense of proportion he's always shown, but the fact is, he could only do what his body asked of him. Not wasting a second more, he answered, 'Well, look, I know how to do this'. He stood up and, very seriously, rolled up his shirt sleeves, clapped his hands together, stared hard at the scrawny man and, after stamping hard on the office floor, let out from the depths of his lungs a tremendous flamenco *quejío* – aaaaayyy! – that seemed like the howl of a poor beast getting its throat cut. Outside, in the passageway, there was total silence. He rolled down his sleeves, bent to pick up his bag and helmet, and headed out into the street.

The moral is that, if we haven't already completely lost the sense of what a dignified (working) life could be, of what meaningful work might entail, we have no choice but to protest, if necessary, through flamenco *quejíos*, through howling and stamping, the process of allocating tasks and jobs in our societies – that is, when they are allocated, because we can hardly ignore rising structural unemployment levels. What do we think 'meaningful' work might be? What (kinds of, in plural) work are we willing to do? In what proportions? And in what conditions? All of these are questions that should be answered by us, that is, very far from the disdainful arbitrariness of supposed employers for whom we are mere means. We can't dance to the sound of bullets being shot at our feet, leaping, scared and frantic from one scrap of activity to another. This isn't life. And, of course, it isn't democracy either.

9

Basic Income and the Democratisation of Work

So, yes, we're talking about democracy. But what can we understand by *democratic* social relations in everything pertaining to the realm of work? In other words, what is economic democracy? By *economic democracy*, I mean the individual and collective ability to decide 'what to do' in terms of production, reproduction and participation in community life, whatever the legal nature of the spaces in which we act, for example environments administered through private property, self-managed cooperative projects, domains governed by the public powers, homes, and so on. But what does this idea of deciding what to do entail? Two things, basically. We can equate economic democracy with the capacity, first, to decide the kind of work environments in which we wish to operate, which means defining – apart from the matter of whether the activity should be commodified and remunerated or not – what we understand by *us*, by *work* and by *workplace*. Is looking after someone or writing poetry *work*? And second, we can equate economic democracy with the ability to choose who we want to work with, at what pace, how often and to produce what kinds of (im)material goods and social settings, etcetera (Casassas, 2016a).

At the opposite extreme of my friend's *quejío*, which was essentially a bitter cry for a smidgen of economic democracy, an advert I recently found stuck to a lamppost said the following:

Dynamic young German woman offers her services:
- Translations from German to Spanish and Catalan
- Housework, ironing
- Cleaning offices and business premises
- Caring for kids
- Dog walking
- As a waitress or cook
In brief, I am offering myself to work.
If you have some small job for me, please call [phone number].

The loss of control over her life shown by the young German woman in her advert, in which she was literally begging for *any* kind of job (and I'm in no way blaming her for that) is horrific. It's pure submission to the brutality of capitalist labour despotism. Instead of any hint of democracy, it demonstrates open docility. Can we afford such colossal resignation?

As we'll see, nothing of what I'm talking about here is a plea for a world without work. On the contrary. Along with affective relations, work (in the plural) is what can give true sense to life. Well, this is the case when we're talking about freely chosen affective relations and work because, as happens with some 'affective' relations, there are forms of work and division of labour that are unhealthy, and that have nothing to do with a life we can feel is our own, but quite the reverse. And we'll see why.

Let's agree that work can be defined as the set of activities, remunerated or not, that we carry out in order to satisfy our (both individual and collective) material and symbolic needs.[1] So, how do we assign these activities? In other words, what are the mechanisms and procedures we use to distribute the workload? At this point, it's a good idea to establish an unambiguous distinction between the *technical division of labour* and the *social division of labour*. We understand by *technical division of labour* any process of assigning tasks – in the productive unit, in the household, and so on – that takes into account the wishes, skills, inclinations and aspirations of the people who must carry them out. This type of division of labour, analysed and upheld by Adam Smith (1981), gives voice to the actors involved in the workplace and leads to good results in terms of efficiency (as specialisation among the workers gives a higher-quality end product) and personal satisfaction (as a higher-quality end product obtained in inclusive environments where workers have had a say brings greater levels of gratification for all participants).[2]

But, while analysing and celebrating the technical division of labour, Adam Smith, like Marx in the *Economic and Philosophic Manuscripts of 1844*, examines and condemns the *social division of labour*, or the process of assigning tasks and activities in keeping with the social background of individuals. Those who have least – the dispossessed – make do with the most unpleasant, least rewarding positions and tasks, while the relationship of socioeconomic dependence on those who contract them obliges them to abide by stipulations and procedures that their employers see fit to impose; and to shut up about it because there is a reason why there is no exit door.

What is problematic, both Marx and Smith say, is that these processes of assigning activities involve serious difficulties for individuals and societies as a whole. First, those who have had to accept jobs imposed by the necessity that follows upon dispossession – the people who, in this regard, are carrying out 'forced labour' because of the different forms of coercion to which they are submitted (Marx, 1975) – see how their freedom is evaporating, day after day. They can only clutch at straws, which are almost unobtainable and very partial at that. This is pure dependence on the will of others. Second, having to accept activities we don't choose to do but that are thought up and assigned by others very often means losing sight of the whole (Smith, 1978), as we don't know what we're doing or why, which means ceasing to be who we are or who we're trying to be since we don't recognise ourselves either in labour or in any of its fruits. In the last instance, we're 'alienated', a long way from any possibility of self-realisation (Marx, 1975; Smith, 1978, 1981). Third, the social division of labour entails gigantic doses of inefficiency. Capitalist dispossession generates inefficiency because it removes workers from activities in which they can contribute more and better, confining them in spaces where they're unlikely to be able to use their talents and creative abilities. In fact, there are huge amounts of work that is productive and beneficial for society, work that adds value, but it remains hidden away by the need of workers to grab at and 'accept' whatever job is 'offered' to them.[3]

Needless to say, *the sexual division of work* (the process by which care work is assigned to women in the opacity of the domestic sphere, simply because they are women) and the *racial* or *ethnic division of work* (or the set of mechanisms whereby people coming from historically colonised places, as well as their descendants, are made to do the most menial jobs) present the same problems as those I've just outlined above. A long time ago, John Stuart Mill warned of the ill-effects of wasting technical-productive competence and the potential of participation in civic-political life by instituting a division of work that relegated women to the domestic sphere where, to make matters worse, they couldn't make their voices heard (Miguel, 2011).

The processes of allocating tasks and activities, then, shouldn't be based on mechanisms that, like rollers going round and round, crushing any attempt to construct and develop a personal life project, annihilate the freedom of popular classes, dispossessed as they are of the necessary means of a dignified existence. These processes, whether the tasks and activities are remunerated or not by the markets, should aim at the chance, within the reach of everyone, of doing what we'd like to do in order to be something that approximates what we'd like to be, with whom we'd like to be and in the way we'd like to experience it. Hence the interest of the basic income proposal, since it offers a flow of monetary resources conferred *ex ante*, unconditionally, enabling us to hold the gaze of those with whom we negotiate the allocation of (whatever kinds of) work, and favouring the individual and collective unfolding of lives that are free and, therefore, liveable.

But these resources must reach everyone[4] unconditionally, that is, 'predistributively'. Otherwise they lose their emancipatory potential. Beyond the 'technical' advantages that basic income presents vis-à-vis conditional subsidies (which I detail below), basic income contributes towards organising sets of resources that seek to consolidate the possibility that everyone can reject unwanted social relations and can explore the paths they wish, which have hitherto been barred by the material need of submitting to the tutelage of others. There are many 'noes' that must be uttered in order to be able to pronounce and meaningfully administer the 'yeses' of a free life. But let's take things one step at a time. First, we look at the *technical* advantages associated with a basic income, and then we return to the question of *social power* it holds out (Wright, 2006a, 2006b), and that of the effects of this *power* in terms of the democratisation of (all kinds of) work.

By comparison with conditional subsidies, basic income presents several technical advantages. I mention just three. Although these are aspects related with the design and *technical* functioning of income transfer systems, these advantages clearly take on a *political* meaning that is by no means trivial.[5]

First of all, basic income stands out for its administrative simplicity since it only requires that the public administration makes a monthly transfer to the accounts of all citizens and accredited residents of a given geographical space. Naturally, any difficulties this might entail are nothing compared with those of having to set up and manage a costly system of resource monitoring and verifying specific social circumstances.[6]

Second, the unconditional nature of basic income means that recipients aren't stigmatised as getting 'poverty', 'sickness' or 'handicapped' benefits, etc. As Zygmunt Bauman points out, all too often, in the domain of social work, it's evident that one of the most distressing problems of receiving conditional benefits is that (potential) recipients are obliged, at the administration counters, to present themselves as 'incapable' and sometimes even as 'guilty' of not being able to lead an orderly, successful life (Leighton, 2002). To go back to Ken Loach, his *Raining Stones* character Bob, an unemployed worker in the north of England, who is true to his Catholic ways, goes to great lengths to get the bureaucratic apparatus of the social services to register him as 'hopelessly indigent' so that he can get a few pounds to buy his daughter an appropriate first communion dress. The social stigma is so unbearable that (potential) recipients frequently decide not to do the unthinkable and choose to renounce the benefits because they can't face having to give excessive explanations and suffering the humiliating checks and monitoring involved.[7]

Third, the unconditionality of basic income means that it avoids the problem of the so-called *poverty trap*. Recipients of conditional benefits tend to have a powerful disincentive to look for and engage in any kind of paid work because this would mean the loss of benefits. Needless to say, replacing cash benefits with low wages from a precarious and alienating job wouldn't seem to be the most sensible option, so many people prefer not to look for or accept these jobs and, if they work, to do so in the black economy. By contrast, an unconditional benefit such as basic income works as a floor and never as a ceiling. Paid employment doesn't entail loss of the benefit so the disincentive to work disappears. We can simply keep accumulating income from whatever the sources may be and, if this income exceeds certain thresholds, we must thenceforth contribute to society through the taxation system. This is why Yannis Varoufakis (2016) urged people to think of basic income as 'a foundation, not a safety net, a floor on which to stand solidly and from which to be able to reach the sky'. Wouldn't the 'free chooser subjects', whose presence the republican tradition has always longed for, aspire to precisely this?

These, then, are some of the advantages of the unconditionality of basic income. As a result of all this, it would act as a mechanism to prevent poverty and exclusion and not as a strictly curative device. As I've said, preventing poverty bolsters freedom, in the sphere of work too. So let's return to the question of the 'social power', or bargaining power, that basic income confers, and recall Erik Olin Wright, who pointed out that '[c]apitalism blocks the universalization of conditions for human flourishing' (2006b: 3) because large concentrations of private economic power prevent collective decision-making processes by means of which we could all (co)determine what we understand by meaningful work and how we wish to go about it. It is in this sense that capitalism shows its most openly anti-democratic face.

This is why basic income, by uncoupling work from income (since it's received independently of the kinds of work, remunerated or otherwise, we're doing), could become a tool for universalising 'social power', taking the form of better bargaining power of labour against capital, as well as offering better possibilities for decommodifying the workforce and extending myriad forms of the social economy which are difficult to set up today because of the precarious conditions of existence of the working population.

Exit doors are needed, exit doors from markets, households, etc. to reboot social interaction on the basis of truly democratic agreements in which we can all make our voices heard and respected. As we'll see later, in Chapter 13, this ability to 'exit' – and especially to exit the labour markets and to decommodify the workforce – is taken as a variable for ascertaining the greater or lesser levels of freedom and democracy that social actors might enjoy in the economic sphere, and at work in particular. As Wright (2006b: 6) himself says: 'Social power comes from the capacity to mobilise people for cooperative, voluntary collective actions of various sorts in civil society.'

In view of all this, one can realise that basic income cannot be seen as a post-work or an anti-work project. As Gourevitch (2022) rightly points out, it is impoverishing in theoretical terms and bears no relation to what work sometimes is or can become to presuppose that work is always a burden. In effect, there are or there can be many reasons and motivations for people to engage in many forms of work that go beyond the mere instrumental act through which we try to earn a wage and survive: attaining various types of excellence, making a social contribution, gaining social recognition and experiencing community and a sense of individual and collective autonomy (Dejours, Deranty, Renault and Smith, 2018; Gheaus and Herzog, 2016) and even a sense of social transformation. However, thinking and experiencing work as something more than a burden requires that individuals and groups be able to leave all (capitalist) forms of work where work is only a burden, too often a heavy burden (Horgan, 2021).

Gourevitch (2022: 15) suggestively warns of the danger of a certain post-work left-wing literature where 'the [...] promise is not just freedom from capitalist exploitation and domination but from work itself'. Indeed, the republican-socialist approach to basic income I uphold in this book makes crystal clear that gaining control over our own lives can only emanate from the kind of bargaining power we attain when we have our existence guaranteed, which fundamentally aims to control decisive economic processes and shape the realm of (both paid and unpaid) work to turn it into a more democratic domain. Thus, *work – dignifying work –* remains crucial.

In the same vein, the republican-socialist project I advocate here does not try to avoid *any possible* work ethic but mainly the kind of work ethic that is linked to work under capitalism and to all those imaginaries vis-à-vis work that are embraced by those left-wing traditions and social and political movements – including certain forms of unionism – that take capitalist labour relations as a fait accompli and 'simply' try to regulate the ways in which such freedom-limiting forms of work take place. This is why one should agree with Peter Frase when he contrasts the 'need to work for wages' with the freedom to 'explore what it means to take care of ourselves and one another' (Frase, 2016: 48) and with Bryant W. Sculos (2018: 5) when he opposes 'structurally-coerced labor' to 'one's ability to live a (decent) life'; but this does not mean that one cannot simultaneously endorse Gourevitch's claim that a post-capitalist work ethic needs to be nourished if we aim to imagine and put into motion emancipatory forms of work. The main point here is that these emancipatory imaginaries and forms of work cannot emerge from a simple voluntarist impulse, but their presence will tend to respond to the enjoyment of bargaining power emanating from unconditional access to income and other resources, that is, to the fact of having individuals and groups liberated from the need to accept the kinds of work that nowadays capitalist dispossession imposes on them.

'If the Left is to have a future, it cannot give up on work', Gourevitch (2022: 47) asserts. I cannot agree more with this statement. But the kind of work that can give the left a future is meaningful work under non-dominating – and therefore post-capitalist – conditions, and unconditional access to resources such as basic income constitutes a necessary (yet not sufficient) condition for us to leave freedom-harming work and fuel more democratic spaces and work environments.

In sum, as I said in the beginning, what is at stake here is none other than basic levels of real or effective democracy, and this democracy is also – and very crucially – expressed in the sphere of work. This is what my friend piercingly demanded with his flamenco howl in the premises of the temping agency.

10

Why Do We Want Bargaining Power?

What are the spheres in which the bargaining power bestowed by basic income enters into action and expands our republican freedom? To put it slightly differently, in what ways does this bargaining power show its democratising potential in our daily activity? The background of what I am suggesting here is that an adequate structure of rights – and the packages of unconditional resources deriving from them, including basic income – allows us room for the manoeuvring we need if we're to be self-determining in all the areas of life where we're engaged in some kind of work.

Structures of rights, and among them economic and social rights, aspire, by their very nature, to counter the expropriating and dispossessing dynamic that is always capitalism's *modus operandi*. Whatever the myths about the supposed 'bourgeois' origins of rights, including the Universal Declaration of Human Rights of 1948, rights – economic and social rights as well as civic and political rights – are a conquest of mass-based social movements, especially the workers' movement (Domènech, 2004). Neither liberalism nor utilitarianism, which are entrenched at the heart of mainstream economic science today, welcomed the idea of rights, which were seen as a stumbling block to the free functioning of the supposed automatisms of markets. There are social, economic and political rights – wherever they may exist – because there were and are working classes that rose up, and are rising up, to demand the universalisation of the condition of citizenship. There are social, economic and political rights – wherever they may exist – because the universalisation of citizenship required, and requires, assuring for everyone, without exclusions, positions of social invulnerability emanating from legal principles that enshrine a material guarantee that must be won and maintained, through conflict if necessary. Guaranteeing resources for everyone in a finite world always means placing on the table the thorny matter of *distribution* of these resources[1] (Casassas, 2016b). The unconditional guarantee of economic and social rights, including basic income, endows us with a bargaining power of deep political and civilisational aspirations.[2] But bargaining power for what, exactly?

BASIC INCOME AS A RESISTANCE FUND

To begin with, this is bargaining power to question, to dispute and, if need be, to redefine the working conditions of wage workers in modern enterprises. It's not enough to have labour legislation that 'protects' them to a greater or lesser extent. This protection amounts to partially limiting the scope of the various kinds of arbitrary interference to which the dependent working population is subjected, and it means taking for granted the loss of freedom of the wage-earning population as a fait accompli and trying to find ways of mitigating the harmful effects of the great disaster.

If we stop for a moment to think about it, we can immediately see that the slave population can also be helped by some sort of 'labour legislation'. Take the measures adopted by the free poor men's party of the Athenian democracy which, led by Ephialtes, Pericles and Aspasia, achieved the great plebeian-democratic revolution of 461 BCE. The reforms introduced by the free poor men's party 'didn't abolish slavery but they did concede two rights of social existence to slaves: equal freedom of speech in the agora (*isegoria*) and total protection from physical punishment by slave owners (*akolasia*)' (Domènech, 1993: 66). These are measures that could increase the well-being of workers and, in this case, slave workers in the strict sense, but in no way do they abolish the servitude that binds these workers as a consequence of the socioeconomic dependence they maintain with respect to those who acquire their labour power. Republican freedom, then, is conspicuous by its absence.

The same is true of wage labour when we turn to it because dispossession leaves us with no other option. When we are forced to cede our decision-making capacity about the what and the how of our possible (different kinds of) work, our freedom evaporates. As with the slaves of the mid-fifth century BCE, contemporary labour legislation regulates the types and degrees of arbitrary interference we might have to deal with today, and it's well known that present forms of wage labour can be true sources of the physical and mental deterioration of our bodies, so that new forms of *akolasia*, when they appear, are a help. Likewise, regulatory frameworks promoting certain levels of *isegoria* – of 'voice', to use Hirschman's expression – for workers today might be introduced. But, as happened with the ancient world of slave owners, neither raising one's voice in a job centre nor protection against the physical and mental damage caused by wage labour is a mechanism designed to put an end to the liberticidal effects of openly asymmetrical social relations. Where there is dependence on the arbitrary will of another, there can be no freedom even when there are well-intentioned 'employers' who, though they might be willing to listen and to be as lenient as possible with punishments, might also not be willing if that's how the mood takes them.

But things change with a basic income because it works like a kind of disaggregated trade union 'resistance fund' that is equally and permanently within the reach of everybody (Casassas and Raventós, 2003, 2007; Van Parijs, 2013). If there is conflict in the labour relationship, the more vulnerable party is equipped (as happened with the principle of the old 'resistance funds' that trade unions established on the basis of quotas paid by their members) with resources that can sustain workers' claims for some time – and it's well known that, in the process of negotiating, success depends to a good extent on the standby capacity, on the ability to stick it out – with resources that must make it possible, thenceforth, to keep proposing and, if necessary, imposing the terms and conditions of this working relationship.

It's worth digressing here to note that it's precisely the fact that this 'resistance fund' is not controlled by union headquarters but 'disaggregated' (or distributed to the pockets of each and every worker) which has set off alarm bells in some trade union organisations because they say they fear the individualising effects of basic income. Many analysts from union backgrounds say that, since it's an individual endowment, basic income could atomise labour relations and undermine collective bargaining (Vanderborght, 2006). However, scares such as this are somewhat surprising in a world where fragmentation of the productive unit combined with the difficulties facing the selfsame union organisations when it comes to dealing with new socio-labour scenarios have *already* ensured that labour relations are highly atomised, and collective bargaining is *already* badly eroded if not in tatters.[3] As noted before, it might be more effective if the unions saw basic income as one more tool for designing new strategies of collective bargaining (Haagh, 2018), since the fact of being individually received in no way excludes the possibility of struggles being coordinated by union headquarters which could turn out to be more combative and successful precisely because of the awareness that the working population they represent would now have a cushion to fall back on, and is not dead but well and truly alive.[4] This is what the American trade union leader Andy Stern, president until 2010 of the powerful Service Employees International Union and fervent basic income supporter, seems to have observed, while also openly showing his opposition to the job guarantee proposal, which he sees as a mechanism that would be highly intrusive in people's lives – how would it be possible to entrust government agencies with the decision of what work is valuable and what isn't? – and also criticising minimum-income schemes which, besides entailing enormous administrative costs, tend to stigmatise and discipline working populations that are precisely those that should be able to shake off all forms of despotism and subjugation (Stern, 2016).

The possibility of credibly threatening rupture, or 'exit' from the relationship, gives working people better possibilities for (co-)determining their use of time, remuneration and other non-monetary rewards and, in general, for organising production as a whole. To give just two examples, first, if our material existence was guaranteed, how many of us would be willing to engage in an activity that is not at all or barely gratifying unless we were given a significant pay rise (Wright, 2010)? And, second, critical voices coming from business circles are often raised against the problem of absenteeism in the workplace, which supposedly means abandoning one's job and/or responsibilities; but how many people talk about *presenteeism* or the decision, dictated by fear of losing one's job or any of its rewards, to turn up and stick at it, sometimes for weeks, months or years when a whole range of circumstances – among them, those related with physical and mental health[5] – recommend the exact opposite? It seems reasonable to think that a basic income could help to put an end to such phenomena which are so alien to the social extension of forms of interdependence that are truly respectful of the freedom of each and every one of us.

To return to the 'exit' and the 'voice', this isn't about forcing anyone to leave the world of wage labour, and neither is it trying to get people to take paths they don't want to take. After all, it's true that there might be people who *prefer* to do wage work for others because they want to avoid the ups and downs of adrenalin rushes and headaches involved in setting up a business. It's about everyone, without exception, *being able to* leave the world of wage-earning work because, if we decide to remain there, this ability to leave it feeds into a vitally important bargaining power if the aim is to ensure that wage-earning work is compatible with effective freedom. To quote Van Parijs and Vanderborght (2017: 123): 'Not forcing all to work but allowing each not to work is then the best way not of abolishing capitalist exploitation, but of reducing its extent and shrinking what is most objectionable about it: its obligatory character.'[6] Everyone's awareness that no relationship is given forever, since we can all 'exit' them if we deem it appropriate, forces all parties to listen to all voices to turn wage-earning work scenarios into suitable places for a truly liveable life for all.

DECOMMODIFICATION OF WORK,
COOPERATIVISM AND OTHER ENDEAVOURS

In an interesting film called *Smoking Room* (2002), the directors, J. D. Wallovits and Roger Gaul are doubly able to offer a period piece about what it must have been like to be employed (with a wage, of course) as an office worker in Europe at the beginning of the twenty-first century while also framing their account in a context that makes this wage-earning work in typical offices seem like the spectre of something that exists and will continue to exist, even when revealing its barefaced ignominiousness, and when it seems it's starting to cry out to be overthrown.

The plot is simple. An American company takes over a Spanish business, where people have always smoked. But the Americans come in with their fine ways and all sorts of adjustments. The new bosses decree that smoking inside the premises is banned. If workers want to smoke, they must go out into the street. In this situation, a worker called Ramírez decides to collect signatures demanding the conversion of an unoccupied office into a smoking room, so that smokers can relax with a cigarette without leaving the building. It may be in the south of Europe, but it also gets cold.

The fantastic part comes with a memorable scene which is shot on the building's roof terrace. Ramírez and another employee, whom we'll call López, open the door and come outside. Ramírez is trying to persuade López to sign his petition. López listens for a while, says alright he'll sign, that he agrees, OK, yes, it's important for people to be able to smoke in peace where they've always smoked. But then López freaks out and explodes. He looks as if he's about to burst a blood vessel. Beneath this bit of paper that Ramírez is obsessing about, beneath this roof terrace where they are talking, a whole world of arbitrariness and submission is hiding, a world of contempt and toadying, and of continuous disregard and humiliation. You can't plan anything. They don't tell you why you're doing what you do, or why sometimes it's good and other times it isn't. They don't respect your time, or your life, or anything else you might have outside the office walls. 'A smoking room? Blow the whole thing up, that's what we have to do!', López comes to exclaim. But in the end, you have to calm down – you have to calm down? – so López tries to calm down and looks at the petition again. A smoking room, OK.

One thing is clear. In the company where López and Ramírez work, nobody has this 'awareness' I just mentioned – that 'no relationship is given forever since we can all *exit* if we deem it appropriate'. And nobody was aware of this for the simple reason that facts are facts. It's not easy to leave the company where you work. Hence the arbitrariness and domination by those at the top. Hence the fact that what made Ramírez so indignant was merely the absence of a smoking room. And hence the fact that Ramírez's greatest ambition was getting someone to kindly listen to his 'voice' and make the unoccupied office available. This is a (part-time) slave's mentality. He keeps repeating that he's going to submit a *petition*. But is it really true that nobody was aware that maybe it would be better to *leave*, that is, to 'exit'? I think that López must have had this bee in his bonnet for quite a while.

But how to leave? And where to go? Blowing the whole thing up because we can't take any more, as López says, is a fairly pre-political project. But we should also recognise that a big explosion, metaphorical though it may be, also means a possible *reset* for openly democratising ambitions. Recall that at the beginning of Part III, *economic democracy* is described as the ability, first, to decide – apart from the question of whether or not there is remuneration in the markets – what we understand by *work* and by *workplace* and, second, the ability to choose who we want to work with, at what pace, how frequently, to create what kinds of (im)material goods and social milieus, and so on. Basically, it's nothing that López wouldn't have thought about, nothing strange to him. But where do we go from here to enjoy higher levels of economic democracy?

To start with, it's a good idea to revive the distinction made by the plainly republican Roman civil law between *locatio conductio operis*, which is equivalent to the contemporary independent producer's 'contract for a specific output' (by means of which individuals sell previously agreed upon goods and services for a price) and the *locatio conductio operarum*, the contemporary correlate of which is the wage worker's 'contract for services', whereby individuals sell their labour power in return for a wage (Zimmerman, 1996). In keeping with republican concerns and perspectives, Roman civil law establishes that this second type can't be a contract between free citizens because wage workers are obliged to partially alienate their freedom, which then makes them subjects of alien law or *alieni juris*, as Cicero argues in his *De Oficiis* (Domènech, 2004; Domènech and Bertomeu, 2016). The thing is, with a basic income in their pockets, the Lópezs of this world could aspire to labour relations in which the prevailing element would be independent work, the *locatio conductio operis*, and where wage labour, or *locatio conductio operarum*, would be carried out in institutional conditions that favour the social extension of republican freedom by protecting workers from the potential or effective arbitrariness of their employers.

To take another step, this 'independent work' doesn't have to be done alone. It can be done in cooperative spaces where workers freely associate and manage production in keeping with democratic procedures. The bargaining power conferred by a basic income makes it possible to transcend the salary society by decommodifying labour power and bringing it into the world of cooperativism. In other words, besides negotiating better working conditions in the capitalist enterprise, basic income also enables us to question the nature of the productive unit and eases the transition to working environments in which we can cooperatively make decision-making processes more horizontal.

Cooperativism appeared decades ago and is here to stay, but no one's ignorant of the fact that, however successful it's been in some domains and sectors, and however much it continues to grow, enormous quantities of willpower and resources are needed for cooperative entities to come into being, develop and endure over time. It's extremely difficult to urge workers – the immense majority of them with lives terribly damaged by the hostility of capitalist job markets that take their time, sap their energy and use up their material and symbolic resources – to attempt cooperativism, to stop the whirlwind and set about imagining and engaging in alternative productive projects. Yet a basic income would equip us with the necessary 'social power' to stop the machine, raise our heads and spend as long as we need to think, probably with others, about what direction to take and how to free ourselves from the bonds of dependence and power relations that are currently preventing us from taking the paths we might choose. Accordingly, basic income has been presented on several occasions as a lever that can activate cooperative forms of managing social and economic life (Casassas, 2011; Wright, 2006b, 2010).[7]

In sum, it would certainly be a mistake to reduce the effects of a basic income to its immediate impact in the labour supply side of labour markets since, by granting bargaining power and drastically reducing levels of uncertainty, basic income would also make it possible to embark on joint projects in the sphere of cooperativism (Stern, 2016; Van Parijs and Vanderborght, 2017). This has been demonstrated in pilot projects carried out mainly with women's associations in the Indian state of Madhya Pradesh (Davala, Jhabvala, Mehta, and Standing, 2015; Standing, 2017).

At the end of the day, we're talking once again about a whole possible exodus, a slower 'exodus' in the case of the sedimentation of new worlds, or faster in the case of an accelerated rushing into acts of defiance, which are nevertheless an *exodus*. Italian workers' autonomy and the spaces and

traditions it has carved out for itself have worked and are still working on
these questions lucidly and perceptively. As Marina Garcés writes (2016: 59
and 67):

[R]ejecting [wage-earning] work has its own traditions. From the pica-
resque and avoidance through to the collective organisation of exodus
from the factory [and office, one might add] through to searching for
alternative and more autonomous forms of life. [...] Rejecting work isn't
just a practice of struggle and sabotage but also the expression of a political subjectivity in defecting from all forms of entrapment, both at work
and politically.

But rejecting (waged) work 'Italian-style' – the 'exodus' proposed by Virno
and company as an emotional act of flight and resistance against the powers
that be (Virno, 2003) – although it has importantly drawn attention to a left
that is all too often acritical about the matter of wage labour when not smug
or merely contemplative, takes on anti-institutional overtones that should be
questioned. The *institutional* isn't necessarily a Weberian iron cage that must
close off any horizon of possibilities in an inevitable teleology that is inertly
and mechanically unfolding.

To go back to basic income itself, this isn't an institutional device that has
come to terminate the contingency of a life that has all of a sudden spontaneously appeared. On the contrary, it has come so we can use it as an
instrument to trace out a path that, of course, won't be recognised and taken
if it isn't walked, very often groping along the way, in the indeterminacy of
what is still possible, of what is not yet defined, this being the very reason
why we need a compass and footwear. But basic income is pure institution-
ality. We're talking about nothing more or less than resources collected by
the taxation system and made available to the public powers so that, every
month, they end up in the pockets of citizens. Is it possible to imagine a
more institutional(ised) mechanism? Hence, we can state that basic income
takes from the autonomous Italian and European traditions – because,
in the first instance, it does so from the bulk of the republican tradition,
which always took these same paths – a vindication of the unforeseen that
suddenly rises from the ashes of a world of despotism and forced obedience
to authority that we might want to see going up in flames. But basic income
also calls for the need for these green shoots to be rather more than episodic
and reserved for a handful of genuine but maybe naïve voluntarists (when
they are not posh people with good intentions and sufficient free time), but

a whole horizon of possibilities that is genuinely open to each and every inhabitant of the world in which we live. In other words, basic income has come to guarantee, politically and institutionally, the universalisation of the possibility of 'exiting', a possibility we grant ourselves so that everybody can embark on 'enterprises' that are truly born from us and that can grow with us, without our having to ask permission from anyone (Barry, 2005).

The question of a possible 'workers' council-based democracy', which could be the result in terms of economic governance of the social extension of the cooperative principle, is not far from what we are now discussing. Recently, Nicholas Vrousalis (2019) has argued that a commitment to workplace democracy that is based on republican normative principles entails the opposition to private property and the promotion of independently constituted workers' councils that share the control over the means of production with democratic parliaments. Leaving aside the whole debate about whether the problem is private property itself or the fact that capitalist modernity has settled on an absolutist, privative and exclusive vision of private property (Casassas and Mundó, 2022), it is worth considering that unconditional access to resources such as basic income, among other measures, can help to consolidate and reproduce in time and space, without a lesser risk of falling into problems of technocratic authoritarianism, the 'social power' that is needed to nourish those processes of societal empowerment aimed at creating and socially extending multilevel networks of workers' councils, whatever form they might take. Here, then, is a sociopolitically ambitious concretion – a clearly post-capitalist one, in fact – of the idea of 'social entrepreneurship' that we are assessing.[8]

But 'enterprise'? Recently, many voices have rightly been raised against the discourse of entrepreneurship and the enterprise and everything they bring in terms of the disciplining power they exercise over the lives of the working population. As Jorge Moruno (2015) and Dejours, Deranty, Renault and Smith (2018) note, the figure of the *entrepreneur* is understood as the epitome of a neoliberal culture that creates labour suffering because it atomises everything and puts it up for sale on the shelves of the supermarket that human life has become. We try to make ourselves so we can make a living, try to be employable assets so that the owners of capital see us as an exploitable commodity, we continually strive to reinvest in ourselves, going into debt if need be so we can stay in the competition and, finally, we bear the burden of shame and guilt when we don't triumph in the implacable rat race that is the *winner-take-all society* (Frank and Cook, 1996), where the winner, which can only be one or, at most, a few – the *oligoi*, the usual *few* oligarchs – get all the prizes.[9]

As often happens, when a term that is a long way from being a neologism and that once designated desirable realities acquires connotations that are so damaging to life, two possibilities appear. The first is jettisoning the term: if it's damaging to life, we don't even want to name it. The second is trying to discover when, where and how the sense changed, to undertake the clearly political task of recovering it and to reveal the ignominy of the attempt to disfigure it. In the case of entrepreneurship, the second option can be highly fertile, because *enterprise* can be highly gratifying in many ways. The tragedy is that the right to enterprise (also related with 'entrepreneur', from the French *entreprendre*, to undertake) has become a privilege reserved for a few. The rest of us are deprived of this possibility and, to add insult to injury, the mythology of *entrepreneurship* in the neoliberal individual-enterprise makes us responsible for and even guilty of the injustice that is inflicted on us.

So, we won't throw the baby out with the bathwater. In its classical sense, *enterprise* is something we can't renounce because it has the sense of 'project'. It is the act of *undertaking* any initiative or project in the spheres of work, remunerated or not, and business that we might wish to engage in, and get into circulation, individually or collectively. Why should we give up on the idea of the pleasure of setting up an establishment, company or enterprise that would contribute to satisfying needs, that would be gratifying and fulfilling, and that would even bring in income we might like to earn?

The problem, as Moruno (2015) and other analysts (Casassas, 2016a, 2016b; Standing, 2017; Van Parijs and Vanderborght, 2017) have mentioned, is that capitalist dispossession and the material dependence resulting from it tends to prevent acts of entrepreneurship from happening, from succeeding and, most of all, from generalising because, as is well known, getting a business off the ground requires initial resources that allow us to hold out until reaching the break-even point, relational–social capital that provides us with a whole network of contacts and solidarities and, finally, the ability to pick ourselves up and keep going when coming up against obstacles and setbacks. Could a basic income contribute towards consolidating the socioeconomic security we need for an enterprise? As Standing (2017: 179) observes, 'people need basic security to develop their talents, potential and vocation. [...] A basic income would allow more people, and not only the well-to-do, to pursue their passions.' He goes on to quote the succinct rendition of the same question by the British writer John O'Farrell:

Anyone who ever created anything did so with a modicum of financial security behind them. That's why Virginia Woolf needed 'a room of her own and £500 a year'. For centuries we have tapped the potential of only a small proportion of the British people; the rest have been powerless to initiate or discover where their true talents lay.[10]

It seems clear enough, then, that the old refrain that where there's a will there's a way is a highly questionable fantasy. Anyone who doesn't agree should ask all those who work hard to pursue some kind of artistic or creative project without being able to count on economic and social-relational resources to begin with. The artistic *enterprise* can become a titanic task, almost certainly condemned to failure or opacity when the socioeconomic conditions are not in place to assure that the project can be nourished and sustained over time. Could a basic income be this lever for activating the most varied forms of artistic work?[11] Bertrand Russell also echoed the intuitions of the socialist tradition and, perhaps especially, its anarchist dimensions when he recalled the need for introducing institutional designs so that artists could reduce the working day without becoming destitute and, accordingly, devote themselves without anxiety to their own projects (Russell, 1966). Guy Standing (2017: 59) suggests that 'a basic income would increase both the amount and the productivity of "work", and could also increase the quality of "leisure", in the ancient Greek sense of *schole*. This term, from which the English word "school" is derived, meant being free from the necessity to labour, which Aristotle argued was a necessary condition for full participation in cultural and political life'. And, finally, Van Parijs and Vandenborgh (2017) propose that we should think about the extent to which robotisation, combined with a basic income, could help to generate spaces for the kind of 'leisure' that is needed to nurture creative projects.

Given all this, we shouldn't throw away the idea of *entrepreneurship* because enterprise in the right conditions can be part of a set of activities we associate with a worthwhile life. Hence, not shunning the notion of *enterprise* but, instead, embracing it would also enable us to say that, in the capitalist world, there is no 'right to entrepreneurship', which is the same as saying there is no 'freedom of enterprise', and that the much-vaunted right to 'private initiative', which shouldn't be discarded either – because who said that the ability to set out, alone or in company, along autonomously chosen productive paths is reprehensible? – is also conspicuous by its absence.

The same thing happens with the famous *culture of effort*. We're bombarded with it, and accused of not making enough of it when what's really happening is that we're dispossessed of the possibility of making an effort in the activities we really love and that partially, for this very reason, tend to be the ones that contribute most and best to society. What, then, should we do about the culture of effort? Rid ourselves of it because it's manipulated to become a weapon aimed squarely at the very heart of our lives? No, we mustn't. We must also reappropriate effort, effort that makes sense. We want to be able to make an effort!

TIME, LIFE AND WORK

At this point, it might be unnecessary to say that we need to free ourselves from the myopic identification between *work* and *employment*. The latter is merely a subset, as large as one likes, of a much bigger set: that of *work*. In other words, there are many kinds of work which, to simplify matters, we could divide into three: remunerated work, domestic or care work, and voluntary work (Raventós, 1999, 2007).[12] In turn, remunerated work includes, together with other kinds – as capitalist or cooperativist partners, as freelancers, and so on – wage labour or *employment*. The range of possibilities in terms of the forms and varieties of work is considerable. Hence, we often speak of *different kinds of work* rather than *work*.

Once again, this implies the question of the need to introduce institutional mechanisms, such as a basic income, that would enable us to decide, individually or collectively, what kind of remunerated or non-remunerated activities we want to do and in what proportions. This is a matter of common sense and also of justice. In the processes of the division of labour, which are essential in complex societies such as ours, we don't all aspire to do everything, but all of us have particular desires and inclinations that should be respected. Likewise, we all need to be co-responsible for the socially necessary set of tasks that are required for our lives to be sustainable. These are sometimes gratifying and sometimes not.

Again, conflict looms. Who should do what? And with what system of rewards and penalties? Since basic income universally offers bargaining power, it could be a tool for fostering – maybe in ways that are indirect and decentralised but never atomised – a distribution of tasks and life-sustaining responsibilities that most and best respects what we all legitimately aspire to be (Haagh, 2018). Let's look at this question in four closely interconnected areas of crucial social and civilisational importance: distribution of work in a world with high levels of structural unemployment and rampant automation; uses of time and caring for life; the material and symbolic organisation that is needed so that we can embark on a just eco-social transition; and the work, normally voluntary, that we carry out in the civic-political domain.

Sharing Out Work in the Age of Robots

It's no secret that, in most of the planet's economies, contemporary capitalism goes hand in hand with high levels of structural unemployment. In the case of Spain, in the 40 years between 1978 and 2018, the unemployment rate was higher than 15 per cent in 28 of them. Contemporary capitalism has also brought labour counter-reforms and wage devaluation policies that have led to the phenomenon of the 'working poor' (wage earners whose income is below the poverty line), and a continual widening of the gap separating permanent and temporary workers. If that wasn't enough, the effects of robotisation could be devastating in terms of job destruction. According to a suggestive study by Torrens and González de Molina (2016): 'Even taking the most cautious figure suggesting that 12% of jobs can be automised in Spain, thus affecting most severely those that require fewer qualifications [...], one can expect a deepening of the patterns of duality, polarisation, and the chronic structural unemployment of the Spanish labour market.' And Spain is far from being an exotic rarity, since its economy, with all its peculiarities, is highly representative of the types of capitalist economies that are consolidating today.

The existing literature about the effects of automatisation on the future of employment offers widely differing lines of analysis. But some data are clear. Several studies suggest that, in the United States, approximately 47 per cent of jobs are at high risk of automatisation in the next two decades, the most affected sectors being logistics and transport, administrative jobs and those in the service sector. Others say that, in the European Union, the threat of automatisation is even greater, as 54 per cent of jobs are extremely vulnerable. Finally, other studies say that, on a global scale, as many as 45 per cent of jobs might be automised.[13] Whatever the figures we're working with, what seems to be beyond doubt is that a net breach is opening up between jobs wiped out by technology, especially routine work of low added value, and the new employment generated by it.[14]

It wouldn't be superfluous at this point to recall the prediction about the future of work that Keynes made in 1930. If the evolution of technological development continued at the same pace it was then, he said, people would be working 15 hours a week by 2030.[15] How wrong was he? At first glance, many would say he was a long way off the mark. But there is one highly revealing datum, which is that, in Spain, the total number of hours worked by the population aged between 16 and 64 was, on average, 19.96 hours! (Torrens and González de Molina, 2016). It wouldn't seem rash to imagine that, by 2030, this figure might be around 15 hours. The problem we will most likely have in 2030, and that we most certainly have today, is these hours of work can be extremely badly distributed. Some people work very few and even no hours for an income while others have to work an exorbitant number of hours every day.

All this is why basic income could be a most valuable instrument, but not to save our skins so we can sadly languish in a dystopian technological world that banishes us from paid work and strips us of the ability to imagine ways of life and working. Basic income could be effective and helpful in giving us the necessary bargaining power to find a proper balance in the distribution of paid work and, more importantly, to obtain for men and woman combinations of remunerated and non-remunerated work that are much more harmonious and closer to what a life worth living is all about. Everybody should have access to better proportioned combinations of productive work, reproductive or care work, and voluntary work.[16]

The processes of robotisation, then, need not be presented by sounding the alarms of an apocalyptic spirit. On the contrary, the democratic management of automation processes, mediated by a basic income, could give rise to parallel processes of reduced working hours that could only be welcomed as something that is normatively desirable (Frase, 2016). First, such processes could spare us from doing (some of) the wage-earning work that we find unedifying or downright disagreeable.[17] Second, they could contribute towards paving the way for the societal debate, which I've already mentioned, about this urgent matter of co-responsibility in socially necessary, paid and unpaid, tasks.

Along these lines, one of the possible positive effects of a reduction in working hours prompted by the presence of a basic income in contexts of large-scale automatisation is that women would be more able to propose and, if necessary, force a more egalitarian distribution of productive and reproductive work. Freed from the need to find a job to save – but also spoil – their lives, men and women receiving a basic income can sit down together and think about how much productive and how much care work they want to do, and nobody will have to feel belittled. First, 'a better job offer resulting from the reduction in working hours would facilitate women's entry into the job market' (Torrens and González de Molina, 2016), if this is what they want. Second, a basic income would allow men to distance themselves from the stale image of 'male breadwinner' and engage in activities that are perhaps non-remunerated but also highly valuable for a life that makes sense.[18] It's also clear that it would help to avoid the notorious problem of 'double presence' that appears when women who join the workforce and enter the labour market still have to shoulder the burden of the family tasks and responsibilities for which they've always been responsible (Moreno Colom, 2016).

'Work less (for pay) so everyone can work.' This is a slogan that has been popular among the European left since the late 1980s and early 1990s (Aznar, 1994) (and 'make us *all* co-responsible for reproductive tasks, normally unpaid', I'd add).[19] What I want to suggest here, together with Torrens and González de Molina (2016), is that one of the aspirations of the basic income proposal is to make this idea effective.[20] In fact, the reduction of working hours can be legislated and introduced as a mandatory measure through its inclusion, for example, in the Workers' Statute (in the case of Spain) or other labour laws, but there would always be loopholes open for negotiation, collective or otherwise, between employers and workers. Moreover, who knows whether well-conducted negotiations, backed by a basic income, could lead to even more desirable situations than those that might be envisaged by law (Van Parijs and Vanderborght, 2017)?

It's evident, therefore, that a reduction in working hours should be accompanied, if not induced, by a basic income, not only to compensate for possible reductions in income but also to give workers, men and women, proper conditions for undertaking any negotiating processes because the forms of the reduced working day that are normally considered, however attractive they might be, leave the way open for high levels of conflict which workers can't deal with unless they have material guarantees. An account of some of the measures explored so far is sufficient to demonstrate the extent to which this is the case: a working week reduced to 35 hours (or even 21 (New Economics Foundation and Ecopolítica, 2012)), a four-day working week or 'Friday off', longer holiday periods, sabbatical years or semesters every so often, longer maternity and paternity leave, earlier retirement age, voluntary reversible changes in the working day made by the worker which the enterprise is obliged to accept except in cases of *force majeure*, encouragement of job sharing between two or more individuals, etc. (Torrens and González de Molina, 2016). Needless to say, achieving any or some of these measures would require negotiating strength that would allow workers to 'hold the gaze' and stand their ground in order to come to a satisfactory agreement.

Be that as it may, the link between basic income and automatisation shouldn't be missed. Basic income isn't *only* a solution for the unemployment caused by the destruction of jobs due to automatisation. If this was the case, we'd be faced with a highly contingent defence of basic income that could lead us to say that no basic income would be needed in a world without technological unemployment. Basic income is needed, above all, so that we can remove ourselves, if we so wish, from the world of employment which, as I described when giving an account of the republican critique of wage labour, entails the high doses of submission and servility that are expected of the 'part-time slave', of the dispossessed who act 'with the frenzy of the desperate', as Adam Smith put it. Accordingly, if basic income is to be supported it is because, besides protecting us from possible technological unemployment, it allows us to opt out – perhaps even by resorting to robotisation (Srnicek and Williams, 2015) – and to look for other spaces and relations.

Caring for Life

To return to co-responsibility, it must be noted that sometimes responsibility isn't *born* but must be *forced*. This might be why Carole Pateman (2006) presents basic income as a kind of 'domestic counterpower' that women can rely on to suggest or, if necessary, impose other uses of time, other distributions of work (paid or unpaid) and other ways of relating. As I have said, material independence isn't the necessary *and sufficient* condition for republican freedom. There are other important factors of a symbolic nature involved, not least of which is the set of cultural representations on which patriarchy rests, which can undermine any effort that is made to empower social actors materially. Yet material independence continues to be at least a *necessary* condition for achieving effective freedom. After all, there'd be little point in gaining a whole cultural and symbolic hegemony over what might come to be a somewhat freer life – in this case for women, historically confined to the household – when there still exist bonds of material dependence acting as veritable straitjackets. In this regard, the fact that basic income also upholds the principle of individuality so that it is received by individuals instead of households couldn't be more reasonable from the feminist perspective because households harbour power relations and forms of despotism that must be done away with in order to benefit the group that is usually the most vulnerable: women and especially poor women (Pateman, 2006; Raventós, 2007).

Let's make a small yet important digression. Wouldn't it make more sense, then, to give a cash grant directly to people, usually women, who carry out domestic work? In a world deeply scarred by the patriarchy such a conditional grant, while making care work more visible, could be interpreted as due compensation for services provided by women in the place where they 'naturally' belong: the household. Moreover, as happens with all conditional cash benefits, leaving the household would mean loss of the 'domestic wage' in question, which would end up confining women in their 'natural' space. In contrast, an unconditional benefit such as basic income, received by both men and women regardless of the kind of work they do, would give women greater freedom in deciding the extent to which they want to stay in (or return to) the home, and the extent to which they want to construct a life outside the household, and how they want to do this. In this sense, the demand for a basic income is better aligned with the feminist perspective, since it destroys economic dependency to a greater extent and better achieves the twin objectives of increasing women's autonomy and social power (Weeks, 2011). However, the 'Wages for Housework' campaign 'was an implicit argument for an unconditional, individual, and universal basic income':

> Its identification of unwaged housewives as workers, its extension of the concept of the housewife to precarious workers in the globalized economy, and its identification of the strategic deficiencies of mainstream working class and feminist movements are critical to contextualizing contemporary debates on basic income and to the development of successful strategies for contemporary working-class movements. (Zelleke, 2022: 1)[21]

But let's go further, because what's really at stake, what really needs to be combatted, are the barefaced, perverse processes of the social construction of femininity and masculinity (Pérez Orozco, 2014), because the bulk of the sexual division of labour rests on these processes. I'd put it this way. Imagine a horizontal line. This line represents the surface separating the visible from the invisible, the observed from the subterranean. Now imagine a vertical structure whose lower half is below the horizontal line and upper half is above it, over the surface. The vertical structure, which could be imagined as a sort of skyscraper, represents the traditional sexual division of labour which, needless to say, has endured until today. What do we observe in this structure?

First, the female population is beneath the surface, in the underground basement where the cooking is done and the machines are kept running.

The female population carries out tasks which, however valuable they are for society,[22] remain invisibilised and undervalued, which is why they're rarely remunerated. Sometimes women gain access but not without effort, for the stairways are high and steep, to the upper part of the structure, to the sphere of visible and socially recognised jobs, but they always do this weighed down by the burden of the jobs 'below' which, evidently, are hard to escape from. Hence the expression 'double presence'. So, the injustice suffered by women in these processes of the division of labour are twofold. First, the 'female' space beneath the line is associated with sacrifice and abnegation, immolation to benefit others, with everything that can't be seen, obscured and unnoticed, concealed in the domestic sphere, the true basement and backroom of life. Second, women are denied the right to decide what work they want to do. It's common knowledge and it is said in many ways, directly or indirectly, that their place is below the line, running the machinery. It's their place to keep quiet. The history of capitalist accumulation, as Silvia Federici (2010) shows, can't be understood without taking into account the mechanisms of control and punishment reserved for women who resist occupying the lower part of the structure or, still worse, dare to question its vertical nature, for women who refuse to discipline their bodies to keep (re)producing and caring for other bodies, usually male, which were and are those who had to be and have to be ready and able at the entrances of productive units.[23]

And what about men? To start with, the roles and activities above the surface, sometimes (not always!) with beautiful large-windowed offices, belong to a 'masculine' life. These are jobs that are visible, that sometimes even have glamour, that are valued, and everyone knows what self-sufficient (self-sufficient?) men are capable of doing (and woe betide anyone who isn't!) and that they're frequently applauded. But we should also understand that hetero-patriarchal capitalism is bad for men too. In hetero-patriarchal capitalism, men share with women the lack of freedom to decide what sort of activities they want for their lives. The figure of the male breadwinner prevails, and how! The figure of the male breadwinner obliges men to enter the markets, to survive therein, to win prizes, to stay in the limelight as long as possible, and so on, as well as renouncing a whole world of caring which, though it shouldn't be romanticised, does contain some of the most rewarding and meaningful activities that can be part of a human life. It is very difficult to move up in the building, but it's also really hard to move down. And the lifts don't work.

Basic income aims to blow up the whole skyscraper structure that is the embodiment of the sexual division of labour as a whole. What is the point of rigidly defined divisions of 'male' and 'female' tasks? Basic income aims to blow up these processes of social structuring by unconditionally providing tools so that every man and every woman can question predetermined roles, can come together in alternative shared practices and procedures adapted to the uniqueness of our lives, and can set into circulation everything we've been able to imagine.

Social Power for a Just Eco-Social Transition

Likewise, caring for life also means caring for the natural environment we inhabit. In this regard, however we choose to organise such an environment, we are now obliged, by ecological imperative, to undertake radical changes in our form of life (Herrero, 2016; Sempere, 2016). There is a crucial question that should be raised at this point: could a basic income contribute towards an ecological transition guided along ways and by decisions that are autonomous rather than authoritarian?

To start with, it is necessary to become aware that a political action aimed at a just eco-social transition – like any form of political action, as we will immediately see – requires that we think about certain socioeconomic conditions that favour its solidity and a broad social impact. This is why, if we're thinking about the eco-social transition in democratic terms, then we should also consider the precarisation of the conditions of work and life suffered by the large majority under capitalism. Dispossessed, trampled all over, and hammered by the machinery of capitalist exploitation, what space do we have in our lives for thinking about *other* ways of (re)production and consumption? Ecological consciousness, like any other form of 'consciousness', also holds out decisive socioeconomic conditions of possibility. In other words: here, too, social class matters. Could a basic income, by freeing the working population from the 'frenzy of the desperate', help us to stop the machines, to take the time we need, every single one of us, to rethink our lives and, on the basis of that, to embark, all of us, on those major processes of decision-making that are being demanded by the eco-social transition? Could basic income, by contributing towards universalising the ability to take part in this and so many other political processes, democratise access to the eco-social reflection and struggle (Blaschke, 2017)? In sum, combatting precarisation is a necessary condition for popular participation in collective thinking and putting into practice other ways of (re)production and consumption, so that we can avoid damaging the ecological environment. This is why it must be asserted that thinking of and introducing radical changes in the ways in which we relate to each other in the (re)productive sphere requires that, first, we stop machines.

Once there, the presence of unconditional access to resources such as basic income, which makes it possible to contradict capitalist precariousness, can favour the extension of non-commodified forms of (re)production. And this can constitute an important first step towards placing the care for life and the environment, and not capitalist accumulation, at the very centre of socioeconomic life. This implies contradicting, together with 'the capitalist grammar of capital accumulation, the growth imperative and the predominance of the production of surplus values over the production of use values' (Mulvale, 2019: 44). The idea is quite straightforward: not having to keep working and producing 'with the frenzy of the desperate' could open up the doors to individual and societal processes of eco-social education and training, which might help start and nourish environmentally friendly projects. As Howard, Pinto and Schachtschneider (2019: 112) put it along the lines of Van Parijs and Vanderborght (2017), 'a Basic Income could remove the need for continuous growth and job creation while still providing a flexible device for economic stability', which leads us to think that 'Basic Income would therefore be an environmental measure'. In fact, Langridge, Büchs and Howard (2022: 30), in their assessment of a selection of basic income pilots in the Global North, found that 'recipients re-evaluated how their work could benefit their communities', which led the authors to think that 'if an Ecological Basic Income could facilitate exit from labour, therefore, citizens would likely still participate socially in their communities'. It's hard to sum all these ideas up better than Simon Birnbaum (2009: 2) did in a seminal article on the recent discussion of basic income and post-productivism:

> The availability of a universal, work-independent source of basic security and the creating of new forms of meaningful activity and integration beyond the employment contract [would mean that] we no longer need to embrace unsustainable engines of growth in order to achieve full employment at any cost. [Thus,] a basic income would greatly improve the opportunities for people to engage in local and service-intensive activities that rely much less on transports or material consumption. More broadly, many of the non-market activities that would become more accessible and affordable through the basic income could help release a process towards 'cultural dematerialization' [...]. A basic income linked to (and supportive of) the expansion of community-based provision, volun-

teer work, cultural and sports activities, etc., could help offer more direct, resource-efficient and, thus, ecologically sustainable paths to wellbeing.

Guy Standing (2020) expresses the very same idea by resorting to the grammar and metrics of freedom: 'a basic income would encourage a transition to an ecological society by giving people the freedom to shift from resource-depleting (and often boring and demeaning) jobs to resource-preserving care, craft, and community work'. It seems, then, that the basic income proposal could not be more sensibly radical or, if you prefer, more radically sensible. In any case, it should be noted here that sociopolitical settings, with all the cultural and symbolic dimensions they harbour, matter. Without a post-Fordist and post-neoliberal political culture that opens the doors to new imaginaries about the meaning of work – and of life – in contexts in which the essential interdependence of human societies becomes more evident than ever, we can find ourselves facing the undesirable phenomenon that the introduction of basic income does not lead to a reduction in the hours worked in productivist environments (Pinto, 2020a).

Basic income, by itself, cannot deactivate the productivist 'game of chicken' in which we find ourselves, in which it seems that the most diverse forms of short-sightedness and atomised competition of all against all lead us headlong to the precipice of environmental collapse. It is therefore necessary to interpret basic income as a device capable of allowing us a great reset and a collective change of course towards contexts that truly welcome profound changes in the economic structures of our societies. In this sense, the results of the experiments analysed by Langridge, Büchs and Howard could not be more revealing of the need for collectively oriented forms of political association and activism fostering the ecological potential of basic income. According to these authors, it can be stated that 'basic income improves household and community [self-managed] activities'; but it should be added right away that 'an Ecological Basic Income needs to form part of an evolution in community services and not a replacement [by forms of atomistic self-management]', as this would constitute a way to 'undermine collective institutions, reduce community interaction and increase individualism' (Langridge, Büchs and Howard, 2022: 31).

But the civilising hope remains intact: if we manage to give it an adequate direction in emancipatory terms – which includes the sociopolitical basis for a just eco-social transition – the introduction of a basic income can help to move towards a 'steady-state economy', this being understood as 'an economy of stable or mildly fluctuating size that may not exceed ecological limits [in which we might] end our addiction to economic growth and create ecologically sustainable societies that are prosperous and democratic' (Mulvale, 2019: 39, 41). Within this kind of economy, activities that would need to be fostered and socially extended would be care activities, joint projects and cooperativism, reuse of goods and resources, rehabilitation and recovery of territories, etc. (Birnbaum, 2016; Riutort, 2016; Standing, 2017). In general terms, the aim is to make the 'autonomous sphere of the economy' grow, in the sense that André Gorz (1985, 1987) gave to the term: 'purposely activity outside the market and the State spheres [or outside *productivist* markets and states, one might add], [which includes] simpler ways of living, [...] encompassing activities in the household, non-profit organisations, community gardens, and so on' (Howard, Pinto and Schachtschneider, 2019: 115). In this sense, being able to exit those markets that are fundamentally or even exclusively oriented to the accumulation of capital plays a crucial role (Van Parijs, 2009). And the fact is that there is room for responsible optimism: 'transfers [of selected basic income pilot interventions in the Global North] did not weaken motivation to participate in society, instead increasing it. An Ecological Basic Income should capture this motivation and direct it towards ecologically and socially beneficial activities, both in the labour market and, increasingly, in the autonomous sphere' (Langridge, Büchs and Howard, 2022: 33).

Let's move on now to a more micro level of analysis. Could basic income be a mechanism that helps us to redefine our needs, and to rethink what we consider to be 'enough' and worthy of being lived, and thus move towards more frugal lifestyles that are also closer to our most genuine yearnings?[24] According to Carole Pateman (2006: 109), 'by breaking the link between income and the labour market, [basic income] would allow individuals, if they so wished, to abstain from the race to accumulate ever more material goods and help combat the identification of freedom with consumerism'. However, one must immediately acknowledge the risk that the presence of a basic income translates into an increase of consumerism (Pinto, 2020a), especially if basic income primarily leads to the increased consumption of resource-intensive goods and services. But it can be stressed that, by fighting poverty, basic income can encourage more responsible consumption, because (1) people would have more time and room for manoeuver to gather information and make meaningful individual and collective decisions; (2) 'most basic income recipients [would be] non-wealthy and would most likely spend it on necessities, rather than on superfluous goods and services that contribute to over-consumption and waste' (Mulvale, 2019:

40); and (3) ecologically responsible consumption tends to be more expensive, which suggests that the implementation of a basic income could favour its social extension – for example, a basic income could universalise the right to healthy food and diet in a context of rising prices that is expected as a consequence of climate change. It is true that, on average, the wealthy members of our societies tend to leave a bigger ecological footprint, but it is also true that a positive correlation is observed between the fact of having a guaranteed existence and the ability to access time and mechanisms to obtain better information and (to be able) to act more responsibly as economic agents – for this very reason, it is not only socially fair but also ecologically urgent that huge amounts of resources be transferred to (the popular classes of) countries impoverished by the (neo)colonial dynamics that structure contemporary capitalism.

Let's return to the level of macro-political analysis to ask ourselves about the role that a basic income should play – and the dangers that it can help to overcome – given the evidence of the need for a political process of articulation and deployment of a just eco-social transition. Three big issues must be addressed here. First, we must ask ourselves to what extent a basic income can help to avoid any form of eco-fascism. The eco-social transition is inevitable, and this affects more than a few dimensions of our lives, from energy and transport to food and the ways in which we settle in a territory. The big question is the same as before. Will this transition be democratic and popular, or will it lead us into openly barbaric scenarios? We should not discount the possibility of certain forms of eco-fascism into which we could be led by the machinations of allegedly 'green capitalism' – if that formula does not hide a true oxymoron. The idea is quite simple: a small handful of modest measures are used to grace and 'greenwash' the path to higher levels of accumulation and capitalist extractivism and, in the face of the resulting environmental disaster, we witness the attempt to naturalise a division of society between a few citizens that are 'safe' from the harshness of a mostly uninhabitable planet and large social majorities abandoned to their fate in the heart of *Mad Max*-like social and ecological scenarios – when examined properly, we see that we are not too far from this situation. Faced with this possibility, basic income can play a role of crucial importance when it comes to strengthening a vision – and a practice – of a robust and expanded citizenship in which the gap between the 'elite' and the 'people' that so much political deactivation generates tends to dissolve. In this sense, James Mulvale (2019) asserts, following Tony Fitzpatrick (1999), that 'basic income embodies an ethic of common ownership of the Earth's resources and global citizenship which requires and enables everyone to be a steward or a trustee whose duty is to hand on the Earth to the next generation of common owners' (Mulvale, 2019: 40). Faced with the genocidal 'every man for himself' of the anti-democratic solutions to the ecocides that we are beginning to witness and that we will most likely witness in an expanded manner over the coming decades, what is being considered here is the possibility of turning basic income, among other measures, into one of the building blocks of a common politics that aspires to find common paths and answers to a problem that, although it has identifiable culprits, is undoubtedly of a common nature.

Second, the role of basic income within the politics of a just eco-social transition is strongly linked to the principles of decentralisation, traceability and accountability. Let's see why and let's see why this is important. It is possible to venture that basic income allows the decentralisation of jobs and activities, which should be understood in terms of a both eco-physical and social-relational proximity that can promote people's deeper control of the activity of economic and social agents, especially with more and better access to information and more transparency and traceability of this activity, which would probably pave the way for deeper forms of accountability as well. Needless to say, these possibilities open up the doors for popular control over the ways in which humans shape and channel the social-ecological transformation we so urgently need.

Third, and lastly, it must be clearly stressed that basic income alone cannot work (Howard, Pinto and Schachtschneider, 2019; Mulvale, 2019). As demonstrated in Part IV, basic income must be placed within the framework of a broad package of measures including other ecologically imperative policies such as housing, food security, urban land use and planning, transportation, education and health (Mulvale, 2019). To put it succinctly, the driving ideas of these eco-social packages of measures are (1) that other resources are needed for individuals and groups to be able to effectively 'exit' certain productive and work environments, and (2) that educational programmes and processes that increase the critical consciousness of people vis-à-vis the need for a just eco-social transition should be intensely and restlessly fostered. In effect, there is a need to use basic income as a tool – even as an 'excuse' – to generate other imaginaries, narratives and subjectivities vis-à-vis the place and the meaning within our lives of life-centred post-productivist activities promoting a better integration of kinds of work of different natures and a better integration of these conglomerates of activities with our natural environments (Ketterer, 2021). In sum, basic income, thanks to the bargaining power it confers upon individuals and groups, must be tied to an expanded definition of 'societal well-being [that is] focused on the distribution of wealth, but also on the distribution of time and opportunities for the expression of human agency that are not instrumentally tied to labor market status or potential for profit' (Marston, 2016: 165).

But the promise of a basic income that promotes a just eco-social transition is not exempt from limits or reasons for doubt and scepticism, which requires further reflection and clarification. Let's consider four broad items for discussion. First, some analysts (Büchs, 2021; Coote and Percy, 2020) suggest that universal basic services may work better than universal basic income in promoting a just eco-social transition. This would be so because universal basic services – healthcare, education, energy, transport, food, care, etc. – have a stronger decommodifying capacity, since they are collective provision systems and, therefore, avoid the risk of social atomisation, and it is already known that social atomisation can reopen democracy-limiting markets, and that these markets can reopen capitalist accumulation. Besides, these authors add, basic income is only a demand-side measure, while universal basic services can be used to reorganise production. In any case, two comments must be made on this idea. First, Milena Büchs herself concludes that universal basic services and universal basic income can be compatible. In fact, it is not just that they are compatible: the fact that a part of the broad emancipatory package of measures that is needed concretises in 'cash' is something that confers freedom and a margin of manoeuvre for individuals and groups that in no case can be disdained – or should we limit ourselves to uncritically accepting the 'gift-package' that certain political-institutional leaderships are pleased to provide us with? Second, it is true that universal basic services serve as a tool to *directly* organise the production, but universal basic income confers a bargaining power – a 'social power' – that can *indirectly* pave the way for many joint endeavours aimed at collectively taking control over the many ways in which we satisfy our (im) material needs, which includes both state-centred and self-managed institutions, practices and devices.

Second, other authors (Swaton, 2018) have suggested that instead of a basic income, what should be introduced is an 'ecological participation income' or, as it is sometimes called, an 'ecological transition income'. According to this proposal – and in line with that of Atkinson (1996) – the monetary benefit should be conditional on the recipients giving themselves up to the practice of a valuable activity for the environment and the eco-social transition. In this sense, just as Milena Büchs pointed out possible complementarities, Sophie Swaton would amend the entire basic income proposal. And the truth is that the underlying logic of the ecological transition income is fully understandable, but it should be noted that, like Anthony Atkinson's participation income, the proposal for an ecological transition income presents two serious problems: it is discretionary – with what legitimacy and with what levels of information about the results of human action can public authorities, among the myriad activities that are potentially compatible with a just eco-social transition, decide which are and which are not? – and would be hugely complex to manage: having decided what counts and what does not as a 'real participation' in the eco-social transition, if such decision can be made, through what democratic, non-invasive and non-draconian methods can public authorities control whether the contribution in question is being made? As always, given the evidence of the serious problem of discretionary arbitrariness that this type of proposal can generate, some of its promoters suggest the possibility of opening up the concept of what is an (ecologically acceptable) 'participation' as much as possible. However, this entails an exponential increase in administrative complexity and control problems of 'participation incomes': if (almost) everything fits, the army of controllers that the activity requires to be carried out effectively would reach colossal dimensions, and the type of 'enquiries' that such 'controllers' should carry out would move between a Kafkaesque collapse and the theatre of the absurd. In light of all this, if we are really willing to radically expand the concept of 'participation', which would actually make good sense, given the immense variety of forms that the human capacity to contribute to society can take, perhaps it is fairer and more efficient to move towards a fully unconditional basic income and, at the same time, try to ensure that this basic income is interpreted and used ecologically, that is, in ways that are compatible with (and favourable to) a just eco-social transition (Pinto, 2020a).

Third, certain pro-eco-social transition authors and activists have sometimes wondered about the financial feasibility of a basic income that effectively promotes such an eco-social transition. In the end, they rightly say, we need a 'social product' and a system made of taxes and budgets in order to finance basic income and its accompanying measures, whatever these end up being. Might there be some forms of 'productivist pressure' on the economic system so that it can offer the kind of 'sufficient basic income' that is required for all of us to enjoy the kind of 'social power' this book upholds? In other words, might basic income end up being financed through a taxation system implying some forms of 'green growth' (Pinto, 2020b)? Or could an emancipatory basic income – and related measures – be financed through post-productivist taxation methods? It seems obvious that it is of crucial importance that we find ways to finance basic income that do not go through the promotion of material production. In this sense, progressive taxes on wealth and inheritance can play an essential role, with special attention – and the tax burden – on the financial sector and the profits of large companies, which, by the way, are those that tend to be more polluting and environment-degrading. This is why James Mulvale (2019: 45) insists on the importance, among other things, of opting for a 'heavier reliance on taxes [...] on luxury goods and services, in order to curb wasteful consumption, [and] rigorous taxation of revenue derived from the buying and selling of real estate, stocks, foreign currencies, and other financial instruments based on speculative greed and quick profit-taking'.

Fourth, and finally, some analysts and environmental activists sometimes claim that basic income puts an insufficient focus on structural change. As they rightly point out, basic income alone may not address the underlying structural issues that contribute to ecological and social challenges. While it can provide economic security and alleviate poverty, it might not tackle systemic problems, such as unsustainable production models and corporate power – and therefore environmental degradation – that is due to capitalist accumulation. Therefore, comprehensive policy approaches that address these structural factors are necessary for an effective eco-social transition. In no case will we argue the contrary here: the bulk of this book, and Part IV in particular, is dedicated to presenting basic income as 'only' *one part* of a broad and ambitious institutionally plural and pluralistic strategy aimed at undermining the main mechanisms that govern capitalism as a social formation. But it is not an obstacle to point out, once again, that unconditional access to resources – in this case, monetary resources – confers a bargaining power or 'social power' that must allow abandoning liberticidal and dedemocratising spaces and procedures to nurture and socially extend 'other economies' – other property rights, other (re)productive relationships, etc. – that promote greater collective control over our ways of working, producing and living. In this sense, basic income would indeed be prepared to address structural factors and, therefore, to focus on structural change, which cannot but have a positive impact on the possibilities of a just eco-social transition.[25]

Holding the Gaze in the Agora

Finally, being able to take our inclinations and aspirations, our ability to work, where we want them to take root and bear fruit also means taking over the spaces of and ways to civic-political participation. But civic-political participation, whether it is in the heart of formal institutions or in self-managed spaces, is something that also requires socioeconomically grounded personal independence. It's not possible to deliberate and/or negotiate in any kind of political agora we might conceive of with social actors – individuals or groups that have managed to seize large concentrations of private economic power or bureaucratic bodies whose tentacles spread into the most recondite corners of our lives – on whose whims we depend. In such cases, we can't hold the gaze.

The democracy theorists of classical Athens realised a long time ago that a free political life requires the socioeconomic independence of everyone who participates in it because socioeconomic independence means independence of judgement, availability of time and absence of – the mere possibility of – blackmail by other interested parties (Standing, 2017). This might be why classical Athens presented the first formulation – and institutional embodiment – of a cash grant which, guaranteeing the material existence of a once dispossessed population, equipped it for a free political existence. Raventós (2007: 53–4) describes it thus:

> [T]he Athenian democrats had no quarrel (and neither did democratic republicans centuries later) with Aristotle's basic reasoning [that the poor free man, the *phaulos*, could not be free because he had no guarantee of his material existence] but, as democrats, they wanted to extend (universalise) political rights based on a guaranteed material existence to the [free] population as a whole. They considered that political participation by poor freemen could be made possible with the *misthon*, the remuneration that was created with Ephialtes' reforms [arising from the revolution of the party of poor free men led by Ephialtes, Pericles and Aspasia in 461 BCE] for performing specific tasks in the public sphere. Without this public remuneration they would never have been able to participate in democratic decision making. [...] [A century later] Aristotle perfectly captures the role of the *misthon* as a substitute for property [as a guarantee of socioeconomic independence].

Twenty-four centuries later, the young Marx, when reflecting on the reduction of the working day, suggested that such a measure would allow a better balance between wage work and leisure which, in turn, should guarantee that a whole human life wouldn't be reduced to the category of a mere livelihood (Marx, 1959). And why would we want this leisure time?

Marx's answer is clear. So that we can be involved in the political life of our community and exercise republican citizenship (Torrens and González de Molina, 2016).

At a closer look, we're not too far from my earlier discussion of Hirschman's analysis of the relationship between 'exit' and 'voice'. As in all workplaces and households, we also need, in all the possible agorae that are organised and reproduced in our own times, the ability to make our 'voice' heard and to ensure that what we have to say is properly taken into account. But, for this, we need the security of being able to reshuffle the cards and 'exit' if we can see that our words are simply falling like dry leaves or are even a reckless reality that endangers our autonomous social existence because, as Gar Alperovitz (2001: 108) puts it, 'liberty to speak out depends on a *guarantee* that one's means of livelihood will not be undermined'.

A basic income – a flow of income that is at least equal to the poverty line and universally and unconditionally guaranteed, together with in-kind benefit packages, also understood as universal and unconditional measures – could, by consolidating forms of socioeconomic independence for everyone, become the foundation of civil and political rights in the contemporary world (Krätke, 2004). This is why Leticia Morales (2019: 135) asserts that 'a […] model of democracy that prioritizes broad and effective political participation in decision-making processes offers a [...] plausible democratic case for a universal basic income'. The principle of collective self-determination, resting on the conviction that an effective civil society composed of sets of diverse but reciprocally free actors is possible, requires that all members of this collective must enjoy a similar status as socioeconomically independent but not atomised citizens. Hence, we have here the principle of economic citizenship which basic income can help to underpin.

To sum up, why do we say we want bargaining power? Being able to hold the gaze, being able to negotiate, to say no in order to be able to say yes, is the same as being able to give rise to myriad forms of work and life that are presently drowned in the quagmire of generalised dispossession. The right not to work for pay doesn't lead to apathy but is intimately linked with everyone's right to work, paid or unpaid, because it opens the door to the co-responsible and co-responsibilising distribution of existing work in the productive sphere, in the domestic domain and in sociopolitical participation, and to the effective social inclusion of all those people who presently don't work, for a wage or otherwise, but would like to do so.

CONCLUSIONS: WHEN BASIC INCOME BECOMES
A MEANS OF (RE)PRODUCTION

Basic income isn't 'only' income. It can become a true lever to transform money into a means of production and reproduction of life. Since it is unconditional, and thanks to the bargaining power deriving from that, basic income is a special kind of cash flow that can be converted or translated in terms of other resources which are essential for controlling (re)production.[26] Basically, there are three.

First, basic income also means *time* for conceiving and getting underway the lives 'of one's own' that Harrington (1992) associated with the condition of free men. In fact, the possibility of moving forwards with one's own life plans crucially depends on the availability of time, which is to say, the 'capacity to wait' in order to think, persuade, negotiate and, finally, obtain those (im)material resources that we need.

Second, basic income can also be associated with a propensity for *risk* that any person or group of people wanting to embark on their own project must be able to sustain. The positive correlation between the ability to explore alternative options and, where necessary, to accept certain levels of risk and uncertainty and the kind of freedom that stems from robust bargaining power, shouldn't be overlooked.

Third, and finally, the right to a basic income is the same as the right to *credit*, in the twofold sense of right of access to financial resources that are essential for acquiring the means of (re)production, on the one hand, and the 'right to social trust', to 'social credit' and to a trust the community decides to place in its members, on the other hand. A constant flow of monetary resources should be understood, too, as the right to second, third and subsequent opportunities (because we don't always get it right the first time and may need a period of trial and error)[27] to launch and sustain (re)productive projects that make sense to us, that we can work on, rework and feel as our own. The possibility of shaping a genuinely democratic and inclusive socioeconomic environment depends on this.[28]

As Mazzucato (2017, 2018) and Varoufakis (2016) have repeatedly emphasised, a large part of available wealth is socially created, whether it is through direct public investment or an accumulation of (im)material resources of shared heritage, and it tends to be appropriated privately by a handful of actors who have the power to do so and to exclude others. It seems to make no sense, therefore, that the citizenry doesn't establish fiscal and financial mechanisms for the collective reappropriation of these assets to make them available, in the form of a basic income, to all the inhabitants of our societies. The power of negotiation that this unconditional flow of monetary resources, namely *basic income*, would confer[29] would allow individuals and groups to try other kinds of work (in plural), other ways of consolidating and getting into circulation productive and reproductive spaces, and other relations and social environments in a world that is really created in common.[30] Let's explore this idea more thoroughly. To start with, we are assisted by evidence that we cannot ignore: wealth is collectively made. It is, in other words, a 'social product'. For this reason, it should be treated as a commons, which puts on the table the need to think politically – not as a merely private matter – about how that wealth is accessed, managed, reproduced over time and, finally, distributed. But why should we conceive of wealth as a social product? Because everything that gives wealth and, perhaps, satisfies needs comes from collective efforts that take myriad forms and end up in the hands of some and not others as a result of all kinds of chance and social circumstances.

And what 'collective efforts' are we referring to? The effort of working people from whom surplus value is extracted, as exemplified by Jeff Bezos' statement: 'my workers, and also my consumers, have paid for my trip to space'; the effort, mostly carried out by women, underlying care work, which literally makes possible any other kind of existing or conceivable work; the effort of others that we perceive – some more than others – through inheritances and private donations; the effort of others that we receive – some to a greater extent than others – from the common heritage of knowledge and infrastructure accumulated over more than 150,000 years of existence as a species; or the effort hidden in public aid to corporations and private entities, both to the cyclopean and, sometimes, to those who are not so – tax discounts, state bailouts of private institutions that are thought to be 'too big to fail', delivery of the results from public investment in basic science and technology to business organisations that are ready to 'internalise' (to privatise) the profits derived from this research and development spending, as shown by Mariana Mazzucato (2018). This is how the emergence and consolidation of economic phenomena such as the tech giants, which include Google, Amazon, Facebook and Apple, must be understood.

If this is so – and at this point in the game it is convenient to avoid absurd denialisms – it seems common sense to introduce a 'social dividend' that can be understood as a way of giving access to (at least a part of) the share that corresponds to all of us of that collectively generated wealth. For what purpose? With what ethical and political ambition? That the public realm, by allowing us to recover and socially distribute the collectively generated wealth that, nowadays, is fundamentally in private hands, guarantees a dignified life for the entire population and, from there, empowers everyone, without exclusions of any type, to insist on the search for paths to participate in economic life in sensible ways that truly add meaning.

This is how Thomas Paine saw it at the end of the eighteenth century (Tena Camporesi, 2021) and this is how Guy Standing (2019, 2022) is nowadays forcefully suggesting it in his proposal for 'common dividends'. The idea is quite straightforward: given that the commons belong to everybody in identifiable communities, which may or may not be the 'state', then (1) our right is to enjoy them, which requires a whole 'bundle of rights' (Ostrom, 2015; Coriat, 2015) that allows us to duly take care of them and project them in good condition into the future; and (2) if particular interests take or are given any commons, the beneficiaries, as a matter of common justice, should be required to compensate the commoners. Given that a true plunder of the commons has been taking place in the era of neoliberalism and rentier capitalism that has dug deeply into the longstanding capitalist history of encroachment, enclosure, privatisation and commodification, Standing states that a 'commons capital fund' must be created through a system of levies on all actions that gain from the commons[31] and all actions that deplete the commons, so that 'common dividends' can be equally distributed to all those deemed to be the commoners and to do so equally, as an economic right. This way, the right to a decent free life, whatever this might end up meaning and however this might end up concretising, would be guaranteed to both current and future generations.

11

Our Flexibility Is Our Freedom

As I've already said, the value of flexibility has frequently been embraced by employers' organisations whose sole aim is to cut costs by eroding legal and institutional mechanisms for the protection of employment and living conditions of working populations. Accordingly, the flexibility discourse has often been seen as a dubious strategy at the very least.

Nevertheless, it's true that humans need to have flexible lives in which we can autonomously engage in different tasks in keeping with our needs, which keep changing over our lifetime. When and how can we do certain kinds of jobs? And how much time do we want to spend doing these kinds of jobs for each period of our lives? These questions can only be answered by the people, individually and/or collectively, which means that the old Fordist imaginary of one job to last your whole life must be challenged. In fact, it is challenged by contemporary social movements that see in the (unlikely) return to Fordist existences, which are secure but monolithically focused on *one* single activity, a clear sign of a serious absence of economic sovereignty (Casassas et al., 2015; Standing, 2014). We return to this in Part IV.

Needless to say, flexibility has been and is terribly hostile because it is increasingly turning us into weathervane roosters looking here, looking there, for whatever blows our way, even if it's only a straw to clutch at. It's getting more and more difficult for growing numbers of us to be able to look back and recognise in our own paths a ductile yet meaningful journey, one we can describe and explain to others and ourselves (Sennett, 1999).[1] It's becoming increasingly difficult to recognise ourselves in what we do.

Yet, at the same time, we're increasingly finding large sections of the population who have experienced and, in all probability, suffered flexibility but who also seem disinclined – and I insist on this – to re-establish the living and work conditions that were typical of the old post-war Fordist consensus. This is a mostly young working population that appears to aspire to combinations of different kinds of work that give more consideration to uses of time and the always-changing situations which *we men and women* might keep wanting and deciding throughout our lifetimes. Thus, far from the Fordist rigidity of ultra-structured lives revolving around the axis of our *sole* occupation, but also far from the thousand splinters of lives shredded by the workings of precariousness, how would it be possible to think about and embark upon diverse, multi-active lives that are as flexible as reeds in the wind, adapting to *our own* changing needs but never breaking or ceasing to be what they are (Casassas, 2016b)? In other words, how can we individually and collectively govern our (re)productive lives? How can we co-determine them and how can we be self-determining in them?

As Kathi Weeks (2011: 33) says, a basic income allows us to 'raise broader questions about the place of work in our lives and spark the imagination of a life no longer so subordinate to it' – or no longer subordinate to the resigned acceptance of the allegedly unavoidable fact that capitalist dispossession imposes exploitative forms of work on us. Once again, the unconditional nature with which resources, including a basic income, are delivered when they act as guarantees of economic and social rights makes it easier for individuals and groups to take control, effectively and securely, of *their own flexibility*, which then expands their freedom to decide what and how many kinds of work to do, how, with whom, in what proportions, and so on (Vercellone and Harribey, 2015). In a well-known passage from *A Critique of the German Ideology*, Marx and Engels (1968 [1844–5]) showed that they shared this aspiration:

> For as soon as the distribution of labour comes into being, each man has a particular, exclusive sphere of activity, which is forced upon him and from which he cannot escape. He is a hunter, a fisherman, a herdsman, or a critical critic, and must remain so if he does not want to lose his means of livelihood; while in communist society, where nobody has one exclusive sphere of activity but each can become accomplished in any branch he wishes, society regulates the general production and thus makes it possible for me to do one thing today and another tomorrow, to hunt in the morning, fish in the afternoon, rear cattle in the evening, criticise after dinner, just as I have a mind, without ever becoming hunter, fisherman, herdsman or critic. This fixation of social activity, this consolidation of what we ourselves produce into an objective power above us, growing out of our control, thwarting our expectations, bringing to naught our calculations, is one of the chief factors in historical development up till now.

If the use of a term as badly connoted today as *flexibility* can be disheartening, we need to realise that we're really talking about *self-management*, and this can be understood as a whole set of individual and collective actions aiming at taking control of the material, symbolic and time-use dimensions of our (many kinds of) work. It happens, however, that this idea of self-management immediately goes back to a principle of flexibility that we can't bypass and, much less, hand over to those who, as we have seen, are ready to pervert it and turn it into ammunition to blow up the paths we might have chosen.

Flexibility is too important to be sold short. We mustn't let it slip away. Flexibility based on the security conferred by unconditionally guaranteed resources – a basic income but also other, equally unconditional in-kind benefits – is all we need to bring into being all the kinds of work we had to abandon when we were clutching at the straws of jobs imposed by capitalist dispossession, all of them the kinds of work that are nowadays hidden away several metres below the ground and that we need to rescue. So, there is a whole archaeology of our own appetites, talents and inclinations that must allow us to find, unearth and rehabilitate everything that was once ours but is now left behind. And this 'everything' is very diverse, which means that we must be able to manage our own timing and spaces in an inventive and flexible manner, so that the inevitable hiatuses and overlaps, including many kinds of activity (frequently unpaid) of a life worthy of being lived aren't turned into precariousness or overburdening, or both since they can go together (Han, 2012). But inventiveness and flexibility aren't enough. We also need security. And this is what economic and social rights (including basic income) must permit: first, a 'great rehabilitation' and, then, the 'great explosion' and propagation of everything we had and have within us and wish to spread into spaces where we want to have a presence so that we can inhabit them and do things in them.[2]

We're living in times of rampant precariousnesses. We're living in times of shattered lives: shattered jobs, shattered wages, shattered subsidies, shattered rights and shattered social services.[3] All of this is turning large social majorities into masses and hordes of true 'supplicants' of some measure of benevolence from others (Standing, 2011, 2014): from employers, from bureaucrats who might be good enough to listen to them and tick the box they really need, and from people with whom they coexist who can, at any point, genuinely or capriciously, lend a helping hand.

In such contexts, one disturbing and yet suggestive reality appears: the precarious population also presents a growing lack of occupational identity (Dejours, Deranty, Renault and Smith, 2018). As we've already seen, it is ever more difficult for people in a precarious situation to construct a coherent narrative about what they do, about the whys and wherefores of the deci-sions they make – *they* make? – regarding the guiding ideas of personal and professional trajectories which, not without some tweaking, we try to recog-nise and keep alive. And this phenomenon which, for better or worse, was absent in the Fordist enterprise and in the guilds of the precapitalist world, is causing frustration, alienation, anxiety and high doses of despair born of anomie. These are not exactly halcyon days.

This whole state of affairs feeds into another phenomenon that we can't ignore since it is of the greatest sociological and political interest. The pop-ulation that is already precarious or about to become precarious (if not the famous 99 per cent, which is a pedagogical exaggeration, then at least a large majority of the society, who are either already part of the precariat or under the Damoclean sword of falling into it) also shows an open symbolic dis-tancing from the world of employment which, having been removed, has ceased to be part of the little group of certainties that consolidated some small degree of stability.

On the one hand, loss of occupational status – for example, after a long time without being able to sell insurance from the comfort of a secure job – is prob-lematic because it means, *inter alia*, an interruption of income flows, which in the capitalist system come from employment, and the loss of other benefits associated with wage labour as well. But, on the other hand, the loss of occu-pational status can help affected people start to suspect something and decide to take the red pill of *The Matrix*, unplug themselves from the beastly parasitic machine and start becoming aware of how alienating capitalist wage labour has been and is. For Marx, it's total 'wage slavery'; for Aristotle, pure 'part-time slavery'. It is in this sense that Standing (2014) asserts that the precariat is less likely to develop the 'false consciousness' of those who uncritically value the undignified and indignation-provoking traditional jobs as bringing com-plete happiness. In brief, the precariat is much more lucid when it comes to the old refrain of 'work dignifies'. Work dignifies? *What* kind of work digni-fies your life? – the precariat wonders, stunned. And the simple act of posing this question is like a contagious virus that can spread beyond spaces that are strictly inhabited by precarious and excluded workers and reach the whole of society, which is what is starting to happen, including those who 'enjoy' or aspire to 'enjoy' a 'traditional' job. Needless to say, this social scenario has an emancipatory potential that we shouldn't ignore.

The precariat, says Standing (2011, 2014), is not made up of people who are only victims because many among them, closely watching how freedom is slipping through their fingers, have shown that they are capable of questioning the work ethic of their parents, to understand and to express, and thus denounce, the fact that while it may be true that they worked in jobs with high levels of well-being, the condition was that their parents had to renounce any hope they might have had of controlling (re)production and thereby to live, in essence, a free life.

Flexibility linked with the precarisation of the living conditions of the working population has had devastating effects: broken lives, interrupted careers and all sorts of fragmentation and discontinuity, etc. But precarious workers occupy, perhaps very much against their wishes, a privileged position for reviewing the situation and recovering a somewhat broader perspective on what capitalist social and labour relations represent, and to send out a loud, clear message to the working class as a whole: we are, all of us, even those who believe they are on firm ground, true 'part-time slaves', and often very part-time. Precarious workers can then experience the flexibility associated with their working conditions as a stimulus to ask and wonder: is this what we really deserve? Does the alternative really entail a desperate attempt to recover the employment-centric rigidities of the Fordist worker who ended his days having grown up and retired in the bosom – or behind the bars – of the same productive unit? Is the aim really about trying to (re)dignify an impossible to dignify 'part-time slavery'? Couldn't we be interested in other kinds of work, other kinds of existences? Could we aspire, as André Gorz (1985, 1987, 1997) suggests and David Frayne (2015) somehow evokes, to work for a wage only intermittently and live a 'multi-active' life in which professional work and non-remunerated activities complement and nourish each other? Could the world of self-management and public-common institutions that might arise from it, on the one hand, and unconditional packages of public policy measures including a basic income, on the other hand, bring us into environments in which we are truly able to act as subjects and collectivities that really choose their lives?

Perhaps it will be good to close these reflections by grounding them in empirical evidence extracted from basic income experiments that can help us glimpse, even partially, the kinds of social transformation that the introduction of universal and unconditional public policy schemes, such as basic income, can entail for our lives.[4] At this point, it is useful to define three broad areas to evaluate the effects of such experiments: the reduction of anxiety derived from deprivation and social exclusion, the increase in the ability to negotiate better working and living conditions, and the availability of resources and mechanisms to define and specify the kind of 'multi-active lives' that have been upheld.

First, it must be stressed that most pilots have shown that people would be able to breathe easier, to live with higher levels of material relief, thanks to the reduction in precariousness and the most pressing forms of social exclusion. In the experiments carried out both in the United States and Canada between 1960 and 1980 and in Europe, Canada and in economically developed Asian countries such as South Korea in recent times, relevant phenomena that can be observed are a reduction in financial stress, a greater facility to pay the mortgage or the rent, an improvement in the nutrition of the working classes and, in general, an expansion of psychological well-being. Likewise, in developing countries such as India or Namibia, experiments carried out well into the twenty-first century show a decrease in poverty and inequality that materialises in a reduction in malnutrition and crime. Also, the intervention that took place in Madhya Pradesh (India) between 2012 and 2014 and the one that has been taking place in Kenya since 2017 show positive effects in terms of individuals' ability to reduce debt, avoid debt and escape debts bondage, and in terms of households' and communities' ability to invest in essential assets.

But it's not just about having a better chance of survival. It is also about being able to do so by dignifying the working and living conditions that accompany us. In this sense, a second set of results points to greater freedom to reduce working hours[5] – in the case of the Madhya Pradesh pilot, it is even possible to observe the disappearance of forced labour – to force increases in the wages of the working population and to manage to incorporate certain levels of consumption of goods and services that are compatible with a just eco-social transition or that are linked to the realm of culture and arts. These processes of dignifying people's living conditions have a gender dimension that cannot go unnoticed: the higher levels of intra-household female empowerment such as those observed in Madhya Pradesh not only result in a greater capacity for women to make decisions that affect the daily running of the environments in which they live, but also in an increase in the divorce rate – as occurred in the North American experiments of the 1960s and 1970s – which allows us to say that the environments themselves, in the event that individuals (in this case, women) have a guaranteed material existence, can be questioned and even abandoned.

Let's focus for a moment on the possibility of turning down jobs that are to be carried out under abusive conditions. According to David Calnit sky (2017), the working population that participated in the 1970s Canada experiments dared to make it explicit that they aspired to stop working under too harmful or alienating conditions, which forced Dauphin employers to raise wage offers to keep or attract workers who now had a decent alternative.

Third and finally – and we're placing ourselves at the very heart of one of the main contributions of this book – the results of the pilot projects show a promising increase in the ability to articulate, deploy and reproduce over time the 'multi-active lives' which, as has been seen, emerge when we count on the possibility of gradually incorporating tasks and responsibilities of a very diverse nature that adjust to what we are or wish to be. In many of the experiments carried out in Europe, North America, Asia and Africa since 2008, we find recipients who express having experienced an increase in personal autonomy, having had a greater ability to train individually and/or generate community ties to undertake paths of their own within the economic sphere – in the case of Madhya Pradesh, it is essential to highlight the importance of female empowerment that resulted in the extension of cooperative businesses in the textile sector – and having been able to open up more easily to the world of voluntary work and, above all, to care work.

Once again, in order to achieve all this, it was and has been very important (to be able) to reduce the labour supply. For instance:

[T]he results of Canada's Mincome trial in the town of Dauphin conclude that the cash transfer led to a reduction in labour participation of approximately 11 percentage points. Nevertheless, it is important to note that individuals, far from leaving the labour market for leisure, were engaged in care work, training or had health and disability problems. [Similarly,] a reduction in labour participation of 9.5 percentage points is found in the 2017–2019 Barcelona intervention, known as B-Mincome [which] is explained by a reduction in the labour participation of individuals living with children, suggesting a substitution of formal work in the market by informal care work [as well as by formal and informal educational programmes]. (Borrell-Porta, de Quintana and Segura, 2023a: 23)

All these realities are expressions of the human propensity to incorporate, in an autonomous and flexible way, different types of activity that form changing conglomerates that can adapt to the evolving needs and circumstances that accompany every singular life cycle – and I insist that 'flexibility' in no case should be interpreted here as 'precariousness'. Can we endow ourselves with resources that give us the necessary bargaining power to make genuine and autonomous decisions and effectively put them into circulation, always in the direction of this plural expansion of the ways in which we externalise our abilities and desires? It seems that, at least to some extent, most basic income pilots suggest that this may be the case.

PART IV

The Dream Is Over: Post-neoliberalism (or Why a Basic Income *Now* and *How*)

Broken windows and deserted factories in post-industrial Detroit. Rusted chimneys, surprising undergrowth sprouting from cracked walls and crumbling asphalt in what was the world's automobile capital. Near the city of Tarragona, a woman in her eighties dies in a fire caused by the candles she used for light. She was threatened with eviction for non-payment of rent. Two months earlier the electricity company had cut off her power supply, also for non-payment. In Santiago de Chile, a post-adolescent girl in a city-centre supermarket is waiting for a tip for putting the customers' shopping into plastic bags. Her salary? Another case of non-payment. From the high-speed train linking Madrid and Barcelona, you can see kilometre after kilometre of partly constructed buildings that were abandoned before the walls were closed and windows fitted. The bubble burst, leaving buyers and their homes in a state of utter ruin. Something like this occurred with the ghost cities of hyper-industrial China. It all happened so fast that the cities were closed down before they were even inaugurated. The 'wetbacks' from Latin America keep crossing rivers and borders to make a living and also sustain a country that would sink without them. 'America for the Americans' may not be exactly what Monroe had in mind, but they're there, from south to north, hidden away, and without anybody recognising them. In the Mediterranean, those who arrive sell their lives too cheap. Others don't arrive.

There was a time when the causal forces that shape capitalist societies, which have never operated outside the will of humans – or at least a few of them – laid the bases for a 'reform' of the system which, while it left intact the disciplinary mechanisms used on the working classes, did ease the rigours with which these devices had come to be used historically. This was the time of the 'social pacts' that came into being with the end of the Second

World War, with effects at both the state level (e.g. the regulation of labour markets, the development and strengthening of tax systems) and the global level (e.g. the structuring of a monetary and financial system that would ensure the subordination of speculative capital to productive capital[1]). It was the 'golden age of capitalism' in which increased productivity always came with equivalent and even greater increases in real wages. It was the time of the spread of welfare regimes which, in the Global North, came with certain sets of certainties in most households and, in the South, worked as a sort of horizon of expectations and possibilities (and, in some cases, of fulfilment, however partial it might have been), and structured the political action of governments and a wide array of sociopolitical movements. These were also the years of the Cold War when the lengthy shadow of a possible philo-Soviet alternative took decades to fade away, even in the bosom of the most 'advanced' capitalist economies.

But *The Spirit of '45*, which Ken Loach so well documented in his homonymous film of 2013, had been melting into air since the early 1970s. The 'reform' of capitalism that had entailed an attempt to effect the famous 'euthanasia of the rentier' proposed by Keynes (2007) in response to the barbarous spectacle of the unbridled capitalism of the 1920s and 1930s was followed by a counter-reform of the system that can be understood as the full-blown revenge of rentier oligarchs who, logically enough, had been loath to accept the regulatory frameworks that emerged in the second post-war period (Domènech, 2015).[2]

The term *neoliberalism* has become a catch all that is difficult to manage analytically and historiographically. It's been so bandied about that it sometimes seems to name everything and refer to nothing. But, given definitional and empirical precision, it's very useful for portraying the reality referred to here. By *neoliberalism*, I mean the whole set of intellectual and media references, on the one hand, and of political-institutional practices, on the other hand, which aim to lay the foundations of the regime of capitalist accumulation that emerged especially after the mid-1970s; a regime that was set on abolishing the mechanisms which, in this golden age of capitalist 'reform', provided social protection to the working classes and exercised some political control over large concentrations of private economic power. This it did, not by 'deregulating the economy' (because, as we'll see, there is no such thing as a *deregulated economy*) but by (re)regulating it in favour of the previously hampered rentier capitalism.

But oligarchic (re)regulation of capitalism generates big doses of unease that spread everywhere. Hence, the history I'm telling here (in lower case because history is always the work of humans) is pushing us towards post-neoliberal times. The suffering must come to an end. Will we be able to exit neoliberalism in a direction which, far from leading us to greater doses of barbarism – a possibility that really exists and shouldn't be overlooked – allows us to civilise the processes and the spaces where we decide to settle our lives? And what role could a basic income play in this project? We'll now look at this from a historical perspective.[3]

12

'Wanting Everything Back': Basic Income in Contemporary Social Movements

As is well known, the so-called *post-war social consensus* or *Fordist pact*[1] established, on the one hand, that the working classes could count on sufficient levels of socioeconomic security by means of guaranteed stable employment and reasonable wages for working males,[2] recognition of collective bargaining and the role of trade unionism in structuring job markets, and the introduction of public policy to meet social needs arising in the always possible situations of misfortune. These took the form of *welfare states* that can be understood as regimes that reinforce citizenship through supposedly inviolable social rights, for example those to housing, health and education.[3] It goes without saying that this achievement, with long roots in trade union struggles and anti-fascist movements that enjoyed considerable social and political prestige, represented a victory of the working classes as they had managed to reduce the harshness of labour markets and the conditions of life imposed by capitalism. Yet the post-war social consensus obliged the selfsame working populations to explicitly renounce the old core aim of the contemporary workers' movement: control of production. The struggle for property and over managing the organisation of work within the productive unit was wiped from the agenda of the social and political movements of the working classes. This was evidently an enormous defeat for the workers' movement because aspiring to control production, to democratise management of workplaces as a whole, had always meant aspiring to decide together what kind of life they wanted to live. In other words, this social pact meant an enormous loss of economic sovereignty (Casassas et al., 2015).[4]

But the pact is broken today. In fact, it has been unilaterally broken by the neoliberal extractive elites since the mid-1970s. To make matters worse, the dispossessing nature of this turn of capitalism has intensified with the oligarchic management of the crisis that hit in 2008. In effect, neoliberal policies have involved labour reforms that have undermined the capacity of workers to look ahead, plan and make progress with stable life projects; they have entailed the loss or erosion of social rights; and they have given rise to increased precariousness.[5] In this context, economic security is no longer guaranteed by participation in labour markets, whether it's because we have no access to them thanks to fast-rising levels of unemployment, or because we no longer earn enough to live on and to sustain our nuclei of coexistence. This scenario inevitably leads to the increased subordination of women because less social rights in the social sphere means more exploitation in the domestic domain where women tend to be in charge of the in-kind benefits that the states were supposed to provide.[6]

That the pact is shattered is evident in several kinds of data and facts. To begin with, there is the decoupling of growth in productivity and growth in real wages. According to the Bureau of Labour Statistics in the United States, between 1950 and 1970 the rise in real wages was slightly higher than productivity in the most important sectors of the economy but, by 2010, real wages were at the same level as those of the mid-1970s while productivity had doubled during the same period (Sorscher, 2012) owing to, among other reasons, the use of new technologies, foreign investment and intensification of working hours (Harvey, 2007; Varoufakis, 2011). Furthermore, the last four decades have seen a dismantling of the welfare policies and devices that underpinned the extension of significant levels of social protection.[7] All of this has resulted in thoroughgoing inequalities of wealth and power that are visible on the global scale. In the words of Boaventura de Sousa Santos (2017: 24):

The publicly available data are alarming. Twenty-eight companies from the finance sector control 50 trillion dollars, which is to say three-quarters of the world's wealth that is accounted for (world GDP [gross domestic product] is 80 trillion dollars, and there are another twenty trillion in tax havens). The great majority of these institutions are registered in the United States and Europe. Their power also derives from another source: the profitability of (industrial) productive investment on the global scale is, at most 2.5%, while that for financial investment can be as high as 7%. This is a system for which the sovereignty of two hundred potential regulators [states] is irrelevant.[8]

As I said, social and political 'history' is written in lower case. There are no metaphysical forces that inform or shape it. Its nature and direction are guided entirely by worldly human hands. And the breakdown of the post-war social pact can't escape this fact. Indeed, it wouldn't have been possible without a (clearly human) Reaganomics which ushered in tax cuts and exemptions for the highest-income earners, dismantled or slashed social spending programmes, and abolished many of the restrictions on Wall Street that had been introduced during the 1930s and 1940s (Varoufakis, 2011). Similarly, the breaking of the post-war social pact wouldn't have been possible without the (clearly human) decision of Margaret Thatcher to vent her rage on the 'counter civil society' of workers, combatting trade unions and the slightest hint of any focus of material or symbolic resistance the workers might have been able to muster.[9] Finally, it's worth of looking at the (not remotely metaphysical) way in which J. P. Morgan's think tank, at the height of its all-out attack on the constitutional foundations of the post-war social pact, expressed the situation in 2013:

> The political systems in the periphery [by which the authors mean the south of Europe] were established in the aftermath of dictatorship, and were defined by that experience. Constitutions tend to show a strong socialist influence, reflecting the political strength that left-wing parties gained after the defeat of fascism. Political systems around the periphery typically display several of the following features: weak executives; weak central states relative to regions; constitutional protection of labor rights; consensus building systems which foster political clientalism; and the right to protest if unwelcome changes are made to the political status quo. The shortcomings of this political legacy have been revealed by the crisis. Countries around the periphery have only been partially successful in producing fiscal and economic reform agendas, with governments constrained by constitutions (Portugal), powerful regions (Spain), and the rise of populist parties (Italy and Greece). (Barr and Mackie, 2013: 12–13)

In the Spanish case, the attack on the legal underpinnings of the post-war social pact took the form of an amendment to Article 135 of the Constitution in August 2011, whereby payment of the state's public debt was to be given priority over social spending. In Pisarello's words (2014), this was nothing less than a 'deconstituent' coup against welfare regimes which, however compatible they might have been with capitalism, had attempted to limit the scope of its depossessing dynamics.

That was the end of the dream. It ended in the sense that the secure lives that characterised the halcyon days of the Fordist consensus – secure, but with the 'conditional freedom' of all the rigidities of a productive model that was designed *inter alia* to restrict the economic sovereignty of workers – are no longer possible. They have been damaged, if not totally stymied by the introduction of cuts and the neoliberal precarisation of living and working conditions. Hence, the promise of full employment as a guarantee of socioeconomic inclusion has already been revealed as nothing more than a pipedream; the domain of labour is being (re)regulated to favour the 'employers'; the safety nets of social protection and provision of services linked with welfare regimes are well into the processes of dismantlement; and regulation and control of the most powerful economic actors (the big investors and the 'super-rich' of all stripes) is being done away with, thus allowing a thoroughgoing process of financialisation of the economy in the framework of increasingly speculative capitalism in which rentierism has free rein (Bello, 2009; Harvey, 2007; Standing, 2016; Varoufakis, 2011).[10] Yes, the dream is over. And the pact is kaput.

The big political and civilisational question that now arises can be summed up as follows: what can we do when a pact is broken? More precisely, what can the injured – the *betrayed*, if you prefer – party do when it becomes aware that the pact has been *unilaterally* broken by the other side? As I said, every pact entails both a victory and a renunciation and, in the case of the social pact after the Second World War, the contents of this victory and this renunciation were very clear.[11] So, given the fact that the conditions that gave rise to the post-war social pact are all but irretrievable since the elites are hardly disposed to go back to the tax regimes and public policies that characterised the agreement, the injured betrayed party – the global working class – can feel legitimised in trying to revive what it had to renounce as a consequence of the signing and introduction of the old pact. I refer to control of production – and reproduction, it must be added – that is, the control of the many ways in which humans work collectively to satisfy our needs.

It's pathetic to beg for what we're not going to be granted. And, in this case, it's pathetic to try to resuscitate a Fordist–welfarist pact that's never going to happen, basically because the capitalist class isn't going to appear at the negotiating table. To put it simply, the rentier oligarchy is busy with 'other matters' and, for these 'matters', it would seem they have less and less need for support from the old disciplined and accommodating working class. And, as happens with couples that break up, friendly advice must be given by an external but close and loyal observer who can tell them that, after a certain amount of time, continuing to implore and pining to try to recover what's impossible is simply degrading and unhealthy. This doesn't mean that the global working class can't or shouldn't struggle to maintain and, if necessary, to reconstruct and even expand the remains of the welfare state arrangements that came out of the post-war pacts. But the global working class would do well to understand that this 'defensive' action must be part of an overall political culture that aims at rearming and taking the initiative to move into fresh terrain in order to leave behind the logic of a consensus that is denied to us, and to attempt an 'offensive' that once again brings us closer to fighting for command of the control panel.

History is, then, pushing us to a post-neoliberal constituent moment, once again urging us to aspire to absolutely everything. Failure to do so is tantamount to ignoring the magnitude of the blow inflicted by the predatory rentier turn of capitalism; is tantamount to ignoring the need to come up with a proportionate response, as a matter of dignity but also and especially as pure sociopolitical strategy. The ashes of the neoliberal conflagration, the chaos of the wreck, can be the new seedbed for the rebel cultures of new working classes which, as E. P. Thompson (1991) suggested, are capable of 'making themselves', as authors and agents of their own condition as classes of workers who are no longer *proletarian* but *having and exercising republican freedom.*[12]

But how can we approach the question of control of (re)production from the circumstances of the present? What I'm suggesting here is that the sets of resources guaranteed as the economic and social rights that constitute our condition as citizens can help us to place the control of (re)production once again at the centre of the social and political agenda because they will allow us to regain something of what the working populations lost as a result of the old Fordist pact: bargaining power. In effect, by unconditionally guaranteeing a sphere of autonomous social existence for everyone, economic and social rights confer on social actors the ability to reject lives they don't want to live and to define forms of work they feel are right for them. At least, this is how it has been understood and expressed in many of the social movements – Spain's 15M among them – that appeared in response to the crisis of 2008 and neoliberal management of it (Casassas et al., 2015). As said in the Introduction, Marco Revelli (2010) couldn't have put it more clearly when he cited the graffiti he saw on a wall of the Polytechnic Institute of Turin: '*Ci avete tolto troppo, adesso rivogliamo tutto*' ('You took too much from us and now we want everything back again'). Could economic and social rights, among them the right to existence in the form of a basic income, come to be tools that help us to conquer this *everything*, whatever we might want it to mean?

What seems to be beyond doubt is that a lot of the social movements that appeared in the wake of the crash of 2008 and to which we owe a Polanyi-style 'double movement' of 'self-defence of society' aren't limited to drawing attention to the unsustainability of the present situation but also point to a 'constituent' response that would allow the popular classes to recover their lost economic sovereignty, or at least significant parts of it, in the attempt to take control of their own lives. Movements such as that of the students in Chile, 15M, Occupy and Nuit Debout can be seen as attempts to defend the institutional mechanisms of welfare regimes that are presently under attack – high-quality public health and education, for example – and, at the same time, as ways of overthrowing welfare state capitalism itself as this was a project that was intentionally aimed at limiting the people's sovereignty in the economic sphere (Domènech, 2015; Rawls, 2001). In other words, what we are seeing today is a struggle for new practices and social relations that will help us not only to contradict the anti-democratic nature of the neoliberal turn of capitalism but also to construct new (re)productive arrangements that will transcend the logic presented by capitalism in its organisation of social and economic life (Casassas et al., 2015). This explains the emphasis of social movements, such as those I've mentioned, on the need for different forms of self-management and mutual aid that will enable the development and reproduction of broad sets of common goods (Coriat, 2015; Mattei, 2011), on the one hand, and fully democratic public policy schemes that are subject to citizen control and that will unconditionally empower the population as a whole so that everyone can participate in social and economic life with effective individual and collective freedom, on the other hand (Standing, 2011, 2014).

As for income policies, the coexistence, which isn't always easy, of what could be called *containment and resistance strategies* and *constituent strategies* (Casassas and Manjarín, 2013) is surprising. The former aspire to deal immediately with pressing situations of social emergency. In many cases, these strategies, which aren't opposed to thinking about basic income as a medium- or long-term goal,[13] include proposing higher amounts for present minimum-income benefits and introducing cash benefits with somewhat weaker conditionality, or at least conditionality that is less strict than that established by the income policies that are presently in force. However, it's interesting to see, at the same time and in a wide range of social and political movements, the emergence of basic income, always with the *constituent* vocation of post-capitalist scenarios in which it is seen as a tool that can help to construct new social consensuses that will give greater freedom for manoeuvre for most of the working population when it comes to co-determining the spaces where we produce material and immaterial goods and reproduce life. In effect, the universal and unconditional nature of basic income can be a particularly effective measure for obtaining the bargaining power necessary to obtain hitherto unknown levels of economic sovereignty. Do we dare?

And the truth is that we must dare, because measures such as basic income can act as a point of support for a whole strategy that proves itself capable of opposing the advance of the far right by resorting to a whole policy that is based on effective freedom for all, on the experience of desire and meaning in relation to the practice of activities of many kinds – productive and reproductive, paid and unpaid – on the sense of belonging to a community that truly accommodates us. In addition, the principle of universality of basic income could promote a solidarity that, today, is hampered by public policies that establish deep tensions and divisions between workers with medium and low wages, and the unemployed and recipients of social assistance. Indeed, the presence of a basic income could favour the generalisation not of equal lives – this would in no case be desirable – but of understandable and comparable lives, and similar life experiences are essential to facilitate communication and solidarity: according to Marx, the similarity of life within the walls of the factory was what galvanised solidarity (Calnitsky, 2017). In this way, even if it does not actively promote solidarity, basic income can break the rigidities of current social benefit systems and thus it can reduce those barriers to alliances between groups of workers and groups of the poor and excluded that generate so much damage in sociopolitical terms (Birnbaum, 2016; Standing, 2011). As Zygmunt Bauman puts it in his conversation with Daniel Leighton (2002):

> Targeted assistance splits and antagonises: it sets 'people who give' against those who 'take'. [...] Basic income is, on the contrary, an idea of effacing the division between givers and takers and dissolving the very distinction between giving and taking in the vocation of the citizen. It is meant to make us all 'stakeholders' of the state-national community. It is meant to unite, not to divide, and above all to make public issues into genuinely shared issues. [...] This is what I mean by insisting that basic income is [...] a way to the restoration of a fully-fledged, vigorous, engaged citizenship; and to the recognition that the country is a shared property of all its citizens.

13

Societies *of* the Market or Societies *with* Markets?

At this point, it shouldn't be surprising that markets aren't presented here as a blight. Why not turn to them as *possible* spaces in which to exercise the economic sovereignty gained by means of being endowed with economic and social rights, and especially with a basic income? Why not situate in commercial environments (some of) the resources and activities pertaining to lives that are freed from the compulsion of working for others? Polanyi himself pointed out that markets are necessary institutions for resolving the problems of coordination typical of complex societies (Baum, 1996). But do we retain the ability to decide, individually and/or collectively, when and how we want to occupy commercial spaces, and when and how we want to stand outside of them? As Polanyi says (1944), the truly degrading phenomenon that capitalism brings with it isn't so much the presence of markets as the fact that this ability to decide has been vanishing after being subjected to the 'dark Satanic mills' that crushed everything and churned it all out into the logic of commodity exchange. The question that needs to be asked at this point has to be this: can a basic income help the popular classes to recover this power of deciding about the limits and nature of markets? Markets or no markets? And, if yes, what should they be like?

To begin with, it would be a good idea to introduce a small conceptual digression. All too often, we hear mention of *the market*, or *the state* in the singular, which is to say in abstract terms. People sometimes ask or consider the question, do we want societies with a bigger presence of the market or more influence of the state? The problem with this kind of approach is that it starts out from an ontological impossibility or, at best, a gross mystification because, in reality, *the market*, in singular or abstract terms, doesn't exist. What do exist are different forms of historically shaped markets as derivations of political options or sets of options (Joerges, Strath and Wagner, 2005). In other words, all markets are the result of state intervention and/ or of other institutional bodies that are able to impose norms and enforce rules. All markets are the result of the sedimentation of layers and layers of legislation with greater or lesser degrees of formality, but they're always the result of some or other political orientation. In turn, this 'political orientation' responds to a certain way of channelling, also in the commercial domain, class struggle and the correlation of forces existing in any given society. It therefore doesn't make sense to place *state* and *market* in opposition. There is no market that hasn't emerged as the result of some kind of intervention by the state or other bodies established for collective control of economic life (Casassas, 2013). This is why I said in Part I that the famous *laissez-faire* is a myth of propagandistic intent.

In this regard, it's worth noting that the early social movements in revolt against capitalist plunder and dispossession in late medieval and proto-industrial England weren't against extending markets (in fact, markets had been present in the continent of Eurasia since the Bronze Age (Goody, 2006)), but they did oppose the methods used by the capitalist class when politically shaping English and European markets during the modern era. When E. P. Thompson (1991) refers to the 'moral economy of the crowd' which, in England and the rest of Europe, appealed to a 'plebeian' sociopolitical culture that rose up against capitalist expropriating 'rationalisations', is referring to sets of rules and procedures that aimed precisely at achieving the regulation of modern markets that would be favourable to the interests of the popular classes. This moral economy of the crowd problematised, denounced and, to some extent, prevented the presence of intermediaries, hoarding practices, the ways that rumours were spread in order to alter the prices of things, haggling, monopoly and oligopoly, speculative buying and selling of the same item, and so on. Did this mean that the moral economy of the crowd was an attempt to restrict the emerging supposedly 'free market'? No, it wasn't. The moral economy of the crowd was a way of curbing the predatory practices of these nascent *capitalist markets*[1] and to consolidate the conditions for the possibility of an 'effective free market' that might not be capitalist.

To go back to the question of predistribution, if basic income is of any interest as a predistributive policy it's because of its potential in terms of decommodifying the workforce and other resources and activities. Owing to the ubiquitous nature of markets, starting with labour markets, any political strategy aiming at improving social justice must offer, first of all, the power to decide whether (or not) to enter markets; and, second, should markets be chosen, the ability to co-determine the nature and functioning of these commercial spaces.

It's surprising, therefore, that most of the foundational literature on predistribution overlooks the question of decommodification – or, to be more precise, that of the *capacity to decommodify* – which is surely a major omission in any normative debate about social justice in the modern world. Why? Because this amounts to giving markets, starting with labour markets, the central role in the processes of structuring our societies. Jacob S. Hacker (2011: 36), for example, states that the aim of predistribution is 'a well-functioning *market*[2] democracy', which requires the public powers to focus on 'market reforms that encourage a more equal distribution of economic power and rewards even before government collects taxes or pays out benefits' (2011: 35). In effect, according to Martin O'Neill and Thad Williamson (2012a), Hacker's project is to 'engineer markets to create fairer outcomes from the beginning'. Hence, the rules of the game may be modified to make it more strife-free, but it seems that the game itself – the establishment of exchanges in capitalist markets – can't be questioned. In some sense, it's as if we were to declare that the treatment of slaves by their masters must be regulated (and, as we've seen, the radical Athenian democrats of the fifth century BCE did just this), while taking it for granted that the institution of slavery should remain legally in force. Similarly, the Labour leader Ed Miliband claimed to embrace the cause of predistribution by proposing measures such as raising the minimum wage and including workers' representatives on committees where company pay scales are decided (O'Neill and Williamson, 2012a). Meanwhile, Lane Kenworthy (2013) outlined the predistributive policy agenda in the following terms: boosting the industrial sector, strengthening unions, raising the minimum wage, desegmentation of the labour market, a fairer distribution of corporate profits and, ultimately, increased employment.

It's true that wage workers can be helped to negotiate better pay, that it is possible to work on labour legislation that will offer them better protection, and even that collective bargaining can be improved by giving trade unions a central role, but in no case is there any attempt to extend the republican freedom of the working population if they aren't allowed to autonomously decide for themselves whether or not they want to become *wage* workers.

Hence, what is really striking is the doggedness of some predistribution theorists – Hacker and Miliband again – in trying to find ways to civilise capitalism which, at most, may be reformable or renewable, but it's always intrinsically incompatible with effective freedom. To sum up, it would seem much more fruitful, conceptually and politically, to turn to predistributive mechanisms, not to tame the (untameable) beast but to open up any feasible way of countering the depossessing and hence liberticidal and anti-democratic nature of capitalism. This is why something unconditional such as basic income – which, as we'll soon see, in no way excludes other related measures such as unconditional access to healthcare, education and housing – should be seen as part of a predistributive strategy aimed at giving individuals and groups the effective right to shape their working lives, inside and/or outside of markets.

On balance, the fact that we live in societies with greater or lesser degrees of commercial activity shouldn't worry us too much. But what is of the greatest civilisational and political importance is the possibility, whether it's within our grasp or not, for us to make truly genuine decisions about the decommodification of resources and activities, once again starting with the labour force. Hence, it makes sense to distinguish between 'actually existing (de)commodification', which could come to be something that is highly contingent, and the 'value of *decommodifiability*' or, to avoid such an unwieldy word, the 'power of decommodification'. Clearly, a society that is free in the republican sense can't be one in which the market appears as the only mechanism of social coordination, so it can't be a 'society *of* the market'. Rather, it must be a society in which individuals and groups are able to decide, from any corner of social life, where, when and how to open the doors to markets, and when, where and how to be rid of them. In this sense, it must be a 'society *with* markets'.[3]

The 'capacity' or 'power of decommodification' constitutes, then, the variable that allows us to evaluate the emancipatory, liberating potential of any public policy proposal, starting with income policies. I now analyse six scenarios before concluding.

First, there is no republican freedom when we are thrown into the capitalist labour markets of a world without any kind of income policy and, in all likelihood, with rickety welfare devices. In these cases, we're simply forced to obey the orders that our supposed 'employers' feel like dishing out. Our most elementary subsistence directly depends on them.

Second, our republican – or, if you prefer, 'effective' – freedom is seriously curtailed when public authorities limit themselves to offering unemployment benefits and the 'dole' and other benefits 'for the poor'. Once again, the game consists in obeying heteronomous, externally imposed orders in the labour market and, if the employment relationship is interrupted and we find ourselves in situations of poverty and exclusion, we're offered the chance to save our lives, usually on condition that we show we're willing to rejoin the horror show of a world of labour in which everything is broken to bits, for this is the unabashed perversity of the *workfare* logic espoused by the conditional benefits that are currently in force in most societies.

Third, our effective freedom remains gravely damaged when the public powers agree to relax the conditionality of income policies while still keeping wage labour as the central and indisputable mainstay of the social contract. It's to be welcomed if countries marked by temporary employment, job precariousness and rising numbers of the working poor (whose incomes are below the poverty line) opt for income policies that refrain from the cynicism of requiring, as a condition of obtaining benefits, that potential recipients agree to enrol in alleged social and labour reintegration programmes in a world that is incapable of effectively reincorporating a huge part of the working population.[4] Nevertheless, such forms of 'income for the poor with relaxed conditionality' continue to present a serious problem: however much the conditions are relaxed – and in the Catalan proposal it is 'enough' not to reach 664 euros per month – they are still offering a 'poverty income', which means that they're mechanisms that come into play once we've accepted the rules of the game of the capitalist labour market game and, in this inescapable interaction with an arbitrary and predatory status quo, we break our backs and can demonstrate it to administrative bodies. These mechanisms certainly make it easier to bear the exploitation, but in no case do they free us from it. And human dignity shouldn't be so vulnerable to the whims of those who have the whip hand.[5]

Fourth, the presence of 'poverty incomes' coupled with 'employment incentives'[6] does little to improve matters in terms of promoting effective freedom. Once again, the mantra is 'earn your living in a world you don't control, in a world you have no need to control'. The logic is the same, *ex post* aid for the poor and needy who can show that this is what they are, which means that *ex ante*, from square one, what we must all do is accept without complaint the rigours of a world of labour in which we are adrift and dispossessed and hence deprived of bargaining power and of any room for manoeuvre. Initiatives such as the Basque Income Guarantee Scheme do take note of the problems caused by the poverty trap that is associated with the usual conditional benefits[7] and introduce the possibility of receiving part of the allowance as a supplement to a low wage. This is a reward for the disciplined behaviour of those who pick themselves up after falling down and, against all odds, keep trying even in social and economic spaces – capitalist markets – that are a long way from being welcoming or inclusive. But the million dollar question is still the same and, so far, doesn't seem to deserve a satisfactory answer: at what point has the poor worker who is also – how wonderful! – a recipient of complementary cash benefits been able to decide what sort of activities, remunerated or not, he or she wants to do as part of his or her life, and the ways and proportions in which the work should be done? Income still comes *ex post*, whether it comes from the labour market or through the public social assistance system, or a combination of both. Income arrives too late. It comes when we've already lost the last shred of decision-making power on the kinds of social and institutional settings we want for our lives.

Fifth, earned income tax credits have the same problem. If they help to supplement the workers' wages that are below the poverty line, they also presuppose that the lifestyles that are to be rewarded with a subsidy are those that mean not leaving the fold in which people carry out the activities that the labour market *presently* deems valuable and, therefore, remunerable, even if the remuneration is very often pitiful. And where is the possibility for imagining and engaging in other life projects that might even be in the markets? And, moreover, what happens with the possibility of incorporating care work, which usually isn't remunerated, into the set of activities for which we should all be responsible? They're just mere possibilities dumped in the gutters of the world.

Sixth, what has been called the 'participation income', which, as seen before, was suggested by the British economist Anthony Atkinson (1996) brings us much closer to the ability to define, individually and collectively, what we understand by *meaningful work*, although it is still fraught with technical and normative problems. As Atkinson puts it, echoing a certain ethos that isn't uncommon among a certain sector of the left, it makes no moral sense to offer 'something for nothing'. A certain kind of participation in society must be demanded so that people become legitimately deserving of something akin to a basic income. According to Atkinson, this 'participation' should be broadly defined: it could be formally remunerated work but also many types of care work or voluntary work in the domains of education, social and community development, sociopolitical participation, etc. It goes without saying that a project like this enormously expands the range of possibilities when drawing the perimeter of the world we'd like to inhabit. However, the administrative difficulties involved (since this proposal would require the establishment of large and extraordinarily invasive armies of public monitors of our supposed 'participation', in addition to problems of paternalism and incomplete information that the scheme presents, as we shall see in Chapter 15) make it advisable to discard this idea as a core mechanism for social inclusion.

In these circumstances, if what is at stake is to conquer and expand the (republican) freedom to decide the spaces and institutions where we want to spend our lives, which requires, among other things, having the power to open and close the doors of markets in keeping with our desires and aspirations, the public guarantee of universally and unconditionally granted monetary resources couldn't be more crucial, especially when we bear in mind the bargaining power they confer. This 'public guarantee' is basic income,[8] a basic income that must be understood (and this is essential) as just one part, as central as you like, of a much wider array of public policy mechanisms, as I'll now describe in more detail.

14

Grappling with Customs in Common: A People's Political Economy?

Basic income is a mainstay but it isn't sufficient. There are many faces of the political polyhedron that need to be created and reproduced over time in order to transform our world into liberated and practicable terrain for everyone. In this chapter I highlight the need for genuine public-common 'packages of measures' which, grounded in renewed 'customs in common', would enable us to organise what the left wing of the French Revolution, that of Mably, Paine and Robespierre, called a 'people's political economy', namely sets of practices and resources that counter 'tyrannical', dispossessing political economies, and that point to forms of collective control over the material and symbolic bases of our lives. Without such assemblages, the common government of the world we inhabit is in danger. Without such assemblages, we run the risk of constructing a neoliberal dystopia in which individuals equipped *only* with a basic income are driven to a desperate and atomising game of 'every man for himself' in social and economic environments that don't allow them to raise their voices at all and, still less, to break away from the voracious and rigorously commodifying channels of capitalism.[1] Be that as it may, it should be noted that the context matters. Basic income solves part of the Kafkaesque puzzle to which the high levels of conditionality of current social protection systems lead, but this does not mean that its institutional design should not be thought out and foreseen with extreme caution. Issues such as the level of basic income, the geographical-political space in which it is implemented, the financing model and the institutional framework in which it is inserted (e.g. would it replace all the conditional cash transfer schemes that we have today or not?) can have a decisive impact on the effects of such measures (Aerts, Marx and Verbist, 2023). So let's think about these matters from the perspective of the emancipatory basic income that we have been assessing and pleading for throughout all this book. There are four main dimensions that need to be explored if the aims of this people's political economy are to be met. At the heart of these, as the French revolutionaries said, was ensuring the continuance of a dignified existence for all (Bosc, 2016, 2018).

First, basic income doesn't exclude but, rather, requires the development of political cultures for the organisation of free work. There'd be little point in acquiring 'starting' resources if this leaving the fold wasn't accompanied and guided by a whole symbolic dimension that points to specific forms of collective appropriation of living and working spaces. Some writers (Gourevitch, 2016; Raes, 2013) have expressed unease at the possibility that the *individual* nature of basic income might *individualise* our work and our lives to the point of undermining the possibility of a culture of resistance and rebellion against capitalist tyranny which would only be possible if people came together to interpret and work for it in common. And, indeed, these concerns are entirely understandable. Is the democratisation of work and co-responsibility for all kinds of work conceivable in a world made up of thousands and thousands of Robinson Crusoes? However, I should immediately add that the individualisation of our activities and lives is already here, and evidently not as a result of basic income but because of capitalist dynamics, especially in its neoliberal version. Moreover, who said that workers can't use an individually granted basic income as a safety net to strengthen and sustain over time the possible collective struggles for other working environments, including those struggles that can be driven by trade unions? There is no rule that says that the collective struggle for the democratisation of work must come together out of the ashes of the most absolute – and most atomising, it must be said – dispossession. The collective struggle for the democratisation of work, a task taken on by a diverse assortment of sociopolitical organisations, including trade unions, would do well to make use of an instrument such as basic income. This would give us some breathing space and the chance to recognise ourselves as equally damaged subjects, in order to catalyse and replicate this 'republican system of the association of free and equal producers' which, as we saw in Part I, contemporary emancipatory movements have always championed.

Second, a basic income must be *sufficient* to cover the basic necessities of life. With a basic income below the poverty line, individuals can enjoy some areas of improvement in their well-being, but not republican freedom. Why not? Because, as I've said, republican freedom depends on the bargaining power we achieve when we can stand tall when we're with other social actors as we don't depend on them socioeconomically in order to live – I've already stressed that poverty is incompatible with republican freedom. And, if we are to stand tall and hold the gaze, without having to cast our eyes down, we need a basic income that is at least equivalent to the poverty threshold (Casassas and De Wispelaere, 2016).[2] It might seem reasonable to consider a 'partial' basic income as part of a politically realistic way towards a sufficient basic income (and this will always depend on the specific political-institutional context), but it should be immediately warned that this 'partial' basic income will still be below the level at which we start to feel the benefits of the measure in terms of 'social power', or the ability to 'exit' to be able to 'enter' (re)productive environments that are compatible with republican freedom (Lazar, 2021).[3]

Third, there are a quite a lot of reasons for believing that a basic income would only be able to extend republican freedom when it is combined with a wide-ranging set of public policies that include the mechanisms typical of the welfare regimes we have known or aspire to know some day, especially if these mechanisms are able to shed the heavy burden associated with the many kinds of conditionalities that have so often been part of the system. In-kind benefits such as healthcare, education (including training for social reintegration), housing policies, care policies, transport and communication devices, and many other resources and regulatory frameworks[4] have a crucial role to play when consolidating the kind of positions of social invulnerability that are required by the attainment and extension of republican freedom.[5] It's of the utmost importance, then, that the 'floor' provided by the basic income, even if it is of a high amount, should be situated in a framework of robust mechanisms ensuring protection and socioeconomic empowerment (Casassas and De Wispelaere, 2016).[6] A republican defence of basic income must then openly oppose proposals which, like that of Charles Murray (2006), aspire to replace almost all welfare state programmes, present and future, with a 'simple' scheme that unconditionally guarantees income. Evidently, having to obtain all kinds of services from markets with, for example, rising costs of health insurance because of risks resulting from 'adverse selection', would make the basic income almost irrelevant in both accounting terms (because most of it would vanish because of having to buy such requirements) and promoting and extending effective freedom (Haagh, 2011, 2017; Krätke, 2004; Standing, 2017). This is why Aerts, Marx and Verbist (2023) assert, using microsimulation analysis in a comparative two-country setting, that if a basic income replaced existing social protection arrangements, poverty would increase without exception. This isn't just academic hot air. The danger that a neoliberal basic income, now being touted by the likes of billionaires including Bill Gates, Elon Musk and Mark Zuckerberg, could come to be a substitute for other mechanisms of social protection and 'self-defence' is already looming.[7] This mustn't happen. As Standing (2017: 4) says, 'a basic income need not – and should not – be a calculated means of dismantling the welfare state'. Rather, it should be the foundation on which the welfare state rests and from which it brings into service its mechanisms of protection and empowerment, and perhaps even more so than it has done so far. Louise Haagh has presented this question with insight. To start with, she has reminded us that 'in the eyes of postwar economists, income security and services were not strangers to, but extensions of, one another. Meade positioned his support for citizens' dividends in 1935 as a continuation of universal services' (Haagh, 2019: 119). Indeed, the idea was and is to establish a 'societal basic income model' in which public policy institutions and mechanisms cooperate and complement each other to favour the effectiveness of all parties. All this with the express and determined ambition to consolidate 'a large and secure public domain, and an active state. Hence, the packaging of basic income does matter. Basic income can form a part, but not the whole, of a scheme of human development justice and public incorporation' (Haagh, 2019: 148–9). And we know well that effective universal human incorporation in society is profoundly linked to a democratic perspective on how our life in common is to be arranged that can block any attempt to dedemocratise our societies through far-right forms of social fragmentation and ghettoisation. This is why it can be asserted that 'basic income may contribute to greater stability and equality in social relations, thus generating a basis for cooperation in society' (Haagh, 2019: 5).

In fact, the results of various basic income experiments come to support the view that things could tend to work this way. Indeed, many of the North American experiments of the 1960s and 1970s and those carried out during the last 15 years in countries of the Global North and Global South show an increase in social and institutional trust, in sociopolitical and community participation, and in social interaction (Laín, 2023), which means that having the material guarantee of a dignified existence – and the awareness and security that the rest of the members of the community also have it – makes it possible to establish and consolidate meaningful social ties in the fields of (re)production and social and community participation, leading to higher levels of social integration. For instance, the results of the Madhya Pradesh pilot report a positive effect of basic income on social relations in those municipalities where the whole community received the payment

(Borrell-Porta, de Quintana and Segura, 2023a). And this is the reason why the Catalan Pilot Project to Implement Universal Basic Income, whose launch is still subject to reaching agreements between parliamentary forces, considers, in addition to a randomised controlled trial throughout the country, a synthetic trial (or saturation trial at municipal level) that would imply the quasi-universal introduction of a sufficient basic income in two towns of approximately 1,250 inhabitants each. Of course, what it is about is testing the principle of universality in the making of dense, inclusive, participatory societies (Borrell-Porta, de Quintana and Segura, 2023b).

Here I make a brief digression and return to my discussion of the job guarantee from Part I, in order to ask: should a job guarantee be part of the measures that ought to accompany a basic income? As I've said in Parts I and II, the main objective is to establish the bases for the emergence of horizontal orders in which individuals, true 'free chooser subjects', can make 'free choices' and thus decide upon and autonomously proceed with their own life projects. In this situation, it's possible to think that some, and perhaps many, people might give shape to these *freer* decisions by resorting to the state in order to ask for public employment in sectors that they find especially interesting or socially necessary, and doing so in the hope that the state's role as employer would be much more dignified and dignifying than that played by many of today's employers. Indeed, *one* of the alternatives that should be within reach of workers who have been freed by a basic income, and the package of measures to go with it, is that of a possible job in the public sector. But this must be *one* of the alternatives. If we're really concerned about the liberation of the working population, we should aspire to something that includes job creation by the state as a possibility but that also transcends it as the sole nucleus of our emancipatory horizon. What I'm talking about is empowering people so that, over time, they can individually and/or collectively organise, proceed with and reproduce, with or without the state's participation, those 'republican systems of the association of free and equal producers' that Marx spoke of when considering socially liberating possibilities.

Fourth, and finally, however much we have a 'floor' to sustain us, we can give little of ourselves if the social and economic space into which we set out ends up being a swamp that is cordoned off and ruined by the rentier voracity of those who have managed to get vast accumulations of private economic power. A long time ago, John Locke warned that if the aim is to assure the effective freedom of society as a whole, the private appropriation of external resources, besides being non-depriving or not depossessing

– so that 'as much and as good' is left for others' – must also comply with another important normative condition, namely that resources must be kept in good condition and used in ways that don't ruin them or prevent their reproduction over time (Locke, 1982). The matter of the 'floor', then, can't be separated from the idea of a 'ceiling', which is to say a set of anti-accumulation restrictions that would make it possible to proceed to a 'euthanasia of the rentier', as Keynes proposed in the mid-1930s, and thus to the opening of real avenues where popular classes can access (re)productive life without having to overcome entry barriers and with a real capacity to act. The 'people's political economy', of which a basic income would be a part, can't fail to take from the republican tradition its prevention of and fight against the liberticidal strength of the 'economic monarchs'.[8]

The republican-democratic logic of the idea is quite simple. A free life in republican terms requires that there be no concentrations of private economic power capable of contesting the *res publica*'s duty to define and protect the common good (or that they are controlled such that they are not able to do this), which is nothing else than the guarantee to all citizens of the possibility of choosing their own life and deploying it without arbitrary interference. In this sense, the tolerance and the neutrality of the republican state does not consist, as occurs with the liberal state, in refraining from intervening in social life, but in the obligation to do so in order to undo those asymmetries of power whose existence the liberal tradition denies and which, so often – certainly constantly under capitalism – prevent us from forming and deploying life plans of our own. For this reason, the republican tradition, aware that wealth is a social product and has a social function, has considered since time immemorial, and continues to do so today (Bertomeu and Raventós, 2020), the possibility of introducing a *maximum*, that is, a cap on the flow of resources that private economic agents can hoard – or, to put it another way, a 'regulatory ceiling' that restricts the range of possibilities available to the most powerful social actors. It's worth realising that, by suggesting this, we are far from being in the middle of a daydream. As Simon Szreter (2022: 6) explains:

[I]n the late 1970s, the US had been at the end of nearly four decades of, in fact, having in place something close to a maximum income and wealth policy owing to the continuing high marginal tax rates established during World War II (originally at 90 per cent, still running at 70 per cent in the 1970s). [And] these alternatives, such as a maximum income, have [...] become once again sayable in the 2010s, following the spectacular collapse of the complacent neoliberal consensus in the wake of 2008, resulting in the intellectual landmark of Thomas Piketty's anti-orthodoxy economics book, *Capital in the Twenty-First Century*, becoming a best-seller.[9]

But let's systematise things a little bit. What kind of anti-accumulation restrictions are we talking about? Essentially, I refer here to what De Wispelaere and I have described elsewhere (2016) as 'Rousseaunian strategies' or 'Rooseveltian strategies'. The former consist of direct limitations on hoarded wealth (tax payments, regulation of income levels, and so on) while the latter refer to the introduction of regulatory frameworks that preclude the possibility of predatory practices by powerful agents.

First, republicanism tends to share the Rousseau-style diagnosis that income and wealth differentials should be kept within reasonable limits, perhaps proportional to the effort that has been expended. Excessive inequality leads to the fracturing of society because it stands in the way of trust, social solidarity and mutual recognition as the subjects of lives that are more or less comparable and recognisable for all.[10] But we live in a world that is increasingly fractured in this very sense. For example, Pizzigati (2009: 41) gives an idea: 'A generation ago, CEO pay averaged 40 times worker take-home. The gap in 2007: 344 times.' Accordingly, Taylor-Gooby (2013: 40) suggests Rousseau-style 'measures to curb incomes at the top end through reforms to remuneration systems and possibly maximum wage legislation'. Similarly, James Meade's model of the 'associative economy' proposed a comprehensive system, also of the Rousseau type, which included the following four mechanisms: company payments should be determined through profit and revenue-sharing arrangements; wealth should be taxed when passed on to subsequent generations; the community should own a significant share of the state's productive resources; and revenues raised by public-commons funds (e.g. by introducing taxes on the private exploitation of community resources) should be shared equitably among all citizens in the form of a social dividend (Meade, 1989; White, 2012). Finally, Piketty (2014) continues to echo this type of 'Rousseaunian strategy' when he proposes a global tax on wealth to avoid exorbitant inequalities.

Second, the 'Roosevelt strategies' point to measures that allow the presence of certain inequalities while also introducing a 'regulatory ceiling' with the aim of ensuring that these inequalities don't become a source of arbitrary interference in the lives of the working classes. In effect, large accumulations of private economic power tend to go hand in hand with the capacity of a few people to turn economic life into an oligarchic game through entry barriers, predatory price fixing, control of strategic resources, limiting the autonomy of workers in the workplace and other kinds of relations that underpin the significant forms of economic control that some people exercise over others (McCormick, 2011). I mention the figure of Roosevelt here because the United States has a long – and now almost lost – tradition of controlling and regulating the practices of the most powerful economic and social actors in order to prevent them from undermining the republican freedom of the popular classes. One example is the legislation that was introduced during the so-called Progressive Era (1890–1914) when an attempt was made to strengthen the foundations of American democracy by conferring economic power on the lower classes (Beard and Beard, 1939). Similarly, Franklin Delano Roosevelt, using the most explicit language, accused the American 'economic monarchs' of having caused the Great Depression with their prior imposition of a 'new industrial dictatorship' (Leuchtenburg, 1995: 125). One result was the famous antitrust legislation which led to the prosecution of such powerful bodies as General Electric and the Aluminium Company of America (Leuchtenburg, 2009).[11]

It makes no sense to decide ahistorically whether a Rousseau- or a Roosevelt-style strategy, or a combination of both, would be better. This will depend on the contingencies specific to each space and society at every point in time when singular and specific trajectories will be observed and windows of opportunity will be opened. The aim of these paragraphs, and of the chapter as a whole, is rather more modest and has another purpose, which is to recall that basic income is meaningless if it isn't part of a renewed 'moral economy of the crowd', with all the institutional arrangements that this requires so that today's working classes can also strive to 'make themselves' as groups of people who are trying to curb all forms of tyranny and to put into practice forms of live and (re)productive activities rooted in the sociopolitical power that people's movements can manage to attain. We need to avoid political short-sightedness and also 'fetishism of the proposal'. Basic income isn't a panacea that can fix everything at the stroke of a pen. But if it is situated at the centre of a well-designed political-institutional arena, which is to say within a 'people's political economy' that doesn't overlook spaces and flanks where tendencies of domination and despotism can get a foothold and seep in, basic income can contribute towards outlining open and determinedly post-capitalist scenarios and social relations.

15

Leaving the Proletariat and Becoming Free Workers

But hang on, some people might say. The house of cards will come tumbling down if people neglect the social product – the contribution of wealth. And then there is Mandeville, whose satire is based on a fear that isn't new. The bees in the hive ask the gods to endow them with virtue and restraint, but when their wish is granted it only leads to disaster. Virtue brings temperance and the hive is ruined. Nobody can be bothered any more to produce clear wax and sweet honey. Where there was once thriving honeycomb, there is now barren wasteland. Why? The structure of incentives linked with the 'private vices' of opulence and ostentation that drove the bees to produce has been demolished. And where there are no private vices, scarcity takes over.

The basic income proposal would be a slight variation on the same theme. Honey, the social product, is made for two reasons: first, Mandeville's 'vice' of self-enrichment and, second, awareness that only personal effort can afford us such well-being. Without personal effort we are ruined. By contrast, a (pre)distributive political strategy such as a basic income could, at first, mitigate the stresses and fears of a possible shortage of resources but, in the long term, it would make us sluggish and dull the motivations that lead us to act. If we're given honey, why should we develop the industrious spirit that must be cultivated by people who know that they alone are responsible for their own survival? Therefore, by (pre)distributing resources, a basic income would be weakening people's motivations to produce the social product. And without a social product, a basic income can't be financed. We'd therefore be lumbered with an openly unsustainable public policy mechanism which, through unable to reproduce itself, would be tragically self-cancelling.

But we need to remember once again that Mandeville's fable was a satire: a joke aimed at people who believe that reasons for acting don't go beyond self-interest and, moreover, a self-interest that is limited to pure instrumental rationality, a simple means–ends logic. Hence, the supposed basic income 'house of cards' isn't going to tumble down because it isn't a house of cards but a wide-ranging and well-defined structure of rights and resources that must encourage the array of motivations for acting, including self-interest, which are part of an undamaged human life.

All things considered, none of the issues raised in this book would make sense if it didn't include an overview of the human motivational apparatus that might point to this 'motivational pluralism', this account of reasons for action embracing the most diverse inclinations. Nothing in this book would make any sense if we were to assume, with Mises (2007: 591), that '[t]he fact that the tedium of labor is substituted for the joy of labor affects the valuation neither of the disutility of labor nor of the produce of labor. […] For people do not work for the sake of labor's joy, but for the sake of the mediate gratification.' If this were really the case, basic income would present a problem of incentives that would be very difficult to solve.

But this book is closer to the 'Adam Smith school' than the 'Mises school'. Recall Smith's *An Inquiry into the Nature and Causes of the Wealth of Nations* and his famous trio of the butcher, the brewer and the baker. None of them, Smith says, produces out of mere benevolence. In other words, none of the three would produce if they weren't in command of the fruits of their labour so they could use them to improve their own condition. Self-interest? Of course. It would be fanciful to think otherwise. But Smith immediately hastens to add that the three men's decision to produce is also explained by other factors of equal or greater importance: the desire to externalise capacities as a form of self-fulfilment in manufacturing and commerce; a search for peers and fellow people engaged in similar occupations with whom they can share information and interests, which then results in greater possibilities to express one's own identity (and, in a very Aristotelean way, Smith assumes that humans come to be something like what we could come to be when we walk hand in hand with other human beings who are in the same situation of defining themselves); and the tendency to observe those constellations of those social norms which, for good or for ill, help us to shape our own life circumstances (Casassas, 2010). According to Smith, then, there are many reasons for wanting to work (Smith, 1976, 1978, 1981).

Hence, when considering the question about the sense of working in a world where basic needs are covered, Smith urges us to recover the classical ethics of virtue, both Attic (Aristotelian) and Hellenistic (Stoic and Epicurean), in order to understand that having our basic needs covered is precisely what lets us know that we'd want to (and could) devote ourselves to a wide range of activities whose interest transcends but doesn't deny the simple requirement of satisfying our needs or merely the desire to get rich.

In other words, Smith helps us to comprehend the distinction that needs to be made between 'instrumental' and 'autotelic' activities. The former are those whose benefits are obtained *after* carrying them out. We engage in them *in order to* extract benefits that are external to them. For example, producing meat, bread or beer *in order to* obtain some income. In the latter case, the benefits, remunerations and objectives – the *telos* – of autotelic activities are *intrinsic* to them, *within* them; they are to be found *in* the pure act of carrying them out. These are often activities requiring long learning processes that might need certain doses of discipline and self-control (Domènech, 1989) but that also offer much longer periods of pleasure and joy (Dejours, Deranty, Renault and Smith, 2018; Elster, 1986). For example, learning to produce and distribute meat, bread or beer – or software, music, clothes, sustainable buildings or spaces for caregiving and mutual aid – are frequently things we do for the pure pleasure of getting better and better at an activity that makes sense to us, and in which we are more able to recognise ourselves and to feel fulfilled.[1] Hence, in a world with a basic income, the ability to detect and cultivate autotelic activities, or the autotelic components of many of the activities we carry out on a daily basis, would be the engine not only for maintaining the social product but also for enriching it through much more respectful (im)material practices and objects that could even be a catalyst for creating the kinds of worlds in which we might all long to live (Van der Veen and Van Parijs, 1986).

We have arrived at one of the questions of greatest interest in the critical analysis of the basic income proposal. I refer to the disincentive it would supposedly mean with regard to work. This is a criticism or questioning which – almost certainly 'forgetful' of the fact that *work* doesn't necessarily mean *employment* or, more generally, *remunerated work* – has been raised from certain milieus of both 'right' and 'left'.[2]

This 'left-wing' standpoint always emphasises the centrality of work (but such a left usually refers to *employment* in *stricto sensu*) for our socialisation and the development of our identities. In fact, personal identity deploys in settings of social interaction, and work relations are an excellent way of mixing with others. For all these reasons, it is held, 'work dignifies'. It's therefore unacceptable to support an unconditional measure which, like basic income, gives away resources 'for nothing', without anybody having to *work* – be *employed* – to achieve anything.

But I want to go back to something I mentioned in Part III, which is that basic income in no way questions the centrality of work. On the contrary, it's a measure that, by covering the basic needs of life, favours the emergence of work that is really desired and which, under present conditions, is barred to us by the need to grasp at any job, usually temporary and precarious, the labour markets have to 'offer', that is, if there is something on offer, for the reality of unemployment, technological or otherwise, is a serious constraint on this process. Work dignifies? Obviously, a worker will be dignified by work that dignifies. If not, there is no dignity for the worker. To sum up, while capitalism's structuring mechanisms dispossess us and, as a result, compel us to abandon our projects and literally accept anything, a basic income can act as a true lever to activate human activity, whether remunerated or not, that is now blocked by the need to accept this 'anything'. It would be a tool for mobilising work that (we believe) really dignifies, work we really want to do.

And, as we've also seen, this is important not only as a matter of justice and equity, but also efficiency and even (re)generation of economic activity. The need to waste no time and to accept on the fly 'whatever they offer us' disables time and opportunities for creativity and the exploration of new paths and productive relations. In a nutshell, it destroys the productive fabric. Yet an income floor brings us to a space from which we might be able to set out, individually or in common, on all sorts of productive and reproductive projects of our own, with the flow of skills, talents and collective benefits they can contribute.

Now we get to the part about how certain 'rightists' approach the matter of purported disincentives to work generated by basic income. In their language, the problem here is what they call 'parasitism'. The argument, which is well known because it's so hackneyed, and also trotted out to discredit much more modest measures such as unemployment benefits, goes like this: since work is always a hassle or a source of *disutility* (the oft-used anthropological assumption, as we've seen with Mises) wouldn't we be encouraging scroungers with a basic income?

On the strictly theoretical level, but by no means irrelevantly because of that, it could be argued that basic income would actually solve the problem of lack of reciprocity in terms of the (right to) parasitism that pervades our societies, which accommodate a minority, but nonetheless numerous, group of people who *already* enjoy the right to live without working. I refer to the rich and their unearned income[3] that allows them to live without doing anything. In this sense, a basic income could make it possible to universalise a right that already exists – but distorted into privilege – for a small percentage of the population: the right to parasitism. Anyone who cherishes even the most rudimentary egalitarian feelings can't wriggle out of this argument.

On the purely empirical level, we find innumerable situations that make us think that, even with a basic income, this whole plurality of motivations for working, paid or unpaid, which thinkers such as Adam Smith have urged us to consider, would remain unchanged: wage workers who work overtime in order to consume more than their salaries allow; retired people with sufficient pensions who keep working, for example in the domestic or voluntary sphere; rich people who could live without working and yet continue to do so; participants in basic income pilot projects and scientific experiments carried out in such different countries as Germany, Belgium, Brazil, Canada, the United States, Finland, Holland, India, Kenya, Namibia, Sri Lanka and Uganda (Davala, Jhabvala, Mehta and Standing, 2015; Standing, 2017).[4] All of these examples show that the reasons for working, whether for pay or not, go way beyond the desire to obtain an income that is strictly necessary to cover the basic needs of life. Many of these experiments or pilot projects, besides providing resources that offer better access to food, health cover and education with surprising results in terms of, for example, improved mental health, have demonstrated that an unconditional flow of income promotes community-based economic development that can put an end to the exodus from rural areas to the big cities in search of wage-earning work, while it also fosters forms of cooperative and entrepreneurial activities that, as in the case of India, mean greater economic empowerment of women (Standing, 2017).

All of this, and all the preceding examples, suggest that what really concerns 'rightists' who warn of the danger of parasitism and thus oppose the right to a basic income (or, in other words, the right to an unconditional guarantee of material existence for everyone) isn't that we'd stop working but that we'd stop working 'for them'. Without a doubt, the emergence of other types and forms of work and production[5] would allow us to leave the fold that's currently constituted by the presently available spaces and procedures controlled by those who have commandeered and keep commandeering the means we need to organise (re)production. So, for them, this could seem dangerous.

In any case, the role of basic income (and, I stress, the package of measures that must come with it) is that of providing a broad economic environment that would incentivise the whole population to 'enter' less precarious, less hostile (re)productive spaces so that everyone can thenceforth develop whatever he or she can and wants to give of himself or herself. For the main disincentive to employment is employment itself, at least employment as we know it in the capitalist world. How much desire and what degree of motivation can we harbour and maintain in carrying out an activity that not only damages us physically and emotionally but also impoverishes us and puts us in a position of subordination to outside influences? There is no need, then, to take part in Bob Black's anti-institutional rant to be able to understand the deep (common) sense, first, of his protest against employment as condemnation to obligatory production, as 'part-time slavery' (since he, too, resorts to the Aristotelian formulation) and, second, of his joining William Morris, Paul Lafargue and Marshall Sahlins in calling for 'productive play' that would make it possible to redirect the time hitherto given to wage labour into basically non-instrumental activities with significant autotelic components (Black, 2013).[6] The unconditional nature of basic income can offer the possibility to 'exit' from an unfair fate and to revisit and revive landscapes we were forced to leave behind too soon.

However, some people ask if a life that makes moral sense is possible if there is no promise from the person who's living it that he or she will somehow contribute to the social product or satisfaction of the community's needs. This question lies behind Anthony Atkinson's (1996) proposal of a 'participation income' and Stuart White's (2003) idea of a 'civic minimum' income. There can be no civic virtue, but the opposite, open exploitation of the diligent by the lazy would be the case – White said some 20 years ago, although his position has changed over time, bringing him closer to the logic of a basic income – unless individuals make a commitment to offering, in exchange for the income flow, some kind of repayment in the form of work in the interests and for the use of the public. Only thus could access to an income become something that is truly 'civic' or 'virtuous'.[7]

It's evident that this approach presents major problems in both normative terms and vis-à-vis institutional design. To begin with, the moral argument offered by Atkinson, White and others is self-cancelling because their proposal leads individuals to contribute *instrumentally* in order to obtain a supposedly *civic* income. Just as it's impossible to force someone to act spontaneously or to oblige someone to have the genuine idea of giving a gift – a wedding gift, for example – because the idea of a gift is only genuine when it springs from oneself, neither can citizens be *forced* to cooperate with others as a *condition* for obtaining the benefits and amenities supposedly accruing to *virtuous* people. Virtue isn't extracted with a corkscrew. Or, better said, if it is, it's not civic virtue but instrumental and even opportunistic behaviour to achieve a goal that is external to us. And, in the domain of income policy, let's not succumb, either, to the blackmail exerted on us by wage labour. Let's not allow others, however good their political intentions might be, to oblige, yet again, dispossessed people to do what they order, knowing that the latter must conform as a matter of survival.

So much for the weaknesses of the Atkinson and White line of argument in the moral terrain. Now I turn to those we find in the institutional domain. Since Aristotle's times, it's been suggested that any genuine contribution people can make to the community is the by-product of a life lived in the tranquillity of knowing that one's material existence is guaranteed. In other words, we can't decide *ex ante* on a blackboard or in a government gazette what genuine and socially valuable participation individuals can really offer when not under duress. This is something that, over time, only they can come to know. However, both the 'participation income' and the 'civic minimum' assume that certain bureaucratic instances *know* and can establish what kind of socially valuable and/or morally virtuous activities we can carry out. This isn't the case, or if it is, it's very partially so. We need to let time speak and, above all, we need to let people show what they can do because they are the ones who know or can come to know this. If not, we run the risk of producing huge doses of paternalism – and resulting invasiveness – or coming up against a tremendous problem of incomplete information, or both things at the same time. What is socially valuable is discovered over time and emerges spontaneously as a by-product of the autonomous conduct of people who have been freed, perhaps by means of a basic income, from the need to go begging to those who force them to 'live only with their permission'. If only.

To sum up, where Atkinson, White and company see problems of (lack of) reciprocity or exploitation, we see a simple equitable distribution of collectively inherited wealth. As Mazzucato (2017, 2018), Varoufakis (2016) and Vercellone and Harribey (2015) have reminded us, today's wealth has been collectively produced and handed down over time and space. Hence, as James Meade (1964, 1989) did, Varoufakis says that each and every one of the inhabitants of the world should have a share of this wealth in the form of an unconditional basic income or 'social dividend'. And, if some people want to use their portion of this collective wealth to lead a frugal or not very industrious life, it is their right to do so. First, whether this frugal and not very industrious life becomes an openly 'unproductive' or 'parasitic' existence remains to be seen. How much time and how many attempts would be needed before a person recognises what he or she really wants and is capable of doing, and then to find the best ways of offering it to the community? We shouldn't jump the gun. We should let things mature, however long it takes. And, second, it's our right to lead a life that's not very industrious for the simple reason that this option of letting things mature, however long it may take, is a possibility that's open to very few. So, why not universalise the privilege and turn it into a right that everyone can enjoy?

Finally, in the unlikely event that the worst-case scenarios should come true and the introduction of a basic income led to a world without enough social product to fund public policies, starting with the basic income itself (and I say this is improbable because of the available evidence of the human propensity to work in meaningful activities), we'd certainly have to come up with institutional designs for an equitable and democratically organised distribution of work deemed socially necessary by the community.

Let's look at this issue in some detail. To start with, we have already seen that the reasons that motivate us to work and produce go beyond the desire to obtain an income that is equivalent, more or less, to the poverty line: the questions of self-realisation, of obtaining a certain 'meaning' or that of social recognition, play a role that cannot be neglected (Gheaus and Herzog, 2016). Likewise, achieving a purchasing power that exceeds what a basic income allows, which should not be equivalent to launching into unbridled consumerism, is something that is highly predictable among very broad sectors of the population. But what if, even so, certain tasks remain undone due to the widespread refusal, by the working population, to take care of them? In this case, three scenarios open up that, although they contain certain complexities, are far from constituting worrisome dystopias – rather the opposite: it is possible that we find in them some of the deepest reasons to claim unconditional resources such as a basic income.

First, the general refusal to carry out unpleasant tasks could go hand in hand with upward pressure on wages and, more broadly, an improvement in working conditions: better uses of time, forms of organising production that are more respectful of the physical and mental health of workers, etc. When one's material existence is guaranteed, one sets conditions to the carrying out of certain types of task. What if, in this sense, basic income was one of the ways to achieve much more reasonable shares between wages and benefits, among many other issues related to productive activity *within* the labour markets?

Second, if these improvements in working conditions fail to incentivise people to get down to the task, unpleasant or otherwise, of producing certain goods and services that are needed by the community – and thus generating the 'social product' that is required to fund basic income itself – 'employers' (which includes the possible members of cooperative companies) could find reasons to promote even more vigorously the processes of robotisation that, as we have already explored, we are nowadays witnessing. We cannot fall into the naiveté of the most apolitical and contentless techno-optimism, but neither can we deny that the automation of monotonous, repetitive tasks that are harmful to the physical and mental integrity of workers is something that should be welcomed. I don't think being able to get out of the hellish assembly line in time and rethinking his relationship with the productive world, which would had been possible thanks to a basic income that would have guaranteed his existence, would have been bad news for the Charles Chaplin of *Modern Times*.[8]

But let's get to the heart of the matter. It seems reasonable to think that the improvement of working conditions and/or the replacement of human labour by robots could solve a large part of the possible disincentives to carry out certain unpleasant yet necessary tasks to sustain life in society. But what if, even so – and we explore now the third scenario – necessary tasks still remain undone, perhaps because they cannot be automated, perhaps because, for whatever reason, certain communities understand that, with guaranteed material existence, under no circumstances is it desirable or recommendable to carry them out? What solution could be found under these circumstances? This study does not propose univocal and universally valid magic formulas, but this study considers it necessary to put on the table that, in these cases, some kind of mechanism (or set of mechanisms) would have to be introduced to articulate democratically managed processes of work sharing and distributing.

In no case can the technical difficulties that something like this would entail be denied – although advances in the field of computing could facilitate their resolution – but it should be noted that these kinds of 'coordination problems' are much more desirable than the 'problems of exploitation and oppression' that we find within the (capitalist) world we inhabit, and it must be outlined that these 'problems of exploitation and oppression' go hand in hand with massive and costly 'coordination problems' in terms of social control and socio-labour disciplining (Jayadev and Bowles, 2006; Wacquant, 2009a, 2009b). Indeed, under capitalism there is *already* a huge problem of disincentives in relation to tasks that are unpleasant or simply necessary for the community: a huge number of people have very little desire to do them. However, capitalism finds a 'solution' for this problem whose effectiveness cannot be denied. It is, in fact, a 'solution' that constitutes the very backbone of its functioning as a social formation, namely: material dispossession of the great social majorities. In effect, dispossession 'allows' them to strive – and even fight among themselves – to take care of those tasks that nobody wants to do. Thus, through the social (and the sexual, racial, etc.) division of labour, capitalism guarantees that it is the poor who carry out the tasks 'that belong to the poor' or 'to the *chavs*' – and women, those 'belonging to women', and racialised population, those 'of blacks', 'of Andean Indians', and so on.

For all these reasons, it is deeply desirable in normative terms that everyone, not just the usual 'few', who do it daily, but also the poor, the women and the racialised population, have the capacity to refuse to perform those tasks that, in the context of their collectivities, it is understood that, with material existence guaranteed, under no circumstances is it desirable or advisable to carry out. This would force everyone – yes, *everyone*, including the usual 'few' – to sit down and talk. Yes, to *talk* and to find decent, practicable and shared solutions. The democratisation of social and economic life – in other words the transition towards social formations of a post-capitalist nature – is a project that cannot rest only on words, good reasons and tidy intentions: sometimes it has to be imposed, and the fact that all of us, without exclusions, count on unconditional resources guaranteeing our existences can open up wide avenues for such a project to come to fruition, no matter who likes it or not.

As Gourevitch (2022: 9) rightly recalls, 'socialists have imagined a free society as one of shared labor. Some labor is necessary, but that does not make it a mere burden. We can distribute it so that it becomes an expression of our human capacity or free cooperation.' And the point is that it is convenient to see basic income as a tool that has to help us to do so, since (1) it allows us to reject the work that we do not want at all – that is not desirable; (2) it allows us to negotiate and tend to obtain forms of work and life that we crave to a greater extent; and (3) in the (unlikely) event that the abandonment of socially necessary tasks becomes widespread, it allows us to push *the society as a whole*, without oligarchic and classist – and racist and sexist – self-exclusions, to seek democratic ways to share responsibilities regarding this socially necessary work.

In effect, faced with a possible (yet unlikely) generalised rejection of socially necessary work as a result of the universal guarantee of the right to existence, human beings can seriously consider, perhaps for the first time, the question of the 'collective responsibility for the organization of [necessary] labor [or, more generally, "work"] through democratic control over the economy. This way of sharing labor [or, more generally, "work"] would free everyone from being forced to work, free anyone from being condemned to hard labor their whole lives, and allow necessary labor [or, more generally, "work"] to become something each could do freely, in the sense of a freely accepted duty rather than mere necessity or external imposition' (Goure-vitch, 2022: 9). As has already been said, in these scenarios it will obviously be necessary to have a democratic, 'centralized way of deciding what counts as necessary labor' and what counts as social product (Gourevitch, 2022: 25). And what is expected of these democratic ways and mechanisms is that 'even necessary labor, when organized properly, can be something done freely' (Gourevitch, 2022: 48). Be that as it may, it is convenient to go back to the start: for this to become a reality, it is convenient that we find ourselves *ex ante*, unconditionally equipped with resources guaranteeing our existence, so that we are all able to reject those forms of work and life that are imposed on us today and, in the event that something – or much – remains undone (which, I insist, is unlikely, but it is a possibility that we should not rule out) it is convenient that we find ourselves *ex ante*, unconditionally equipped with resources to be able to push in the direction of a democratic distribu-tion of socially necessary work.[9]

We are not discussing here any academic quip that is disconnected from crucial societal debates and those massive social movements that fuel such debates. Let's think about the bulk of feminisms. All feminist trends, which so often diverge from each other for many complex and multifaceted reasons, agree when it comes to establishing that care work, despite not being paid for – such is the case on most occasions – cannot be made invisible, because, under certain circumstances, it can become intrinsically valuable and, also, because it constitutes the necessary condition for the existence of any other kind of work, paid or unpaid. For this reason, feminisms affirm, it is con-venient for all of us, women and men, to look for mechanisms to share responsibility with respect to a type of work that is so absolutely necessary for the maintenance of life in common. Isn't this a way that is present in our daily life to concretise the question of the collective duty to think and walk the paths so that nothing that is really necessary is left undone? And is it not reasonable to think that unconditional resources such as basic income can help this reflection on (and this opening of) ways to carry out socially neces-sary tasks to take place effectively, if necessary, with all the doses of conflict that this may entail?

Some analysts might raise a concern that is related to all that is being sug-gested here, but from the point of view of the fiscal stability of basic income: what if people start to perform socially useful but unpaid (and therefore untaxed) labour? As I said, this question puts us back at the centre of the analysis that is being carried out in these pages. In effect, if this socially useful yet unpaid (and therefore untaxed) labour is not enough to cover our needs (and, furthermore, tax revenue shrinks and collapses to the point that a basic income cannot be financed), we will have to resort to taxes on great accumulations of wealth and capital gains, especially those originating from the financial sector. Looked at properly, resorting to tax figures that tax great accumulations of private economic power, especially those originating from the processes of financialisation of the economy, is highly desirable in terms of social – and fiscal – justice, even if people do *not* start to perform unpaid (and therefore untaxed) labour. But let's push the line of reasoning a little bit further: what if the widespread rejection of capitalist exploitation – let's assume that unconditional measures such as basic income might induce this – caused these concentrations of private economic power to dilute to the point of ceasing to exist, at least under the form they have today? And what if, at the same time, people placed themselves in an effective and prolonged way in the world of socially useful yet unpaid (and therefore untaxed) labour? In such scenarios, it would be necessary to return to the assertion of the need to articulate democratic processes of the public-common assignment of those tasks and responsibilities that are necessary for the maintenance of life in society, with the advantage that broad layers of the population would *already* be carrying out socially useful activities *on a voluntary basis* and that a deep political culture would have been forged aimed at rejecting freedom- and democracy-limiting work and social relations and at promoting ways of sharing socially necessary work that would allow it to be seen, as was said a moment ago, as 'a freely accepted duty' rather than the result of 'mere necessity or external imposition'.

But it is convenient not to permanently situate our thinking in frontier positions: the most probable thing that will happen as a consequence of the introduction of unconditional measures such as basic income is that people will try to continue working (but not at any price!) to sustain certain levels of consumption and to relax the financial stress that today drowns them (but not at any price either!); that people will fight for an improvement in working conditions, inside and outside the labour markets; and that people will push automation processes that make certain forms of work history. All of this could happen within the framework of inclusive and diverse economies that are compatible with worthy human life on our planet. In fact, these economies can become widespread thanks to the universal guarantee of unconditional resources allowing us to reset our lives and open paths that are truly of our own.

But let's resume the discussion about the political role of basic income under today's circumstances by going back to the start. The dream is over.

As I said in Chapter 12, the dream is over, first of all, in the sense of the expectations raised by the post-war social pact, in the sense of lives which, constructed with materials that were too rigid, that admitted no gestures of autonomy while guaranteeing a certain set of securities, have been irredeemably damaged, if not shattered. But the dream has also ended in the sense that it terminated the lethargy induced by a pact that protected but also sought to stifle the rebellious spirit of generations upon generations of working men and women who struggled for genuine democratisation of productive and (in today's terms) reproductive relations. And the hostile social circumstances characterising the neoliberal turn of capitalism are today working towards reviving – paradoxically, if you like – these same defiant longings: 'You took too much from us and now we want everything back again', as the graffiti Marco Revelli made popular said. Do we dare to try for this 'everything'?

Epilogue: Unconditional Freedom at the Frontiers of Capitalism

Do we dare to try for this 'everything'? Would we be able to live outside the zoo? Born in captivity, non-human animals can't be freed into nature because they haven't developed the skills to survive and live in it. Would we be able to slow down, calmly look around us without getting too dizzy, and make for ourselves a culture and set of practices that aim to reappropriate the right to decide our own lives?

The world of wage labour is a sort of Ferris wheel going round and round and never stopping, so it's hard to get off without breaking your neck. It's also difficult to climb on board. The passenger cars are full and speed past us. It's a big wheel that both swallows you up and expels you. To make matters worse, those who go round and round in the crowded capsules tend to feel proud to have a foothold in the whirling beast. At the amusement park you feel happy and can even enjoy yourself, but that's just a matter of time. After days, weeks, months and years, staying trapped in the grounds can turn into a nightmarish horror story. Yet we have the odd habit of applauding the supposed achievement of getting locked into the horror show grounds of wage labour. This is the kind of 'false consciousness' it can come to feed.

Basic income isn't about destroying amusement parks and Ferris wheels but about pulling down the gates of the enclosure and letting us pull the lever to stop the infernal spinning. Leaving the proletariat means this: being equipped with resources so that we can leave behind capitalist dispossession and, after that, decide when to stop and when to set rolling the gears of the different kinds of paid and unpaid work we might want to do in our lives. Hence, leaving the proletariat in no way means ceasing to work or denying that we are working people. On the contrary, leaving the proletariat, being able to deproletarianise ourselves, means opening the doors to forming new groups of free workers who, as such, can choose the kinds and processes of work that they feel are truly theirs. In capitalism, the great disincentive to work is employment itself and the conditions under which it happens. Freeing ourselves from the need to accept the jobs that are offered today, if they are offered at all, basic income allows us to recover and reformulate incentives to work by empowering us to do so in the spaces and ways we believe are consistent with who we are or who we're trying to become. The worlds of work (of many kinds of work) and the worlds of affection (of many kinds of affection) are the spaces in which our lives acquire meaning. We mustn't let them take away our desire to inhabit them.

Here, pride is essential. But we mustn't project it wrongly. We can't show compliance and even enthusiasm about belonging to classes of people who've been proletarianised by the juggernaut of capitalist dispossession. African Americans who rose up, and still rise up, to demand their civil rights, and women who organise to break their shackles, acquire, in each case, a 'pride of belonging' but not one that's understood as a mere chant of shared vulnerability that is seen as insurmountable (which would stifle any attempt to make these voices heard). This pride of belonging is explained because there is a dynamic perspective not, of course, in ceasing to be African American or women, but in no longer belonging to a subaltern population that is diminished because of ethnic group or gender. Where there is domination, no group pride is possible without a horizon of expectations that holds out the possibility of self-dissolution as people who are crushed by despotism and constant subordination. The same thing happens with the proletarian population, subjugated thus because dispossession has left no alternative. It would border on pathos if we felt proud of being sheep locked in the fold, animals caged in so many zoos, giddy passengers in the cars of Ferris wheels or, in other words, part-time slaves. The pride of class belonging takes on all the sense in the world when it comes with the open defiance of those who want to leave the sheepfolds, the zoos and the passenger cars of the big wheel, that is, of those who want to 'undo' themselves as a proletarian class, in order to occupy spaces of work that are rooted in the nerves and muscles of people's power, the power to 'make themselves' as the class – or, better said, as the 'group' – of effectively free workers.

We can't live with the 'frenzy of the desperate' that Adam Smith spoke of. And Mises' assertion that workers and capitalists need each other with the same degree of urgency, with no asymmetries of power, with nobody obliging anyone to do anything, isn't true. Yet it is true that lives damaged by proletarianisation, as the traditions of Gramsci and Pasolini saw all too clearly, are marked by the loss of control of all kinds of knowledge, starting with what we do every day in the workplace. Producing or trying to produce with the 'frenzy of the desperate', clinging to the edge of the passenger car of the big wheel, we become unable to remember the difference between a pea and a cabbage, a rooster and a lizard, winter and summer, hammering a nail and making a groove, turned on and turned off, heavy wind and smoke from motors, programming and being programmed, and standing tall and shrinking away. And losing control of what's known, letting it drop into oblivion, is the same as letting a whole life slip away.

This is why it's essential and urgent that we should take the red pill of *The Matrix*, get a good idea of where we are and become aware of the quagmire we're in, of all the possibilities and chances of life that are being taken from us. And we need to arm ourselves with whatever forms and mechanisms of rebellion and solidarity we can find so that we can all create and care for worlds we can coexist within lastingly. The caps become important once again. Basic income, like other unconditional measures, aren't designed to make us go *cap in hand* but to give us 'caps' *with* which we can create an interdependence that is compatible with freedom. It depends how you see the cap. For example, the bargaining power stemming from the unconditional nature of basic income equips us to create and care for worlds that have a place for markets and property, but they'd be worlds in which we could all keep the ability to decide when and how we want markets to emerge and develop, if we want them to some extent, and what specific forms of property we reserve for our social relations. The possibility of doing jobs we choose to do and of organising mechanisms to be jointly responsible for them crucially depends on whether things can be thus.

Basic income doesn't inevitably lead to social scenarios of a post-capitalist nature. But it is capable of deactivating one of the main disciplinary mechanisms of capitalist societies, including those that incorporate welfare mechanisms: the obligatory, forced nature of wage labour. And herein lie the potentials of the proposal in terms of combatting the dispossessing and commodifying dynamics of capitalism. In effect, the compulsory nature of wage labour has blocked and keeps blocking myriad autonomously made (re)productive settings that can only appear when work and income are uncoupled, and unconditionally conferred resources open the way to all kinds of projects and forms of life. More than a few social movements can see this and urge us to grab our times by the lapels and shake them up to make visible what was hidden or hopelessly blurred over: that now, with the acute malaise brought on by the neoliberal turn of capitalism, with an old Fordist pact unilaterally broken by the elites, and with indignation rooted in a profound sense of betrayal fuelling social and political ambitions that are unparalleled in the last seven decades, a proposal such as a basic income can help us to break with the discipline of capitalist markets and create forms of work and life that are unquestionably freer.

Some people have suggested that, if we had the correlation of forces that is needed to attain a world where there was room for a basic income, it might cease to be necessary because, in this case, we could aspire to 'something' that would take us even 'further'. The political viability of the basic income would therefore make it a directly unnecessary mechanism. But hang on, what is this 'something'? And, still more important, what 'further' are we talking about? Throughout these pages, I've avoided presenting some kind of emancipatory 'end of story'. However successfully high levels of economic democracy might be attained, and however well we find ways of politically materialising forms of common government of the means of production – and reproduction – we'll still, first, be inhabiting conflictive environments, characterised by the presence of scarce resources and conflicting interests, since healthy human societies are essentially diverse; and, second, we'll keep being able to and needing to use social institutions such as markets and very diverse configurations of property rights, institutions without which life in complex societies would be unsustainable. And this requires that we all keep being equipped with the bargaining power we need so that in every socio-institutional context, in every corner of social life, we'd be able to decide what form, if any, we want to give these institutions so that we'd be able to shape, individually or collectively, lives 'of our own'.

Basic income then appears as a necessary measure both *within* capitalist social formations, because it helps us to combat its intrinsically depossessing dynamics and thus to make our lives more liveable, and, precisely because of that, also *outside* the frontiers of the world we're used to inhabiting, as it allows us to keep shaping the possible work and life spaces of a truly democratic essence, that is, of a post-capitalist nature. In this regard, always within the broad 'popular political economy' in which it must be inserted, basic income can be seen not as the 'capitalist road to communism' that Van der Veen and Van Parijs described almost 40 years ago, but as a Polanyian and therefore openly democratising and anti-capitalist path to a world in which we could, in effect, receive according to our needs and, thanks to that, finally give according to our real abilities.

Capitalism isn't natural and inevitable. It can crumble, especially if we can give it a push. Indeed, as Marx pointed out a century and a half ago, and as Silvia Federici recalls today, its appearance back in the sixteenth century was due to the hysterical reaction of some European oligarchies which organised a true counter-revolution to put a stop to what they saw as unacceptable advances being made by the masses in terms of 'social power'. Basic income aspires to walk that path once more, rethinking and reinstituting such forms of social power. To borrow Walter Benjamin's idea, the democratic-revolutionary potential of basic income lies in the possibility of bringing the locomotive of history to a halt and thinking about another kind of modernity – a non-capitalist one in which everyone without exclusions can enjoy a freedom in which no one is subjected to blackmail and conditions.

Because freedom has conditions. In fact, most of this book has been devoted to exploring the ways in which a basic income could guarantee some of the material (and perhaps symbolic) conditions of freedom. But access to this 'freedom with conditions' can't, in democratic and democratising contexts, be subject to any kind of condition: in this regard, it should be *unconditional freedom*. As Thomas Paine, the first to include a basic income proposal in contemporary democratic-revolutionary republicanism, might have said, it's simply a matter of common sense.

Notes

INTRODUCTION

1. See Ben Stein, 2006, 'In Warfare, Guess Which Class Is Winning', *The New York Times*, 26 November. www.nytimes.com/2006/11/26/business/yourmoney/26every.html.
2. Spanish Minister Alberto Ruiz-Gallardón on the radio station Cadena COPE when he was asked about protests in legal circles and by citizens about the so-called 'law on fee policy', of 12 December 2012.
3. As we shall see in Part I, a conscious approximation to the idea of 'liberalism', in both historical and political terms, helps us to understand this tradition as one which – unlike republicanism and the various forms of socialism that are its heirs – tends to obscure the link between freedom and access to resources that guarantee a decent existence. In other words, it disregards the material and also symbolic conditions of freedom and citizenship. In these pages, then, 'liberalism' isn't a synonym of 'progressivism', as it tends to be in the United States. Neither do I associate 'liberalism' with the type of 'secular progressivism' that inspired the 'egalitarian liberalism' stemming from the appearance of the work of John Rawls, which could be seen as an academic oddity of the late Cold War years whose political translation is closer to republicanism (and even some forms of socialism) than to liberalism, understood in the historical sense.
4. See, for instance, Leipold, Nabulsi and White (2020).
5. It is not by any chance that Bruno Leipold (2020) speaks of 'Marx's Social Republic', that is, of a 'radical republicanism' leading to 'the political institutions of socialism', as the title of his chapter in the edited volume on 'radical republicanism' reads. See also Gourevitch (2014).
6. Cited by Domènech (2004: 125), emphasis added.

PART I

1. *Rerum novarum*, 1. www.vatican.va/content/leo-xiii/en/encyclicals/documents/hf_l-xiii_enc_15051891_rerum-novarum.html.
2. Ibid., 19.
3. Needless to say, the repertoire of ideas and normative projects that the modern world has known is much more diverse than that presented here, giving rise to political-practical projects that are vastly more complex and heterogeneous than this triangle seems to suggest. Nevertheless, it would be helpful to have a good understanding of the three vertices because they isolate sets of ideas that, working together, have been able to promote recurring political horizons.

4.   Later I explain why it makes conceptual and historical sense to associate the 'liberal' tradition with this overlooking of the material and symbolic conditions of freedom, where freedom is understood as a given and apparently assumed to be endowed by the (supposedly) spontaneous nature of social reality. Needless to say, authors who are often and perhaps too hastily associated with 'liberalism' – including John Stuart Mill and John Rawls, and long before them John Locke, Adam Smith and Immanuel Kant, among many others – have little in common with this *classically* liberal conceptual and political framework.

CHAPTER 1

1.   *Rerum novarum*, 3.
2.   Ibid. This had also been established in the Holy Scriptures. 'Neither shalt thou desire thy neighbour's wife, neither shalt thou covet thy neighbour's house, his field, or his manservant, or his maidservant, his ox, or his ass, or any thing that is thy neighbour's' (Deuteronomy 5:21, King James Version).
3.   For a reconstruction of Locke's treatment of the question of property, which shows clear isomorphisms with what other authors of republican inspiration have also said, see Mundó (2015, 2017).
4.   *Rerum novarum*, 8.
5.   Ibid., 38.
6.   Romans 13:1 (King James Version).
7.   *Rerum novarum*, 19 and 24.
8.   Scheler, cited by Domènech (2004: 268–9).
9.   *Rerum novarum*, 58. I won't yet enter into a systematic analysis of the conceptual distinction, which is so crucial for both scholarly and ethical-political points of view, between *work* and *employment*. In Part I, the word 'work' refers to remunerated work, usually wage labour. This will do for the time being.
10. In part VIII, chapter 26, volume 1 of *Capital* (1976 [1867–94]) on 'so-called primitive accumulation', Marx warned that the long process of capitalist dispossession was especially repressive and 'bloody' because there was a message that had to be loud and clear: the pauperised majority were to be put to work without complaint in the nascent capitalist enterprises. Hence, the legislation against beggars and vagabonds in modern England, which Marx describes in detail. Begging was seen as a way of eluding a destiny that was the inexorable lot of the emerging proletarian class as a whole.
11. That the old dictum of Leo XIII is still fully valid today is evident in the words pronounced by pope Francis on 5 November 2016 in his closing address summing up the Third World Meeting of Popular Movements, held at the Legion of Christ Seminary in Rome. Attending the meeting were 'some two hundred activists from among the poorest people on earth' (rag-pickers, rubbish recyclers, street vendors, landless peasants, indigenous people, unemployed, shanty dwellers, residents of squatter settlements, and so on). In his speech, the Pope declared that he was genuinely upset to learn of the levels of barbarism reached by the tyranny of money, and exhorted the 'organisations of the excluded' not to 'fall into the temptation of the straitjacket, which reduces you

to being extras off-stage, or worse, to mere administrators of existing misery'. www.vatican.va/content/francesco/en/speeches/2016/november/documents/ papa-francesco_20161105_movimenti-popolari.html. But how can this misery be avoided, if it is to be avoided at all? Pope Francis' answer couldn't be more faithful to the dictum of Leo XIII: 'dignified employment for those excluded from the labour market; land for *campesinos* and the native peoples; housing for homeless families'. Land, work and housing. The poor will be poor but they are *our* poor and therefore can't be separated from the main structuring mechanism of the great stratified pyramid. What is needed is (decent) work for others, and the appropriate forms of succour to the obedient people accommodated in each niche of the pyramid. The description of the meeting has been taken from Ramonet (2016: 1, 12).

CHAPTER 2

1. Antoni Domènech (2004) has revealingly documented the fact that the terms 'liberalism' and 'liberal', in their political acceptance, which goes beyond the classical psychological-moral sense related with 'generosity', is a neologism that did not appear until the Cortes de Cádiz (Spanish parliament of Cadiz) of 1812, after which it came into popular use, especially in France.

2. It's also worth emphasising that thinkers who – *in the nineteenth and twentieth centuries but not before* – were turned into the 'founding fathers' of the liberal tradition, for example John Locke, Adam Smith, and Immanuel Kant, have little in common with the liberal conceptual framework that appeared at the beginning of the nineteenth century with the expansion of the juridical-political logic of the Napoleonic civil codes. None of them does; indeed, hardly anybody else does before the nineteenth century. I repeat, 'liberal common sense' took shape in the first two decades of the *nineteenth* century. Situating it in earlier times is a serious anachronism. None of these writers would have assumed that a poor person depending on the will of others can be considered to be free. Freedom, Locke, Smith, and Kant state, requires important socioeconomic conditions for its existence, and each society must make the entirely political decision as to the social scope this freedom (understood in republican terms) should have. For John Locke, see Mundó (2015), for Adam Smith, Casassas (2010, 2013), and for Immanuel Kant, Bertomeu (2017).

3. Neither should we forget that some of these self-proclaimed 'liberals' (and in the case of Rawls this is obvious) have used the term 'liberalism' because, in their world (the United States of the latter half of the twentieth century and through to the present day) it has a 'progressive' meaning. In other words, it aspires to show a distance from 'really existing socialism' (and the shadow of the Soviet bloc spread far and wide in those earlier decades) and from the many forms of servitude of the *also* 'really existing' capitalism of the West. The semantic nuance is important. While, in Europe, being '(neo)liberal' tends to mean being a supporter of capitalism governed by the interests of a ruling minority, in the United States since Roosevelt's day, being 'liberal' means advocating more or less

intense market regulation so that large social majorities can become full participants in social and economic life.

4. *Selfish* should be understood here, not as something malign or springing from envy, but as pure indifference or, analytically speaking, as denoting the mathematical independence of the utility functions of each and every bee.

5. For an interesting discussion of *The Fable of the Bees*, see Kaye (1997).

6. Well into the twentieth century, Samuelson, the heir and continuer of this neoclassical economic analysis which totally ignores the power relations between actors with conflicting interests, had the following to say: 'In a perfectly competitive market, it really doesn't matter who hires whom: so have labour hire capital' (Samuelson, 1957: 894).

7. For a more detailed analysis of the possible causes, both epistemological and political, of the marginalist shift in economics, see Casassas (2010).

8. It should be noted that this assumption of consumer sovereignty when it comes to defining desires and seeking ways to satisfy them implies the absence of any notion of human nature and any objective theory of needs. And it should be noted that this supposition, which is at the heart of neoclassical economics, has no place in the descriptions of human action we are given by 'classical' writers such as Smith and Marx. Smith says in *An Inquiry into the Nature and Causes of the Wealth of Nations* (I, viii, 33): 'It is not because one man keeps a coach while his neighbour walks a-foot, that one is rich and the other poor; [and, here, we would have a synthesis of the theory of revealed preferences: the rich man is rich because he *prefers* to be rich, and we discover that he prefers this because he has a coach, while the poor man is poor too because he *prefers* it, and we discover that he prefers this because he travels a-foot] but because the one is rich, he keeps a coach, and because the other is poor, he walks a-foot [and it is more comfortable and satisfies our objective needs better to travel by coach than to tire oneself by walking]'.

9. Emphasis added.

10. As a sign of the presence and social penetration of the pluralist ontology in our own times, it's worth noting the success of Moisés Naím's recent book *The End of Power* (2013). Its subtitle, *From Boardrooms to Battlefields and Churches to States, Why Being in Charge Isn't What It Used to Be*, is more than revealing. Paradoxically, or perhaps not so paradoxically, one of the most powerful men in the world, Mark Zuckerberg, placed the book in the number one spot of essential books for his global reading club, A Year of Books, and invited his 31 million 'friends' to immerse themselves in it.

11. For a brilliant analysis of the reception of Dahl-style pluralist political science by the kind of methodology pertaining to Rawlsian political philosophy – consider, for example, the ingenuous idea of the so-called *overlapping consensus* – see Bertomeu and Domènech (2005).

12. For a discussion of the uses and abuses of the idea and practice of 'social innovation', which is also very appetising for neoliberal rhetoric, see Pradel and García (2018) and Riutort (2016).

CHAPTER 3

1. The bishop and theologian Jacques-Bénigne Bossuet and other apologists for absolutism also used to urge us to leave things as they are, which is to say, in the monarch's hands.
2. Cited by Domènech (2006: 349).
3. Emphasis added.
4. Emphasis added.

CHAPTER 4

1. *Rerum novarum*, 19.
2. Smith (1981 [1776]: I, viii), emphasis added.
3. The term *common* comes from the Latin *communis*, with the prefix *con-* which is associated with the Indo-European root **kom* ('next to' or 'near'), giving us *koine* and *koinonia politike* ('political community' or, better, 'civil society') in Greek.
4. Smith, (1981 [1776]: I, viii).
5. Aristotle, *Politics*, 1260b. www.perseus.tufts.edu/hopper/text?doc=Perseus%3A text%3A1999.01.0058%3Abook%3D1%3Asection%3D1252a-.
6. In Part III I stress the distinction, which is also enshrined in Roman civil law, between 'contract for a specific output', which republicanism considers to be compatible with freedom, and 'contract for services', where one individual is at the beck and call of another individual (as in the wage labour contract that Aristotle compared with slavery), which republicanism has always seen as harmful to the worker's freedom.
7. Republican understanding of the basic income proposal will be duly detailed in Part II.
8. Cited by Domènech (2004: 125).

PART II

1. For a brilliant reconstruction of Kant's approach to the matter of taxes, which is part of an exhaustive analysis of the incompatibility of poverty and freedom, see Bertomeu (2017). Along similar lines, the constitutionalists Stephen Holmes and Cass Sunstein (2000) have offered a detailed argument as to why taxes, far from being an obstacle to freedom, constitute a necessary condition for its existence. Moreover, Raventós and Wark (2018) have emphasised that charity, including in its postmodern manifestations, is a long way from being a selfless gift. The act of *giving* or *offering* entails reciprocity, that is, the presence of a living bidirectional social relationship that allows for two-way travel. Otherwise, the act of *giving* lies outside the logic of an interdependence that respects the autonomy of each party, and charity becomes yet another manifestation of the class structure of our society: a sterile, unidirectional act that only aspires to maintain the status quo of the neoliberal order.

CHAPTER 5

1. Emphasis added.

2. In Philip Pettit's seminal work on republicanism as a 'Theory of Freedom and Government', the question of the material foundations of freedom is mentioned only once and then somewhat vaguely: 'if a republican state is committed to advancing the cause of freedom as non-domination among its citizens, then it must embrace a policy of promoting socioeconomic independence' (1997: 158–9).

3. Of everyone? As said before, this point needs clarifying because, though there is no republicanism that would define freedom differently from the way it is presented here, there are more than a few historically existing forms of republicanism that choose to restrict this freedom to a certain number of people. In this case, we refer to *oligarchic republicanism* (recall Aristotle, Cicero, Jefferson or Kant). However, when this republican freedom is understood and presented as non-domination that must (tend to) include the population as a whole without any kind of exclusion (recall Pericles and Aspasia, Robespierre or Paine), we're talking about democratic forms of republicanism or *democratic republicanism*. For an analysis of the distinction between democratic and oligarchic forms of republicanism, and a reading of Marxian socialism as a way to update democratic republicanism, see Domènech (2004) and Roberts (2017).

4. In no way am I embarking on a detailed discussion of the whole diversity of approaches of all these authors, with all their minutiae and meanderings. But I do think it's necessary to acknowledge the existence of this rich, fertile debate and to clarify what I think should be an epistemologically sensible and politically fruitful position with regard to some of the basic elements that have been put forward. For the 'structural domination' perspective, see Gädeke (2020), Gourevitch (2013, 2014) and Roberts (2017). Moreover, Philip Pettit (2012), who isn't prone to finding continuities between republicanism and socialism, has recognised the presence of unintended or 'structural' components in social domination. I'm grateful to David Guerrero and Julio Martínez-Cava for our enriching conversations on these matters. However, any inaccuracy or omission is strictly my responsibility.

5. Cited in Martínez-Cava (2020: 86). Available in English at: www.marxists.org/archive/marx/works/download/pdf/condition-working-class-england.pdf.

6. I refer to the onslaught by Marxist historian E. P. Thompson (1978) against the dead ends of Louis Althusser's structuralist Marxism and French post-structuralist Marxism of the 1960s and 1970s. Needless to say, today's 'radical republicanism' theorists, who are highly attentive to real causal mechanisms that act as the backbone of capitalist societies, are light years from the post-structuralist metaphysics that Thompson was lambasting.

7. In fact, Alex Gourevitch (2013, 2014) has often pointed out that the situation of 'structural' domination is used, and politically (hence intentionally) defended by those who benefit from it, namely capitalists. Accordingly, Mau (2023) asserts that there may be impersonal domination, but the 'economic power of capital' is possible because capital, through defining the exclusionary property relations

that underpin the violent barring of large social majorities from access to the means of subsistence, governs the material conditions of social reproduction. I'd add that it would seem reasonable to assume that these social processes respond, in large part, to the capacity of agency of humans, or some of them. In fact, Mau himself argues that (abstract and impersonal) economic power requires (violent and sovereign) state power for both the 'creation' of the capitalist mode of production and its 'reproduction' over time. In effect, capitalist states are, *inter alia*, agents of codification and legal protection of the economic power of capital.

8. As described below, the working classes can find in the collective struggle for tools like a basic income, among many other mechanisms geared to *unconditionally* guaranteeing lives in conditions of dignity, a fertile means for combatting the forms of domination they find *within the labour markets* and also for decommodifying the labour force, and thence for trying to bring about more democratic productive and reproductive environments *outside the labour markets too*. In this regard, see Bryan (2023).

9. Jan Eeckhout (2021) has recently pointed out that there's a clear chain of cause–effect relations that has enabled big corporations to gain unprecedented levels of market power that go hand in hand with stagnating wages, extreme wage inequality and an undermining of social mobility and economic dynamism. In brief, capitalism as we know it today – as it has always been, in fact – isn't conducive to popular participation in economic life (e.g. in goods and services markets) but, rather, favours the positions of power of large corporations. Eeckhout concludes that safeguarding democracy demands high doses of public regulation and institutional design (of an *intentional* nature, I would add) with the aim of fostering much more inclusive forms of markets – I do not now go into whether or not this is possible within capitalism, even within certain varieties of reformed capitalism.

10. It's not enough to argue that these *structurally* unjust worlds were often 'already there', or 'that's what we've got' and 'that's how things are'. Neither should we simply add that it's difficult to identify who's responsible for the fact that we find ourselves in such a state of affairs. Faced with structurally unjust scenarios, we should be co-responsible for the duty of correcting both mechanisms that operate to generate injustice in social life and their specific results. To resort to a comparison, it's no coincidence that the crime of 'omission of the duty to help' is codified in the criminal laws of so many countries. Failing to correct socially unjust scenarios – the world's patriarchal structure, for example – is tantamount to helping to consolidate them. Not acting in (or when faced with) a certain situation or scenario is, in some sense, an *intentional* way of favouring the naturalisation of such an unjust scenario. Or can the male population just shrug off, at both the political-institutional and personal everyday levels, the social processes that reinforce its positions of patriarchal privilege with the excuse that they're 'already there', or 'that's what we've got' and 'that's how things are'?

11. Indeed, both Dorothea Gädeke (2020) and William Clare Roberts (2017) make the point, with insight and sophistication, that although domination may be 'systemic', it is in no case disconnected from the agency of individuals: 'Systemic

domination does not mean that the system as such dominates, mysteriously, over and beyond the agents acting within it' (Gädeke, 2020: 35).

12. Critics of what has been called 'sufficientarianism' might suggest that this approach suffers from the problem inherent to all 'sufficientarian' schemes: by indicating the importance of a threshold beyond which republican freedom expands, we could be neglecting myriad forms of inequality that appear above that threshold. As will be seen below, especially in Part IV, this book takes an approach to republican freedom for which, even if strict equality of resources isn't required, control of the accumulation of private wealth occurring 'above that threshold' is of vital necessity. Great inequalities tend to pose a serious danger for putting into practice the life plans of less powerful actors. Nevertheless, this doesn't prevent us from insisting on the importance of the 'basic' thresholds above which our personal independence starts to be socioeconomically grounded, which means increased bargaining power. For a detailed analysis of the limits of 'sufficientarianism', see Casal (2007).

13. It's very likely that one of the social movements that has most genuinely understood and reconstructed this framework of republican analysis is the worldwide Independent Living movement. See, for example, Gómez Jiménez (2016).

CHAPTER 6

1. In other words, the act of nurturing broad sociopolitical movements – and also concrete (re)productive experiences, such as forms of cooperative work or mutual support networks – must allow us to move beyond the sad obligation to choose between various types of 'business dictatorship', as González-Ricoy (2014) suggests can happen to those workers who decide to 'exit' from their arbitrarily managed firms. Indeed, that an awareness that the arbitrary management of firms is widespread cannot lead us to assume that there is no alternative to the arbitrary management of firms – in fact, empirical evidence confirms day after day that myriad possibilities in terms of organization of work and production with higher degrees of economic democracy are not free of difficulties, but they are permanently open (Lazar, 2023). What it is about is knowing how to sociopolitically take advantage of the windows of opportunity to access these 'other environments', to these 'other logics', and to extend them socially. Probably, basic income constitutes a measure that contributes to this being the case.

2. Needless to say, this book has nothing to do with the idea of a republicanism that is fully compatible with capitalism, as it is upheld by authors such as Robert S. Taylor (2013) and Frank Lovett (2010). First, Taylor's project is that social actors should be able to exit social relations *within (capitalist labour) markets*, that is, without considering the possibility that such 'exit' places them outside capitalist social relations, which is, according to the perspective that is defended in this book, the most important variable to seize the degrees of effective freedom within contemporary societies. Second, Lovett seems to separate the question of non-domination, which acquires a strongly procedural nature, from the issue of individual and popular access to (im)material resources guarantee-

ing such non-domination. On the contrary, this book suggests that for freedom to be considered 'unconditional', the (*ex ante*) distribution of resources cannot be seen as an issue that is conceptually separated from the social ontology of such freedom. Certainly, a society may harbour the finest procedures in terms of social and political organisation, but it cannot be free while most of its members lack resources to make their freedom effective. I am indebted to David Guerrero for very inspiring conversations on these issues.

3. In this sense, it is interesting to note that the history of the basic income proposal is not exempt from links to political forces that have sought a market-friendly alternative to the post-war welfare state and, currently, with some Silicon Valley techno-populist figures to whom it matters little – rather, they fear – the emancipatory potential of a true liberating basic income (Jäger and Zamora Vargas, 2023). However, it cannot be ignored that the true historical origins of the contemporary proposal of a basic income lie in the left wing of crucial revolutionary movements of the late eighteenth century – let us think, above all, of figures such as Thomas Paine and Thomas Spence (Tena Camporesi, 2021) – and that the old idea, which was already present in these movements, of granting all citizens, for the mere fact of being citizens, a 'social dividend' as compensation for the illegitimate private appropriation of a wealth that must be understood as a social product is at the core of many of the defences of basic income that we have known in the twenty-first century (in part, also the one that is offered in this book).

CHAPTER 7

1. *Sumangali* is a form of contract that is used in the Tamil Nadu textile industry in the south of India whereby children under 16, and especially girls, are recruited to work long hours in factories a long way from urban centres, so they can't leave, even to sleep. Their meagre earnings are divided into three parts. The first, almost half, is sent to their parents or guardian through the contracting agencies that lured them into this situation. The second part, which is almost non-existent, is for their personal consumption. The third is accumulated and received at the end of the contract, which is normally for three years, to be used as a dowry so that the workers can marry (Shadab and Koshy, 2012).
2. In his film *I, Daniel Blake*, which premiered in 2016, Ken Loach offers many powerful examples that allow a full understanding of the conditions of life of these 'supplicants'.
3. Simon Birnbaum (2012) also does this when he states that the unconditional nature of basic income could come to constitute the true socioeconomic foundation of self-respect, which isn't possible when we are submitted to bonds of dependence and a whole range of forms of arbitrariness.
4. Blackstone (1979), volume 2, part II, emphasis added.
5. In *Politics* (1256b), Aristotle says that a good life requires relevant sets of external resources, but then adds that these sets must be finite and limited or, in other words, they must be confined to the function of reproducing the material basis of a dignified human existence. Exceeding these limits makes no sense.

6. In fact, these were the approaches that, at the end of the eighteenth century, inspired the first systematic defence of something like a basic income proposal, by Thomas Paine in his pamphlet *Agrarian Justice*. See Paine (1974), Bosc (2016), Van Parijs and Vanderborght (2017) and Tena (2021). For a study of basic income as an 'indirect strategy' in the recovery of the idea and the practice of collective fiduciary control over the economic realm, see Casassas and Mundó (2022).

CHAPTER 8

1. For a critical analysis of the reasons, probably related to political-electoral strategy, adduced by Hacker and other predistributive theorists for shunning tax programmes, see Casassas and Guerrero (forthcoming).

2. For suggestive republican interpretations of Rawls' late works, see Francisco (2006) and White (2012).

3. As can be seen, the crux of the predistributive proposal is the idea of freedom. Authors like O'Neill and Williamson (2012a, 2012b) suggest that predistribution is concerned with shaping a more egalitarian society. And this is so. But, here, equality has a subordinate role with respect to freedom: equality is important because inequalities tend to undermine freedom. Therefore, it is necessary to prevent concentrations of private economic power that are able to limit the freedoms of others, but this doesn't mean any kind of commitment to strict equality of resources. The moral and political commitment is established with respect to the idea of equality of opportunities to live the kinds of lives that 'free chooser' subjects tend to be able to live. Obviously, this entails egalitarian measures, but they have another, underlying aim: equal (republican) freedom for everyone. For a Marxian take on this core republican – and socialist – point, see Roberts (2017).

4. For a defence of basic income that takes up Rousseau's insight that no citizen should be so poor as to be forced to sell himself to a rich citizen, see Goodhart (2007).

5. It should be emphasised that although public policies are invoked, this isn't the same as saying that the predistributive strategy or the 'property-owning democracy' is limited to them alone. As Stuart White (forthcoming) suggests, there are forms of 'commons-based predistribution' that can also help to create productive – and reproductive – opportunities so that we can be in command of our lives from the very beginning of our social interaction with others. In effect, spaces where resources and activities are produced, managed and used in cooperative and self-managed ways can also function to empower, *ex ante*, individuals and groups and, consequently, increase their bargaining power and, ultimately, their freedom.

6. For a historically conscious and analytically rigorous reconstruction of republican freedom and neutrality, incorporating both the 'positive' and 'negative' dimensions being discussed here, see Bertomeu and Domènech (2005).

7. In this regard, it's surprising that Pettit suggests we should renounce understanding our aspiration to freely operate on shared paths in non-hostile environments

as a creative, positive act. This conceptual shift, he says (1997), would mean an act of 'populist' voluntarism, a veritably meaningless toast to the sun in a world where it behoves us to restrict ourselves to 'negatively' equipping ourselves in spaces affording safety and protection for everybody.

8. This would seem to be the project of Hannah Arendt (1958, 1959), who didn't hide her hostility to the presence of public policies geared to the institutional protection of the most vulnerable social groups.

CHAPTER 9

1. I leave aside evidence that there are many kinds of work that, even if they can bring in some income – hence covering *some* basic needs – are not only a long way from offering society as a whole the means by which we can *decently* and *thoroughly* satisfy these material and symbolic needs, but that they can also become veritable sources of prejudice and great harm.

2. It should be noted that, thus understood, the technical division of labour is compatible with both certain types of capitalist enterprises and possible post-capitalist 'republican' associations of cooperatively grouped free workers.

3. Such efficiency losses are also due to the fact that, under 'forced' labour regimes, because of the need to accept such labour, diminished motivation must be made up for by huge amounts of 'guard labour' (Jayadev and Bowles, 2006) aimed at recruiting, training and disciplining, monitoring and controlling and, finally, rewarding or punishing the conduct of the working population, all of which leads to negative net productivity (Jordan, 1992). As Van Parijs (1990) says, efficiency is closely related with the effective freedom to choose a job but not with having to 'put up with it' on a daily basis.

4. At this point, it's important to note that, although everybody receives the basic income, not everybody benefits in terms of obtaining income. This is because the basic income is settled into the taxation system, which provides the necessary resources for financing it. If it is to be universal, it must go to the population as a whole, including those with most resources but, since it is linked with the taxation system, these people contribute more (and in some cases, much more) than what they obtain as a basic income. In this regard, basic income works like a public hospital where, of course, access to healthcare is a universal right. Everyone, including those with most resources, have the right to go there, and they can use that right or seek private treatment but, on average and over a lifetime, what these people with more resources contribute through taxes to the public health system is greater than what they *take* from it. This is why Aerts, Marx and Verbist (2023) point out that a considerable share of the population would lose out financially from the implementation of a basic income. Of course, what share of the population and which specific groups would lose out is something that will directly depend on the nature of the tax reform that is made to finance basic income. For a scheme that illustrates this logic of functioning when explaining how to finance a basic income, see Arcarons, Raventós and Torrens (2017). For a concise and didactic (and even funny) explanation, see Santens (2022).

5. The analysis here is close to what appears in an earlier study (Casassas, 2017).
6. But all that glisters is not gold, as Shakespeare's Portia pointed out. De Wispelaire and Stirton (2012) have shown that basic income isn't free of all administrative difficulties since it is necessary to register all recipients, design efficient methods of payment and, finally, establish non-clientelistic methods for supervising the payments.
7. For an analysis of the 'punitive turn' welfare policies have taken in the last thirty years, see Haagh (2017). Moreover, Guy Standing (2017) has exposed and denounced the paternalistic and intrusive nature of conditional subsidies which suggest that 'the poor' are still regarded as suspicious individuals who need all sorts of external supervision. Bru Laín and Albert Julià (2022) have studied how information barriers and the administrative logic and functioning regarding the communication strategy used by public institutions play a fundamental role in discouraging potential claimants and therefore increasing the rate of 'non-take-up'.

CHAPTER 10

1. For a demystifying critique of the purported 'bourgeois' origins of the ideas of rights and democracy, see Domènech (2009).
2. Philippe Van Parijs and Yannick Vanderborght have also pointed out that basic income, precisely because it endows the most vulnerable people with bargaining power, becomes an instrument of emancipation with considerable possibilities (Van Parijs, 2013; Van Parijs and Vanderborght, 2017).
3. Needless to say, attacks by neoliberal governments, through labour reforms, against the institution of collective bargaining have dealt the death blow to the forms of social consensus that were the legacy of social pacts which came after the Second World War. I say more about these in Part IV.
4. It's also true that wages are received on an individual basis, but I don't believe that this is why trade unions and collective bargaining in particular are currently at a low ebb.
5. For an analysis of the mental health epidemic in our societies and also the role that basic income could play in combatting it, see Raventós, S. (2011, 2016).
6. We should all understand this because the equitable distribution of relevant doses of bargaining power makes perfect sense in a capitalist environment in which, as Van Parijs (1995) himself points out, having a good job is a matter, in many cases, of luck and arbitrariness or, in other words, of a whole combination of circumstances that are totally out of our control and have nothing to do with our responsibility.
7. It should be noted that these cooperative environments are especially apt for this treatment of property as a fiduciary relationship, as described in Part II. If the main purpose of wealth and property isn't personal enrichment but guaranteeing the basic needs of citizens and organising workplaces in which we can all feel reasonably fulfilled – after which comes personal enrichment – the world of cooperativism would seem to be a means by which this understanding of economic life could be socially extended. Indeed, the democratic principle gov-

erning cooperativism – one person one vote in the framework of inclusive and binding decision-making processes – provides tools with which everyone can take part in acts of mutual trust where we can reciprocally ask each other to carry out tasks and follow up, also reciprocally, the degrees and forms of accomplishing these tasks.

8. For a defence of a model of self-managed market socialism that includes a basic income for all as a means to promote a democratic transformation of workplaces, see Howard (2000).

9. Foucault (2008: 160) and others who came later such as Laval and Dardot (2013) have suggested that the interventionism 'is pursued as the historical and social condition of the possibility for a market economy, as the condition enabling the formal mechanism of competition to function' – yes, you heard right: the neoliberal regime of accumulation would not be possible without huge and cleverly arranged doses of state intervention. The aim is that *Homo œconomicus* should become 'an entrepreneur, an entrepreneur of himself' (Foucault, 2008: 226), ready to compete in all areas of our lives and to be meticulously prepared, from earliest childhood, to accumulate the 'human capital' that will be essential for obtaining minimally acceptable levels of income and profit. Part of the success of the neoliberal turn of capitalism can be seen in the social permeation – in working classes too – of this kind of subjectivity. Will we ever stop receiving insidious invitations from people we don't know to connect with allegedly 'social' networks that have been set up to channel our 'employability'? Or, to put it another way, will we ever manage to achieve democratic control of the information network concerning our desire(s) to work?

10. Standing also notes that a productive economy is that which facilitates an efficient reassigning of talents and increased levels of job engagement, adding that: 'In the US, lack of employee commitment [a lack of commitment for which they can in no way be blamed, given the nature of the markets and workplaces through which they are forced to wander (Horgan, 2021)] has been estimated to cost some $500 billion in lost productivity' (Standing, 2017: 99).

11. For a hopeful response to this question, see Laguna (2017).

12. At this point, I overlook the fact that part of care work or reproductive work is carried out in domestic spaces that aren't those of the people who engage in it, normally women, who are remunerated.

13. All these figures are taken from Torrens and González de Molina (2016). The film *In the Same Boat* (2016) by Rudy Gnutti offers some interesting thoughts on this reality and suggests why a basic income makes sense at this historical juncture.

14. That robotisation is a fact of life is far from being a fantasy of visionary madmen. Take, for example, the following devices: 'driverless cars, machines that can win at world chess or Go championships, big data, Internet of things, artificial intelligence [with features such as machine learning and advanced sensors], 3D printing, nanotechnology, biotechnology, digitalisation, etcetera' (Torrens and González de Molina, 2016). Despite all this, we mustn't fall into the trap of technological determinism. Yes, robotisation is a fact, but there's another fact, namely that humans still have the ability to decide, in accordance with ethical-political

criteria, the point to which we want technology to replace human work, and in which spaces. This is a Polanyi-inspired nuance that can't be dodged.

15. In the same way, it would not be superfluous to recall here that, at the same time, Bertrand Russell (2004) published his *In Praise of Idleness*, a prescient essay in which he suggested that a reduction in the working day to four hours a day would allow people to engage to a greater extent in autotelic activities, which are those that are rewarded in the mere act of carrying them out, which would result in mental benefits – a 'better character' – for those who perform them and in a better satisfaction of the needs of the population as a whole, because when we do not work for strictly instrumental reasons that have to do with our need to survive, the best ideas and the best ways to carry them out and (im)materially concretise them appear.

16. As Claus Offe (1992) says, basic income isn't 'pay without work' but pay for all those people who 'work without pay', which is precisely why they are deprived of the ability to decide on the most natural combinations of the different kinds of work we might genuinely want in our lives.

17. Furthermore, a reduction in working hours, coupled with the benefits of a basic income, would mean lower unemployment rates, and less need to enter job markets to earn a living. As a result, employers wouldn't be able to take advantage of the huge numbers of unemployed people willing to work at any price to further degrade the working conditions of their employees.

18. So, it's not surprising that reducing working hours has been one of the core aims of contemporary emancipatory movements, starting with the workers' movement (Torrens and González de Molina, 2016), because it was understood that this could provide the necessary free time, not only to organise the political struggle of the working class, but also to give shape to less monotonous lives that could embrace activities of the most diverse nature. In fact, this is actually the reason why, at present, authors who are critical of work (but not of any type of work), such as David Frayne (2015) or Kathi Weeks (2011), suggest the need for a link between basic income and a reduction in working hours: the ultimate goal is none other than to open spaces for more critical thinking about what meaningful work can mean and to collectively act to organise work in liberating post-capitalist ways.

19. As Moreno Colom points out, without genuine co-responsibility of men and women, 'work less' isn't only insufficient, but it can also constitute a trap because, '[f]rom a woman's point of view, working less means caring more, or working less in the labour market and more in the household' (2016: 141).

20. As well as those cited (Aznar, 1994; Torrens and González de Molina, 2016), other authors have written about combining a shorter working day with political measures such as a basic income, among them Bregman (2016), Frayne (2015), Gorz (1997) and Mason (2015).

21. For a discussion about remunerating domestic work and the 'wages for housework' movement, see Federici (2013).

22. And they are so valuable! As Pérez Orozco (2014) says, the fact that there can be no productive work without reproductive work should make us question the very existence of the distinction. For a critical analysis of the way in which the

current wage-and-family system miscounts women's economic contributions, see Weeks (2011).

23. Naturally, the fact that women accepted as their own, with the help of coercion, the space for reproduction and caring of life – the life of workers – didn't mean that they stopped 'going up' to the world of wage labour, and this didn't stop them from joining the workforce: 'double presence' has a long history.

24. The basic income experiment carried out in Dauphin (Manitoba, Canada) between 1974 and 1979 produced a non-trivial decline in labour force participation. And stopping working for others means getting a lower income and, therefore, having less, not more, to spend (Calnitsky, 2017). For this reason, one would have to wonder if this reduction in the hours dedicated to wage-earning work, in the event that it responded to a free and autonomous decision, could constitute the gateway to more frugal lives, to lives that were less oriented towards meaningless consumerism.

25. Many enriching conversations with Julio Lucena de Andrés and Àlex Boso have helped inspire these reflections on the possible role of basic income in conceiving of (and fighting for) a just eco-social transition. I can only be grateful to them. Any errors, omissions or inaccuracies are strictly my own responsibility.

26. It can therefore be argued that basic income combined with in-kind benefits and political control of the more powerful actors can open up the way to a world in which individuals and groups would be (unconditionally) provided for according to their needs and, thanks precisely to that, they would (voluntarily) be able to contribute work according to their abilities. For a reinterpretation of this criterion of distribution that Marx proposed for communist societies, see Van Parijs (2013).

27. Appealing to this possible right has nothing to do with building castles in the air. In today's world, it doesn't exist as a *right*, though it is a *privilege* reserved for some.

28. José Luis Rey Pérez (2007) has shown from philosophy of law how basic income can, in this regard, act as a guarantee of a right to work which, far from being understood purely and simply as the right to a job, should be seen as the right to social inclusion by means of engaging in freely chosen sets of activities and developing autonomously defined life projects.

29. For an analysis of the determinants of bargaining power, see Elster (2007), and for an exploratory examination, inspired by Elster's work, of the effects of basic income on the bargaining power of workers, see Casassas and Loewe (2001).

30. It's no accident that most of the forms of socialism, which are based on the conceptual and political model of republicanism (Domènech, 2004), have aspired through a variety of methods and procedures, to establish 'collective property or control of the means of production'. In doing so, they have claimed to be heirs of a pan-European tradition of grassroots struggle which, like the republican endeavour, had and has as its core objective gaining control by everyone, which is to say *collective* control, of all spaces and processes in which we produce material and immaterial goods, where we reproduce life, where we make decisions about how to live, once again, in common.

31. This is the logic behind the South Korean proposal to finance the Gyeonggi Province's 'Youth Basic Income' through taxes on technology and the private use of commons and citizens' data (Langridge, Büchs and Howard, 2022).

CHAPTER 11

1. From the cognitive sciences, Owen Flanagan (1996) observes that this ability to explain (ourselves) and 'self-express' is what can give a certain sense to life.
2. If we're going to keep using 'problematic' but maybe necessary terms, we might say that all this is the same as calling for an *effective flexicurity*. This neologism, which results from the contraction of the terms 'flexibility' and 'security', has been used on too many occasions when talking about making labour markets more *flexible* with the promise that this will come with considerable *security*. Unfortunately, this has been tried this way in a few countries, notably Holland and Denmark. Generally speaking, the flexicurity discourse has brought considerable precariousness because the elements of security that are supposed to accompany flexibility have proven to be absent (Klosse, 2003; Standing, 2009). But this doesn't prevent us from thinking of basic income as a tool that can contribute not only to providing us with 'security' to survive capitalist labour markets but also to exit from them to undertake life projects that 'flexibly' adapt to the kinds of lives we really aspire to.
3. Standing (2014) describes as *denizens* those citizens who are *denied* both socioeconomic and civic-political rights as they are also being denied their status as wage labourers. The French sociologist Robert Castel (1997) uses the term *disaffiliation* to designate the expulsion from the realm of employment and the isolation suffered by the new groups of people who are being excluded from the social contract.
4. The existing literature on the results of basic income pilots already seems endless. In this book, I'm relying on the attempts at synthesis and systematic analysis offered by Laín (2023) and Borrell-Porta, de Quintana and Segura (2023a).
5. But this does not mean that the labour supply *must* be reduced. As shown in the work of Guido Imbens, winner of the Nobel Prize in Economics in 2021, if people do not leave their jobs when they win the lottery, they will not do so because of the introduction of a basic income set at the level of the poverty line – at most, he adds, 6 or 7 per cent of the employees will do so (Imbens, Rubin and Sacerdote, 2001). As always, it is about how the behaviour of the working population, whatever orientation it has, responds to genuinely autonomous decisions.

PART IV

1. To cite one example, the famous Glass–Steagall Act, which was passed in 1933 and definitively overturned in 1999 by the Clinton administration, separated commercial banking from investment banking with the aim of protecting small savers from the 'banksters', as Franklin Delano Roosevelt called them. It goes

without saying that the abrogation of this law was one of the factors that explains the pre-eminence that global finance capital has been acquiring over the last few decades.

2. For a study of the practices and aspirations of this rentier class which, some time ago, decided to operate overtly and unabashedly, see Standing (2016).

3. The next few paragraphs are an updating of Casassas (2016b) and Casassas et al. (2015).

CHAPTER 12

1. My use of the term 'Fordist pact' isn't random, as the origins of the consensus are to be found in the five-year contract signed in 1950 by the powerful United Automobile Workers union and General Motors, which was followed by similar agreements with the Ford Motor Company and Chrysler. The agreement came to Europe after the Second World War under the auspices of the Marshall Plan and, in fact, it was in Europe where it was most developed.

2. It should be noted that the pact ignored reproductive work as a condition for the possibility of any other kind of work, which explains why it never became paid work or publicly recognised. This meant hiding several dimensions of exploitation of women behind the smokescreen of the supposed prosperity of the household. Moreover, it's worth noting that a world of effective full employment would have eroded the bargaining power of the capitalist class because it would no longer have had unemployed workers who would agree to take jobs with worse conditions and lower wages. It was therefore standard practice of the capitalist class to use its capacity for political influence to subvert the goal of full employment, which was equivalent to undercutting the foundations of this social pact (Kalecki, 1943).

3. It's striking to realise that these 'inviolable' rights have so often been linked to participation in the labour market, as is the case, for instance, with the right to a *conditional* income in case of unemployment.

4. For an account of the advent of the pact in both the United States and Europe, see Davis (2000) and Zunz, Schoppa and Hiwatari (2004).

5. In addition, precariousness constitutes a reality that is shared with most of the working class. In fact, being *precarious* doesn't only mean living in effectively precarious conditions – unemployment, transitoriness, little public assistance, and so on – but also being under the permanent threat of falling into the precariousness trap. Do we know many people who can say with certainty that they aren't living under the Damoclean sword of precariousness? The slogan 'We are the 99%' isn't exactly accurate in terms of pointing to well-founded empirical evidence, but it is a metaphor that can be used to designate an indisputable tendency to social polarisation the length and breadth of the planet. Economic security has ceased to be a reality for the great majority of the working population. Accordingly, could being aware of the precariousness in which we live in reality, or that is threatening us, help us to reconstruct the unity of the working class and likeminded political subjects? For an analysis of these transformations

of capitalism and their translation into the 'indignation' that occupied the streets and squares of Spain between 2011 and 2015, see Rodríguez López (2016).

6. David Harvey (2003, 2007), Guy Standing (2009, 2011, 2014) and others have described in great detail how this process unfolded historically and the effects it has had on the daily lives of working populations. For a study from the standpoint of gender, see Pérez Orozco (2014).

7. Evidently, the fact that the key objective of the political economy of neoliberal regimes has been reducing deficit and public debt – and here we only need to think of the Maastricht Treaty, which has been obligatory in much of Europe since 1992 – has done little to help maintain the safety nets of 'reformed capitalism'.

8. And still more, according to the 2016 Credit Suisse annual report on global wealth, the top 1 per cent of adults owns 51 per cent of global wealth, while the bottom half of adults owns only 1 per cent. In fact, the top 10 per cent of adults owns 89 per cent of all the world's wealth (Credit Suisse Research Institute, 2016).

9. And it's well known that as the figures for union membership decline, those for participation of working classes in national earnings also drop, a correlation that has been observable since 1970 (Fairchild, 2013).

10. Marlène Benquet and Théo Bourgeron (2022) call 'authoritarian-libertarian' the regimes that, far from falling from heaven, are intentionally managing the financial assault on democracy that Western societies are witnessing today.

11. Saying that every pact includes a dose of victory and a dose of renunciation isn't the same as denying that, on some occasions, there are 'net victories'. The attainment of universal suffrage, for example, represents a net victory which can't be appealed against or broken down into fragments. Universal suffrage is achieved 'totally' or not at all. Hence, these net victories can't come under the heading of pacts because they are straightforward victories.

12. In this regard, it's interesting to observe that the post-war social pact was harshly criticised by some far-left groups and the so-called Autonomous Workers' Movement for which the concession of renouncing control of production was too onerous in terms of economic sovereignty, and totally unjustifiable because it obfuscated the sense of organised working-class struggles (Katsiaficas, 2006). Indeed, it's doubly interesting to see how a good part of the present groups of today's 'indignados' and 'rebel' insoumis groups are taking up, in new language and with perhaps dissimilar aims, the kinds of criticism the 'other' lefts reserved for welfare state capitalism. 'It's not a crisis. It's capitalism!' protestors exclaimed, for example, when the 15M movement filled the squares of Spain. Actually, it's triply interesting because more than a few political forces and trade union organisations of the 'conventional' left are prepared to recover the awareness that wage labour under capitalism is 'part-time slavery' and, without abandoning negotiations regarding immediate aspects of the labour relation, are starting to open the doors to different kinds of support for initiatives that break with the logic of capitalism.

13. In fact, many analysts and activists suggest that this immediate action, which is 'merely' palliative in cases of poverty and exclusion, should be carried out in

the form of an unconditional universal basic income, precisely because of its enormous (pre)distributive capacity.

CHAPTER 13

1. Adam Smith himself was aware of this: the 'system of perfect liberty' he yearned for and which he linked to the development of manufacturing and commerce was supposed to be the political solution to the stumbling block resulting from the machinations and rentier practices of a capitalist class whose interests, a long way from coinciding from those of society as a whole, meant excluding the people from access to the productive sphere as free actors in the republican sense of the term. Hence his insistence on all sorts of cautionary measures and political-institutional controls to confront any legal steps or proposals coming from these extractive elites (Smith, 1981).
2. Emphasis added.
3. Here, proposals of 'socialism *of* the market' or 'market socialism' coming from authors of a wide range of scientific and political backgrounds, from the revolutionary neoclassicism of Léon Walras (Domènech, 2013) to the political-philosophical analysis of John Roemer (1994) through to Oskar Lange's (1938) interwar model, show an absence of this decision-making capacity. If all these proposals agree on the importance of politically guaranteed initial endowments to all actors, requiring sweeping processes of redistribution of income and property which, it must be noted in passing, include the proposal of a 'social dividend' in the cases of Lange and Roemer (Van Parijs and Vanderborght, 2017), they also coincide in assuming that once these 'corrections' are introduced, social life as a whole should be channelled through markets. By contrast, this book is committed to an analytical and normative scheme pointing to the idea that, if it's a matter of instituting 'socialist' orders or 'radically democratic' systems or whatever name you wish to use, they must be closer to a possible 'socialism *with* markets' than to a 'socialism *of* the market'. For a republicanising defence of this Polanyian capacity of opening doors to the market wherever it's deemed to be a good idea, and to veto this social institution in spaces where its presence is thought to be inappropriate, see Sandel (2012).
4. This is how it was seen, for example, in Catalonia by the promoters of a Peoples' Legislative Initiative for the introduction of what has been called a 'guaranteed citizen income' (Toledano, 2017).
5. Something similar occurs with the so-called 'negative income tax' (NIT), which is often erroneously equated with a basic income. The logic of the NIT is as follows: a minimum annual amount is established below which it is understood that no one should live, and if it is found that there are people who have not managed to reach that amount (through annual personal income tax returns), the state pays the remaining part. Nevertheless, although given the present circumstances, this extra amount would be welcome, it can't hide the fact that the 'supplement' in question is a 'survival supplement', an *ex post* measure to keep people alive who have never enjoyed the *ex ante* possibility of choosing their own lives from the outset.

6. This scheme has been adopted, for example, as a so-called Income Guarantee Scheme in the Basque Country.

7. As we saw in Part III, this is the disincentive to look for or accept what will most probably be a badly paid and unfulfilling job which, moreover, entails loss of the 'poverty relief' that we currently enjoy.

8. Van Parijs and Vanderborght (2017: 109) also see it like this: 'because of its freedom from conditions, a basic income contributes to [...] decommodifying labor power, to boosting socially useful yet unpaid activities, to protecting our lives against forced mobility and destructive globalisation, and to emancipating us from the despotism of the market'.

CHAPTER 14

1. Perhaps this is why the Spanish 15M activists, in the movement's first anniversary celebrations from 12 to 15 May 2012 with the slogan 'Take to the Streets', presented a 'citizens' rescue plan' consisting of the following *set* of measures: ending any kind of bailout of financial institutions, cancelling all neoliberal labour reforms that worsened precariousness and servitude in the labour markets, high-quality public health and education, a fully inclusive stock of public housing that would ensure a roof over everyone's head and, finally, a universal and unconditional basic income that would guarantee the material existence of the population as a whole (Casassas et al., 2015). It's worth pointing out that the word 'rescue' didn't have any assistance-based meaning. It was simply used as a kind of Polanyi-style 'double movement' in which, instead of 'rescuing' the banks, which was precisely what the neoliberal governments were doing at the time (though they tended to use the word 'bailout'), the aim was to rescue people from the wreckage. 'People first', they said.

2. In this regard, basic income can 'be conceived as a step good that contributes to republican freedom in a discontinuous manner. A gradual increase in [basic income] – a low basic income, for instance – may have little or no direct effect on a person's republican freedom until it reaches a tipping point, at which point a 'higher stage' of republican freedom comes about. [A basic income] pitched below such a tipping point or threshold entails that citizens are perhaps better off in terms of well-being, but not necessarily more free in the republican sense' (Casassas and De Wispelaere, 2016: 288).

3. Accordingly, republican theory favours adopting a stricter criterion for defining the amount of a basic income than that suggested by Philippe Van Parijs, whose analytical framework operates within the field of Rawlsian 'ideal theory'. According to Van Parijs (1995), the basic income should be of the 'highest sustainable' amount. For republicanism, however, if the 'highest sustainable' amount of the basic income is too low, it may not be worth the effort of assuring this level, especially if other available measures show that they are more likely to promote republican freedom (Casassas and De Wispelaere, 2012). This said, it should be added that, at the beginning of the twenty-first century, Van Parijs stated that he now believed that 'all the richer countries can now afford to pay a basic income above subsistence' (Van Parijs, 2001: 6).

4. Take, for example, the role that a decent minimum wage could play. Although it's true that the kind of bargaining power given by a basic income *already* allows us to reject badly paid jobs, a good legally defined minimum wage could prevent certain employers from taking advantage of the presence of a basic income to cut wages. If this were to happen, we'd be faced *de facto* with the quite undesirable situation in which part of the worker's revenue *as a worker*, which should all be paid by the enterprise under the form of wages, would be taken from state coffers. Basic income should not take the form of an unconditional wage subsidy for employers – the financial viability of companies should be guaranteed through other means, especially when in no case is it contemplated that profits be totally or partially socialised.

5. It's not just that basic income would be compatible with these 'other' policies but also that many people who are familiar with the everyday management of social and welfare programmes suggest that a basic income could enhance the efficacy of many of these programmes and mechanisms. Coming to them from beneath the Damoclean sword of precariousness is different from doing so with levels of socioeconomic security that provide some real room for manoeuvre when trying to make the most of what these programmes have to offer when defining one's own life trajectory, which may be a long, slow process, but can also be exhaustive and truly effective (Birnbaum, 2016; Haagh, 2017; Ramos, 2011; Standing, 2009; Van Parijs, 2018). This is why basic income, by offering a useful response to structural inequality – provided it is part of a predistributive policy and not simply a cost-saving replacement for other welfare measures – might turn certain public policy-related groups such as 'critical social workers', who are well aware of the extent to which social intervention is encouraged and gains efficacy when the recipients have a decent socioeconomically guaranteed existence, into true supportive allies in campaigning for an equitable and adequate basic income through practitioner activism, professional advocacy and critical pedagogy (Ablett, Morley and Newcomb, 2019). Likewise, the results of many basic income experiments suggest that the unconditional availability of income has a positive correlation with access to and use of social services and policies such as healthcare and education (Borrell-Porta, de Quintana and Segura, 2023a; Laín, 2023).

6. And what would be the role of the sphere of self-management in constructing this protective context? Should this task be the exclusive responsibility of state organs? Not at all. Public policies and self-managed initiatives and spaces have equally valuable and frequently intersecting roles in the provision and reproduction of packages of resources designed with the aim of consolidating a socioeconomic base for everybody. The 'proportions' of both spheres and their possible intertwining and synergistic action depends entirely on the historical trajectories and particular processes of self-understanding of each specific society. But one thing is clear: today, both strategies, the 'statist' and the 'self-managing', will need to respond to an impulse that has been increasingly present in society since the onset of the crisis of 2008, which is to seize, occupy and govern in common the areas and processes by means of which (self-) protective resources and devices are produced and made available to the collec-

tivity. For an inspiring analysis and a proposal of a 'metropolitan welfare', that is, of forms of 'common-fare' or commons-based welfare (housing, education, healthcare, sociality, lifelong learning, etc.), including a currency and financial institutions 'of the commons' as a complement of a basic income, see Fumagalli and Intelligence Precaria (2011).

7. See the report by the powerful conservative think tank the American Enterprise Institute, which favours abolishing the majority of welfare and cash transfer programmes, including Social Security and Medicare, and replacing them with a universal basic income (Jensen et al., 2017).

8. It's true that it could also be argued that basic income constitutes per se a mechanism that tends to equalise since, in a certain sense, it tends to impose a ceiling. First, this is so because its financing entails large transfers of resources from the richest to those who have least, which ends up with better levels of equality which can be seen in the Gini coefficient in the available simulation studies (Arcarons, Raventós and Torrens, 2017). Second, basic income can set in motion equalising dynamics because it would allow those who have least to 'exit' (or refuse to 'enter') productive relationships that aren't only alienating but that also frequently constitute the substratum of great accumulations of private economic power. Hence, these productive spaces would be more limited in their ability to reproduce and expand. Nevertheless, none of these facts exempts us from the need to think more carefully about the 'ceiling'.

9. For a thorough analysis of the reasons why concentrations of wealth pose a threat to democracy and for a case for introducing a maximum wage, see Pizzigati (2018).

10. Ingrid Robeyns (2016) has recently offered a philosophical-political reinterpretation of this position, which she calls *limitarianism*.

11. For an interesting analysis of the disproportionate capacity for influence of the big economic powers in the decision-making processes of public institutions, see Winters and Page (2009). Moreover, Hacker and Pierson (2010) state that, far from being a game in which players are provided with equivalent resources, contemporary political life should be understood as an 'organized combat' notable for a systematic use of force and leverage by the economic elites, and this can only favour *winner-takes-all* outcomes in which a few victors make off with all the spoils. This discussion of Rousseaunian and Rooseveltian strategies that is offered in these pages is taken from Casassas and De Wispelaere (2016).

CHAPTER 15

1. Unless, of course, we're being exploited or are exploiting ourselves, going too far and working many more hours than would seem commonsensical.

2. The following paragraphs rework and develop the analysis offered in this regard in Casassas (2017).

3. These are people who inherit fortunes or amass them thanks to rentier activities that include, *inter alia*, lobbying government bodies and establishing emoluments that are way in excess of the value generated by these recipients (McQuaig and Brooks, 2014; Raventós, 2017; Standing, 2016). Again, according to the ine-

quality analyst Matt Bruenig (2017), the statistics show that, for every ten dollars of revenue produced in the United States, one goes to the pockets of the richest 1 per cent in the form of payments that are totally unrelated to work done.

4. However, the results of the experiments should be viewed with caution, not so much because they might lead to excessive optimism, but the opposite. By definition, these pilot projects are of short duration, a few years at most. But, also by definition, basic income is received without interruption, 'from the cradle to the grave'. Indeed, the reliable nature of payments made at regular intervals until the end of our days is one of the essential features of the proposal (Standing, 2017). Hence, the expected effects of basic income in terms of 'a big reset' of our lives, with great changes in the (re)productive sphere and transformations that would also reach a broad spectrum of internally organised groups, are not readily seen in the experiments (Van Parijs and Vanderborght, 2017).

5. For a study focused on the global south on forms of production that go beyond the 'capitalist canon', see Sousa Santos (2006).

6. James Livingston's (2016) call to construct a world in which we can engage in activities that are meaningful beyond the domain of employment is situated in this same conceptual and political framework. In the same way, but with a stronger interest in institutional ways to collectively organise freer forms of work, William Clare Roberts (2017) recalls how the main objective of socialism was and is to work less *under capitalist tutelage*, where 'work' always tends to become 'excess work'.

7. See also Dagger (2006).

8. Srnicek and Williams (2015) insightfully point to all this, despite the fact that their proclamation about the need for 'a world without work' is something that, as has already been said, must be deeply questioned (Gourevitch, 2022).

9. Stuart White (2003: 171) gives an account of those authors – Ronald Dore or André Gorz in the 1980s – who have suggested a 'citizen service as a complement to a basic income'. Note, however, that, just as these authors present such a 'citizen service' as something that must accompany basic income *under any circumstances*, here it is stated that it must be considered *only if* some necessary tasks remain undone or, in other words, *only if* the social product is insufficient to universally cover the basic needs of the population as a whole. For a discussion of the (quite unlikely) possibility of the need for a 'national service' that is equally demanding for all people regardless of social or individual advantage, see Widerquist (2013, 2023).

Bibliography

Ablett, P., Morley, C. and Newcomb, M., 'Social Work, Human Services and Basic Income', in E. Klein, J. Mays and T. Dunlop (eds), *Implementing a Basic Income in Australia: Pathways Forward*, Cham, Switzerland: Palgrave Macmillan, 2019, pp. 215–35.

Aerts, E., Marx, I. and Verbist, G., 'Not That Basic: How Level, Design and Context Matter for the Redistributive Outcomes of Universal Basic Income', *IZA Discussion Paper Series*, 15952, 2023, pp. 1–33.

Alperovitz, G., 'On Liberty', in P. Parijs, J. Cohen and J. Rogers (eds), *What's Wrong with a Free Lunch?*, Boston: Beacon Press, 2001, pp. 106–10.

Anderson, E., 'Equality and Freedom in the Workplace: Recovering Republican Insights', *Social Philosophy and Policy*, 31(2), 2015, pp. 48–69.

Arcarons, J., Raventós, D. and Torrens, L., *Renta básica incondicional: una propuesta de financiación racional y justa*, Barcelona: Ediciones del Serbal, 2017.

Arendt, H., *The Human Condition*, Chicago: University of Chicago Press, 1958.

—, 'Reflections on Little Rock', *Dissent*, 6(1), 1959, pp. 45–56.

Argemí, L., 'La mano invisible y la divina providencia', in J. Claret Miranda (ed.), *Miscelánea Ernest Lluch*, Barcelona: Fundació Ernest Lluch, 2006, pp. 37–46.

Atkinson, A. B., 'The Case for a Participation Income', *The Political Quarterly*, 67(1), 1996, pp. 67–70.

Aznar, G., *Trabajar menos para trabajar todos*, Madrid: HOAC, 1994.

Barr, M., and Mackie, D., 'The Euro Area Adjustment: About Halfway There', *JP Morgan Global Issues*, May 2013, pp. 1–16.

Barragué, B., *Desigualdad e igualitarismo predistributivo*, Madrid: Centro de Estudios Políticos y Constitucionales, 2017.

Barry, B., *Why Social Justice Matters*, Cambridge: Polity Press, 2005.

Baum, G., *Karl Polanyi on Ethics and Economics*, Montreal: McGill-Queen's University Press, 1996.

Beard, C. A., and Beard, M. R., *America in Midpassage*, New York: Macmillan, 1939.

Bello, W., 'Capitalism's Crisis and Our Response', *Focus on the Global South*, 2009. http://focusweb.org/node/1486.

Benquet, M. and Bourgeron, T., *Alt-Finance: How the City of London Bought Democracy*, London: Pluto Press, 2022.

Bergmann, B. 'A Swedish-Style Welfare State or Basic Income: Which Should Have Priority?', *Politics & Society*, 32(1), 2004, pp. 107–18.

Berlin, I., 'Two Concepts of Liberty', in I. Berlin, *Four Essays on Liberty*, London: Oxford University Press, 1969 [1958].

Bertomeu, M. J., 'Republicanismo y propiedad', *El Viejo Topo*, 205–6, 2005, pp. 85–9.

—, 'Pobreza y propiedad: ¿Cara y cruz de la misma moneda? Una lectura desde el republicanismo kantiano', *Isegoría: Revista de Filosofía Moral y Política*, 57, 2017, pp. 477–504.

—, and Domènech, A., 'El republicanismo y la crisis del rawlsismo metodológico', *Isegoría: Revista de Filosofía Moral y Política*, 33, 2005, pp. 51–75.

—, and Raventós, D., 'Renta Básica y Renta Máxima: una concepción republicano-democrática', *Daimon: Revista Internacional de Filosofía*, 81, 2020, pp. 197–213.

Birnbaum, S., 'Introduction: Basic Income, Sustainability and Post-productivism', *Basic Income Studies*, 4(2), 2009, pp. 1–7.

—, *Basic Income Reconsidered. Social Justice, Liberalism, and the Demands of Equality*, New York, Palgrave Macmillan, 2012.

—, 'Basic Income', in *Oxford Research Encyclopedia of Politics*, 2016. http://politics. oxfordre.com/.

—, and Casassas, D., 'Social Republicanism and Basic Income', in S. White and D. Leighton (eds), *Building a Citizen Society: The Emerging Politics of Republican Democracy*, London: Lawrence & Wishart, 2008, pp. 75–82.

—, and De Wispelaere, J., 'Basic Income in the Capitalist Economy: The Mirage of "Exit" from Employment', *Basic Income Studies*, 11(1), 2016, pp. 61–74.

—, 'Exit Strategy or Exit Trap? Basic Income and the "Power to Say No" in the Age of Precarious Employment', *Socio-Economic Review*, 19(3), 2020, pp. 909–27.

Black, B., *La abolición del trabajo*, Logroño: Pepitas de Calabaza, 2013 [1985].

Blackstone, W., *Commentaries of the Laws of England* (ed. S. N. Katz, 4 vols), Chicago: University of Chicago Press, 1979 [1765–1769].

Blaschke, R., 'Sustainable Ecological Transition Is Impossible without Unconditional Social Security for All People', *Degrowth in Movements*, 2017. www.degrowth. info/en/dim/degrowth-in-movements/unconditional-basic-income/.

Borrell-Porta, M., de Quintana, J. and Segura, A., *Review of Evidence: Universal Basic Income Pilot Project, Review of Literature and Theories of Change*, Barcelona: Ivàlua, 2023a.

—, *Universal Basic Income Pilot Project in Catalonia: Proposed Design Methodology*, Barcelona: Ivàlua, 2023b.

Bosc, Y., *La Terreur des droits de l'homme: le républicanisme de Thomas Paine et le moment thermidorien*, Paris: Kimé, 2016.

—, 'L'Économie politique populaire de Robespierre', in M. Bellet and P. Solal (eds), *Républicanisme et économie politique*, Paris: Classiques Garnier, 2018.

Breen, K., 'Non-domination, Workplace Republicanism, and the Justification of Worker Voice and Control', *International Journal of Comparative Labour Law and Industrial Relations*, 33(2), 2017, pp. 419–40.

Bregman, R., *Utopia for Realists: The Case for a Universal Basic Income, Open Borders and a 15-Hour Workweek*, Amsterdam: De Correspondent, 2016.

Bruenig, M., 'The Rich Already Have a UBI', *Jacobin*, 2017. www.jacobinmag. com/2017/01/rich-universal-basic-income-piketty-passive-income-capital-income.

Bryan, A., 'Structural Domination and Freedom in the Labor Market: From Voluntariness to Independence', *American Political Science Review*, 117(2), 2023, pp. 692–704.

Büchs, M., 'Sustainable Welfare: How Do Universal Basic Income and Universal Basic Services Compare?', *Ecological Economics*, 189, 2021, pp. 1–9.

Calnitsky, D., 'Debating Basic Income', *Catalyst: A Journal of Theory and Strategy*, 1(3), 2017, pp. 62–91.

—, 'Does Basic Income Assume a Can Opener?', *Catalyst: A Journal of Theory and Strategy*, 2(3), 2018, pp. 136–55.

Cameron, D., 'The Big Society', speech, 2009. https://web.archive.org/web/201207 14070101/http://www.conservatives.com/News/Speeches/2009/11/David_ Cameron_The_Big_Society.asp.

Casal, P., 'Why Sufficiency Is Not Enough', *Ethics*, 117(2), 2007, pp. 296–326.

Casassas, D., 'Sociologías de la elección y nociones de libertad: la renta básica como proyecto republicano para sociedades de mercado', *Isegoría: Revista de Filosofía Moral y Política*, 33, 2005, pp. 235–48.

—, 'Basic Income and the Republican Ideal: Rethinking Material Independence in Contemporary Societies', *Basic Income Studies*, 2(2), 2007, pp. 1–7.

—, *La ciudad en llamas: la vigencia del republicanismo comercial de Adam Smith*, Barcelona: Montesinos, 2010.

—, 'La renta básica como vehículo de la democracia económica: relaciones de producción más justas para una ciudadanía sustantiva', in A. Comín Oliveres and L. Gervasoni Vila (eds), *Democracia económica: hacia una alternativa al capitalismo*, Barcelona: Icaria, 2011, pp. 521–8.

—, 'Adam Smith's Republican Moment: Lessons for Today's Emancipatory Thought', *Economic Thought: History, Philosophy and Methodology*, 2(2), 2013, pp. 1–19.

—, 'Economic Sovereignty as the Democratization of Work: The Role of Basic Income', *Basic Income Studies*, 11(1), 2016a, pp. 1–15.

—, 'La centralidad de los trabajos en la revolución democrática: ¿qué aporta la perspectiva de derechos?', in D. Casassas (ed.), *Revertir el guion: trabajos, derechos y libertad*, Madrid: Los Libros de la Catarata, 2016b, pp. 21–41.

—, '¿Por qué la renta básica?', in J. Arcarons, D. Raventós and L. Torrens (eds), *La renta básica incondicional: una propuesta de financiación racional y justa*, Barcelona: Ediciones del Serbal, 2017, pp. 7–18.

—, et al., 'Indignation and Claims for Economic Sovereignty in Europe and the Americas: Renewing the Project of Control over Production', in P. Wagner (ed.), *African, American and European Trajectories of Modernity: Past Oppression, Future Justice?* (Annual of European and Global Studies, vol. 2), Edinburgh: Edinburgh University Press, 2015, pp. 258–87.

—, and De Wispelaere, J., 'The Alaska Model: A Republican Perspective', in K. Widerquist and M. W. Howard (eds), *Alaska's Permanent Fund Dividend: Examining Its Suitability as a Model*, New York: Palgrave Macmillan, 2012, pp. 169–88.

—, and De Wispelaere, J., 'Republicanism and the Political Economy of Democracy', in *European Journal of Social Theory*, 19(2), 2016, pp. 283–300.

—, and Guerrero, D., 'De ingresos y pedazos de tierra: renta básica, predistribución y desmercantilización en el marco de economías políticas populares', *Política y Sociedad*, 59(2), 2022, pp. 1–16.

—, and Guerrero, D., 'Pre-distribution, Basic Income, and the Institutions of Economic Democracy', forthcoming.

—, and Loewe, G., 'Renta básica y fuerza negociadora de los trabajadores', in D. Raventós (ed.), *La renta básica: por una ciudadanía más libre, más igualitaria y más fraterna*, Barcelona: Ariel, 2001, pp. 205–22.

—, and Manjarín, E., 'La renta básica en los ciclos de protesta contemporáneos: propuestas constituyentes para la democratización de la vida (re)productiva', in *Educación Social: Revista de Intervención Socioeducativa*, 55, 2013, pp. 62–75.

—, and Mundó, J., 'Property as a Fiduciary Relationship and the Extension of Economic Democracy: What Role for Unconditional Basic Income?', *Theoria: A Journal of Social and Political Theory*, 69(2), 2022, pp. 74–96.

—, and Raventós, D., 'La renta básica como caja de resistencia: poder de negociación de los trabajadores y libertad como no dominación', in J. Giraldo (ed.), *La renta básica, más allá de la sociedad salarial*, Medellín: Escuela Nacional Sindical, 2003, pp. 107–28.

—, and Raventós, D., 'Propiedad y libertad republicana: la renta básica como derecho de existencia para el mundo contemporáneo', *SinPermiso*, 2, 2007, pp. 35–69.

—, Raventós, D. and Szlinder, M., 'Socialist Arguments for Basic Income', in M. Torry (ed.), *The Palgrave International Handbook of Basic Income*, New York: Palgrave Macmillan, 2019, pp. 459–76.

Castel, R., *Las metamorfosis de la cuestión social: una crónica del salariado*, Barcelona: Paidós, 1997.

Cicerchia, L., 'Structural Domination in the Labor Market', *European Journal of Political Theory*, 21(1), 2019, pp. 4–24.

Constant, B., 'De la liberté des Anciens comparée à celle des Modernes, París, Mille et Une Nuits', 2010 [1819].

Coote, A., and Percy, A., *The Case for Universal Basic Services*, Cambridge: Polity Press, 2020.

Coriat, B. (ed.), *Le retour des comuns: la crise de l'idéologie propriétaire*, Paris: Les Liens qui Libèrent, 2015.

Credit Suisse Research Institute, *The Global Wealth Report 2016*, 2016. www.credit-suisse.com/corporate/en/research/research-institute/publications.htm.

Dagger, R., 'Neo-republicanism and the Civic Economy', *Politics, Philosophy & Economics*, 5(2), 2006, pp. 151–73.

Dahl, R. A., *Polyarchy: Participation and Opposition*, New Haven: Yale University Press, 1971.

Davala, S., Jhabvala, R., Mehta, S. K. and Standing, G., *Basic Income: A Transformative Policy for India*, London and New Delhi: Bloomsbury, 2015.

Davis, M., *Prisoners of the American Dream: Politics and Economy in the History of the US Working Class*, London: Verso, 2000.

De Wispelaere, J., and Stirton, L., 'A Disarmingly Simple Idea? Practical Bottlenecks in the Implementation of a Universal Basic Income', *International Social Security Review*, 65(2), 2012, pp. 103–21.

Dejours, C., Deranty, J.-P., Renault, E. and Smith, N. H., *The Return of Work in Critical Theory: Self, Society, Politics*, New York: Columbia University Press, 2018.

Domènech, A., *De la ética a la política: de la razón erótica a la razón inerte*, Barcelona: Crítica, 1989.

—, ' ... Y fraternidad', *Isegoría: Revista de Filosofía Moral y Política*, 7, 1993, pp. 49–78.

—, *El eclipse de la fraternidad: una revisión republicana de la tradición socialista*, Barcelona: Crítica, 2004.

—, 'El socialismo y la herencia de la democracia republicana fraternal', *El Viejo Topo*, 205–6, 2005, pp. 90–6.

—, 'Ortega y el "niño mimado de la historia": O qué se puede aprender políticamente del uso incongruo de una metáfora conceptual', in R. R. Aramayo and J. F. Álvarez (eds), *Disenso e incertidumbre: un homenaje a Javier Muguerza*, Madrid: Consejo Superior de Investigaciones Científicas and Plaza y Valdés, 2006, pp. 341–78.

—, 'Democracia burguesa: nota sobre la génesis del oxímoron y la necedad del regalo', *Viento Sur*, 100, 2009, pp. 95–100.

—, 'Republicanism, Natural Right, Political Economy and Free Markets: The Astonishing Case of Léon Walras', lecture given at the international symposium 'Cultures des républicanismes: pratiques, représentations, concepts, de la Révolution anglaise à aujourd'hui', Universidad de Rouen, 21–2 November 2013.

—, 'Prólogo', in X. M. Beiras (ed.), *Exhortación a la desobediencia*, Santiago de Compostela: Laiovento, 2015, pp. 9–35.

—, and Bertomeu, M. J., 'Property, Freedom and Money. Modern Capitalism Reassessed', *European Journal of Social Theory*, 16(2), 2016, pp. 245–63.

—, and Raventós, D., 'Property and Republican Freedom: An Institutional Approach to Basic Income', *Basic Income Studies*, 2(2), 2007, pp. 1–8.

Edmundson, W. A., *John Rawls: Reticent Socialist*, Cambridge: Cambridge University Press, 2017.

Eeckhout, J., *The Profit Paradox: How Thriving Firms Threaten the Future of Work*, Princeton: Princeton University Press, 2021.

Elster, J., 'Self-Realization in Work and Politics', *Social Philosophy & Policy*, 3(2), 1986, pp. 97–126.

—, *Explaining Social Behavior: More Nuts and Bolts for the Social Sciences*, New York: Cambridge University Press, 2007.

Engels, F., *The Condition of the Working Class in England*, Moscow: Progress Publishers, 1973 [1845]. www.marxists.org/archive/marx/works/1845/condition-working-class/cho5.htm.

Esping-Andersen, G., *The Three Worlds of Welfare Capitalism*, Princeton: Princeton University Press, 1990.

Fairchild, C., 'Middle-Class Decline Mirrors the Fall of Unions in One Chart', *The Huffington Post*, 18 September 2013. www.huffingtonpost.com/2013/09/18/union-membership-middle-class-income_n_3948543.html.

Federici, S., *Calibán y la bruja: mujeres, cuerpo y acumulación primitiva*, Madrid: Traficantes de Sueños, 2010.

—, *Revolución en punto cero: trabajo doméstico, reproducción y luchas feministas*, Madrid: Traficantes de Sueños, 2013.

Fitzpatrick, T., *Freedom and Security: An Introduction to the Basic Income Debate*, New York: Palgrave Macmillan, 1999.

Flanagan, O., *Self Expressions: Mind, Morals and the Meaning of Life*, Oxford: Oxford University Press, 1996.

Foucault, M., *El nacimiento de la biopolítica*, Madrid: Akal, 2009 (in English, *The Birth of Biopolitics: Lectures at the College of France, 1978 - 1979*, London: Palgrave Macmillan, 2008, translation, Graham Burchell).

Francisco, A. de, 'A Republican Interpretation of the Late Rawls', *Journal of Political Philosophy*, 14(3), 2006, pp. 270–88.

Frank, R. H., and Cook, P. J., *The Winner-Take-All Society: Why the Few at the Top Get So Much More than the Rest of Us*, New York: Penguin, 1996.

Franklin, B., *Memoirs of Benjamin Franklin*, 2 vols, New York: Harper & Brothers, 1839.

Frase, P., *Four Futures: Life after Capitalism*, New York: Verso, 2016.

Frayne, D., *The Refusal of Work: The Theory and Practice of Resistance to Work*, London: Zed Books, 2015.

Fumagalli, A. and Intelligence Precaria, 'La proposta di welfare metropolitano: Quali prospettive per l'Italia e per l'area milanese', *Quaderni di San Precario*, 1, 2011, pp. 224–59.

Gädeke, D., 'From Neo-Republicanism to Critical Republicanism', in B. Leipold, K. Nabulsi and S. White (eds), *Radical Republicanism: Recovering the Tradition's Popular Heritage*, Oxford: Oxford University Press, 2020, pp. 23–46.

Garcés, M., *Un mundo común*, Barcelona: Bellaterra, 2013.

—, 'Trabajo y vidas en común', in D. Casassas (ed.), *Revertir el guion: trabajos, derechos y libertad*, Madrid: Los Libros de la Catarata, 2016, pp. 59–71.

Garzón, A., and Guamán, A. (eds), *El trabajo garantizado: una propuesta necesaria frente al desempleo y la precarización*, Madrid: Akal, 2015.

Gauthier, F., 'À l'origine de la théorie physiocratique du capitalisme, la plantation esclavagiste: L'expérience de Lemercier de la Rivière, intendant de la Martinique', *Actuel Marx*, 32, 2002, pp. 51–72.

Gheaus, A. and Herzog, L. 'The Goods of Work (Other than Money!)', *Journal of Social Philosophy*, 47(1), 2016, pp. 70–89.

Gómez Jiménez, N., 'La revolución democrática será diversa y accesible o no será', in Fundación de los Comunes (ed.), *Hacia nuevas instituciones democráticas: diferencia, sostenimiento de la vida y políticas públicas*, Madrid: Traficantes de Sueños, 2016, pp. 159–74.

González-Ricoy, I., 'The Republican Case for Workplace Democracy', *Social Theory and Practice*, 40(2), 2014, pp. 232–54.

Goodhart, M., '"None So Poor That He Is Compelled to Sell Himself": Democracy, Subsistence, and Basic Income', in S. Hertel and L. Minkler (eds), *Economic Rights: Conceptual, Measurement, and Policy Issues*, Cambridge: Cambridge University Press, 2007, pp. 94–114.

Goody, J., *The Theft of History*, Cambridge: Cambridge University Press, 2006.

Gorz, A., *Paths to Paradise*, London: Pluto Press, 1985.

—, *Farewell to the Working Class*, London: Pluto Press, 1987.

—, *Misères du présent, richesse du possible*, París: Galilée, 1997.

Gourevitch, A., 'Labour Republicanism and the Transformation of Work', *Political Theory*, 41(4), 2013, pp. 591–617.

—, *From Slavery to the Cooperative Commonwealth: Labor and Republican Liberty in the Nineteenth Century*, New York: Cambridge University Press, 2014.

—, 'The Limits of a Basic Income: Means and Ends of Workplace Democracy', *Basic Income Studies*, 11(1), 2016, pp. 17–28.

—, 'Post-Work Socialism?', *Catalyst: A Journal of Theory and Strategy*, 6(2), 2022, pp. 8–48.

—, and Stanczyk, L., 'The Basic Income Illusion', *Catalyst: A Journal of Theory and Strategy*, 1(4), 2018, pp. 151–77.

Haagh, L., 'Basic Income, Social Democracy and Control over Time', *Policy & Politics*, 39(1), 2011, pp. 43–66.

—, 'Basic Income as a Pivoting Reform', *Nature Human Behaviour*, 1(125), 2017, pp. 1–3.

—, 'Basic Income and Institutional Transformation', in P. Van Parijs (ed.), *Basic Income and the Left: A European Debate*, London: Social Europe, 2018, pp. 78–88.

—, *The Case for Universal Basic Income*, Cambridge: Polity Press, 2019.

Hacker, J. S., 'The Institutional Foundations of Middle-Class Democracy', in Policy Network (ed.), *Priorities for a New Political Economy: Memos to the Left*, London: Policy Network, 2011.

—, and Pierson, P., 'Winner-Take-All Politics: Public Policy, Political Organization, and the Precipitous Rise of Top Incomes in the United States', *Politics & Society*, 38(2), 2010, pp. 152–204.

Han, B., *La sociedad del cansancio*, Barcelona: Herder, 2012.

Harrington, J., *The Commonwealth of Oceana and a System of Politics* (ed. J. G. A. Pocock), Cambridge and New York: Cambridge University Press, 1992 [1656–1747].

Harvey, D., *The New Imperialism*, Oxford: Oxford University Press, 2003.

—, *Breve historia del neoliberalismo*, Madrid: Akal, 2007.

Harvey, P., *Securing the Right to Employment: Social Welfare Policy and the Unemployed in the United States*, Princeton: Princeton University Press, 1989.

Heckman, J., 'Promoting Social Mobility', *Boston Review*, 2012. www.bostonreview. net/forum/promoting-social-mobility-james-heckman.

Herrero, Y., 'Apuntes ecofeministas para reconsiderar el trabajo humano', in D. Casassas (ed.), *Revertir el guion: trabajos, derechos y libertad*, Madrid: Los Libros de la Catarata, 2016, pp. 123–33.

Herzog, L., 'Basic Income and the Ideal of Epistemic Equality', *Basic Income Studies*, 11(1), 2016, pp. 29–38.

Hirschman, A. O., *Exit, Voice, and Loyalty: Responses to Decline in Firms, Organizations, and States*, Cambridge, MA: Harvard University Press, 1970.

Holmes, S., and Sunstein, C. R., *The Cost of Rights: Why Liberty Depends on Taxes*, New York and London: W. W. Norton, 2000.

Horgan, A., *Lost in Work: Escaping Capitalism*, London: Pluto Press, 2021.

Howard, M.W., *Self-management and the Crisis of Socialism: The Rose in the Fist of the Present*, Lanham, MD: Rowman & Littlefield, 2000.

—, Pinto, J. and Schachtschneider, U., 'Ecological Effects of Basic Income', in M. Torry (ed.), *The Palgrave International Handbook of Basic Income*, New York: Palgrave Macmillan, 2019, pp. 111–32.

Hsieh, N., 'Survey Article: Justice in Production', *Journal of Political Philosophy*, 16, 2008, pp. 72–100.

Imbens, G. W., Rubin, D. B. and Sacerdote, B. I., 'Estimating the Effect of Unearned Income on Labor Earnings, Savings, and Consumption: Evidence from a Survey of Lottery Players', *American Economic Review*, 91(4), 2001, pp. 778–94.

Jäger, A., and Zamora Vargas, D., *Welfare for Markets. A Global History of Basic Income*, Chicago: Chicago University Press, 2023.

Jayadev, A., and Bowles, S., 'Guard Labor', *Journal of Development Economics*, 79(2), 2006, pp. 328–48.

Jensen, M. H., et al., 'A Budget-Neutral Universal Basic Income', *AEI Economics Working Papers*, 10, 2017, pp. 1–19.

Joerges, C., Strath, B. and Wagner, P. (eds), *The Economy as a Polity: The Political Constitution of Contemporary Capitalism*, London: UCL, 2005.

Jordan, B., 'Basic Income and the Common Good', in P. Van Parijs (ed.), *Arguing for Basic Income: Ethical Foundations for a Radical Reform*, London: Verso, 1992, pp. 155–77.

Kalecki, M., 'Political Aspects of Full Employment', *The Political Quarterly*, 14(4), 1943, pp. 322–30.

Katsiaficas, G., *The Subversion of Politics: European Autonomous Social Movements and the Decolonization of Everyday Life*, Edinburgh: AK Press, 2006.

Kaye, F. B., 'Introducción', in B. Mandeville, *La fábula de las abejas (o los vicios privados hacen la prosperidad pública)*, Madrid: Fondo de Cultura Económica, 1997 [1729], pp. xiii–xxvii.

Kenworthy, L., 'What's Wrong with Predistribution', *Juncture*, 20(2), 2013, pp. 111–17.

Ketterer, H., 'Living Differently? A Feminist-Bourdieusian Analysis of the Transformative Power of Basic Income', *The Sociological Review*, 69(6), 2021, pp. 1309–24.

Keynes, J. M., *The General Theory of Employment, Interest and Money*, New York: Palgrave Macmillan, 2007 [1936].

Klosse, S., 'Flexibility and Security: A Feasible Combination?', *European Journal of Social Security*, 5(3), 2003, pp. 191–213.

Krätke, M., 'Basic Income, Commons and Commodities: The Public Domain Revisited', in G. Standing (ed.), *Promoting Income Security as a Right: Europe and North America*, London: Anthem Press, 2004, pp. 129–43.

Laguna, H., '"¡Mamá, puedo ser artista!" Renta básica y trabajo cultural', *Nativa*, 2017. www.nativa.cat/2017/04/mama-puedo-ser-artista-renta-basica-y-trabajo-cultural/.

Laín, B., 'Política basada en evidencia y experimentos de renta básica: el caso de Barcelona', in J. Ponce and M. Villoria Mendieta (eds), *Anuario del Buen Gobierno y de la Calidad de la Regulación 2022*, Barcelona: Fundación Democracia y Gobierno Local, 2023, pp. 227–66.

—, and Julià, A., 'Why Do Poor People Not Take up Benefits? Evidence from the Barcelona's B-MINCOME Experiment', *Journal of Social Policy*, 2022, pp. 1–22. https://doi.org/10.1017/S0047279422000575.

Lakoff, G., and Johnson, M., *Metáforas de la vida cotidiana*, Madrid: Cátedra, 1986.

Lange, O., 'On the Economic Theory of Socialism', in O. Lange, F. M. Taylor and B. E. Lippincott (eds), *On the Economic Theory of Socialism*, Minneapolis: University of Minnesota Press, 1938, pp. 55–143.

Langridge, N., Büchs, M. and Howard, N. (2022), 'An Ecological Basic Income? Examining the Ecological Credentials of Basic Income through a Review of Selected Pilot Interventions', *Basic Income Studies*, 18(1), 2022, pp. 1–41.

Laval, C., and Dardot, P., *La nueva razón del mundo. Ensayo sobre la sociedad neoliberal*, Barcelona: Gedisa, 2013.

Lazar, O., 'Work, Domination, and the False Hope of Universal Basic Income', *Res Publica*, 27, 2021, pp. 427–46.

Lazar, S., *How We Struggle: A Political Anthropology of Labour*, London: Pluto, 2023.

Leighton, D., 'Searching for Politics in an Uncertain World: Interview with Zygmunt Bauman', *Renewal: A Journal of Labour Politics*, 10(1), 2002, pp. 14–18.

Leipold, B., 'Marx's Social Republic: Radical Republicanism and the Political Institutions of Socialism', in B. Leipold, K. Nabulsi and S. White (eds), *Radical Republicanism: Recovering the Tradition's Popular Heritage*, Oxford: Oxford University Press, 2020, pp. 172–93.

—, Nabulsi, K. and White, S. (eds), *Radical Republicanism: Recovering the Tradition's Popular Heritage*, Oxford: Oxford University Press, 2020.

Leo XIII, *Rerum novarum: sobre la situación de los obreros*, 1891. http://w2.vatican.va/content/leo-xiii/es/encyclicals/documents/hf_l-xiii_enc_15051891_rerum-novarum.html (in English, www.vatican.va/content/leo-xiii/en/encyclicals/documents/hf_l-xiii_enc_15051891_rerum-novarum.html).

Lerner, A. P., 'The Economics and Politics of Consumer Sovereignty', *American Economic Review*, 62(1/2), 1972, pp. 258–66.

Leuchtenburg, W. E., *The FDR Years: On Roosevelt and His Legacy*, New York: Columbia University Press, 1995.

—, *Franklin D. Roosevelt and the New Deal, 1932–1940*, New York: Harper Perennial, 2009.

Livingston, J., *No More Work: Why Full Employment Is a Bad Idea*, Chapel Hill: University of North Carolina Press, 2016.

Lo Vuolo, R. (ed.), *Citizen's Income and Welfare Regimes in Latin America: From Cash Transfers to Rights*, New York: Palgrave Macmillan, 2013.

Locke, J., *Second Treatise on Government* (ed. R. Cox), Wheeling: Harlan Davidson, 1982 [1689].

Lovett, F., *A General Theory of Domination and Justice*, New York: Oxford University Press, 2010.

Mandeville, B., *La fábula de las abejas: los vicios privados hacen la prosperidad pública*, Madrid: Fondo de Cultura Económica, 1997 [1714] (in English: *The Fable of The Bees: or, Private Vices, Publick Benefits*, https://oll.libertyfund.org/title/kaye-the-fable-of-the-bees-or-private-vices-publick-benefits-vol-1).

Manjarín, E., and Szlinder, M., 'A Marxist Argumentative Scheme on Basic Income and Wage Share in an Anti-capitalist Agenda', *Basic Income Studies*, 11(1), 2016, pp. 49–59.

Marston, G., 'Greening the Australian Welfare State: Can Basic Income Play a Role?', in J. Mays, G. Marston and J. Tomlinson (eds), *Basic Income in Australia and New Zealand: Perspectives from the Neoliberal Frontier*, New York: Palgrave Macmillan, 2016.

Martínez-Cava, J., *Gorros frigios en la Guerra Fría: El socialismo republicano de E.P. Thompson*, Barcelona: Universitat de Barcelona, 2020.

Marx, K., 'Instructions for the Delegates of the Provisional General Council: The Different Questions', *Der Verbote*, 10 and 11, 1866. www.marxists.org/archive/marx/works/download/Marx_The_First_International.pdf.

—, *Grundrisse* (translated by Martin Nicolaus), London: Penguin Books in association with *New Left Review*, 1973, www.marxists.org/archive/marx/works/download/pdf/grundrisse.pdf (*Grundrisse der Kritik der Politischen Ökonomie*, Berlín: Dietz Verlag, 1953 [1857–9]).

—, *Manuscritos económico-filosóficos de 1844*, Barcelona: Grijalbo, 1975 [1844] (in English: *Economic and Philosophic Manuscripts of 1844*, Moscow: Progress Publishers, 1959, www.marxists.org/archive/marx/works/1844/manuscripts/preface.htm).

—, *El capital: crítica de la economía política*, 3 vols, Mexico City: Fondo de Cultura Económica, 1976 [1867–94].

—, *Teorías sobre la plusvalía, parte I*, OME 45, Barcelona, Buenos Aires and Mexico City: Crítica-Grijalbo, 1977 [1862] (in English: *Theories of Surplus Value*, 1863, www.marxists.org/archive/marx/works/1863/theories-surplus-value/).

—, and Engels, F., *La ideología alemana*, Barcelona: Grijalbo, 1970 [1844–5] (in English: *A Critique of the German Ideology*, Moscow: Progress Publishers, 1968, www.marxists.org/archive/marx/works/download/Marx_The_German_Ideology.pdf).

—, *Crítica del programa de Gotha; Crítica del Programa de Erfurt*, Madrid: Fundación Federico Engels, 2004 [1875–91] (in English: *Critique of the Gotha Program*, www.marxists.org/archive/marx/works/1875/gotha/cho1.htm).

Mason, P., *Postcapitalism: A Guide to Our Future*, London: Allen Lane, 2015.

Mattei, U., *Beni comuni: un manifesto*, Roma and Bari: Laterza, 2011.

Mau, S., *Mute Compulsion: A Marxist Theory of the Economic Power of Capital*, London and New York: Verso, 2023.

Mazzucato, M., 'Rediscovering Public Wealth Creation', *Project Syndicate*, 2017. www.project-syndicate.org/onpoint/growth-and-public-sector-investment-by-mariana-mazzucato-2017–12?barrier=accesspaylog.

—, *The Value of Everything: Making and Taking in the Global Economy*, New York: PublicAffairs, 2018.

McCormick, J. P., *Machiavellian Democracy*, New York: Cambridge University Press, 2011.

McQuaig, L., and Brooks, N., *El problema de los super-millonarios. Cómo se han apropiado del mundo los super-ricos y cómo podemos recuperarlo*, Madrid: Capitán Swing, 2014.

Meade, J., *Efficiency, Equality, and the Ownership of Property*, London: George Allen & Unwin, 1964.

—, *Agathatopia: The Economics of Partnership*, Aberdeen: Aberdeen University Press, 1989.

Meiksins Wood, E., 'Why It Matters', *London Review of Books*, 30(18), 25 September 2008. www.lrb.co.uk/the-paper/v30/n18/ellen-meiksins-wood/why-it-matters.

Miguel, A. de, 'Participación, deliberación y excelencia. En torno a la filosofía política de John Stuart Mill', *Isegoría: Revista de Filosofía Moral y Política*, 44, 2011, pp. 73–88.

Millar, J., *The Origin of the Distinction of Ranks*, Bristol: Thoemmes Press, 1990 [1771].

Mises, L. von, *Human Action, A Treatise on Economics*, 4 vols, Indianapolis: Liberty Fund, 2007 [1949].

Morales, L., 'The Democratic Case for a Basic Income', *Law, Ethics and Philosophy*, 6, 2019, pp. 120–37.

Moreno Colom, S., 'Trabajo y tiempo: una controversia de género', in D. Casassas (ed.), *Revertir el guion: trabajos, derechos y libertad*, Madrid: Los Libros de la Catarata, 2016, pp. 134–45.

Moruno, J., *La fábrica del emprendedor: trabajo y política en la empresa-mundo*, Madrid: Akal, 2015.

Mulvale, J.P., 'Social-Ecological Transformation and the Necessity of Universal Basic Income', *Social Alternatives*, 38(2), 2019, pp. 39–46.

Mundó, J., 'Political Freedom in Locke's Republicanism', in Y. Bosc, R. Dalisson, J.-Y. Frétigné, C. Hamel and C. Lounissi (eds), *Cultures des républicanismes: pratiques-représentations-concepts de la Révolution anglaise à aujourd'hui*, Paris: Kimé, 2015, pp. 103–16.

—, 'La constitución fiduciaria de la libertad política (por qué son importantes las coyunturas interpretativas en la filosofía política)', *Isegoría: Revista de Filosofía Moral y Política*, 57, 2017, pp. 433–54.

Murray, C., *In Our Hands: A Plan to Replace the Welfare State*, Washington, DC: The American Enterprise Institute Press, 2006.

Murray, M. J., and Forstater, M. (eds), *The Job Guarantee: Toward True Full Employment*, New York: Palgrave Macmillan, 2013.

Naím, M., *El fin del poder: empresas que se hunden, militares derrotados, papas que renuncian y gobiernos impotentes: cómo el poder ya no es lo que era*, Barcelona: Debate, 2013.

New Economics Foundation and Ecopolítica, *Veintiuna horas: una semana laboral más corta para prosperar en el siglo xxi*, Barcelona: Icaria, 2012.

Offe, C., 'A Non-productivist Design for Social Policies', in P. Van Parijs (ed.), *Arguing for Basic Income: Ethical Foundations for a Radical Reform*, London: Verso, 1992, pp. 61–78.

O'Neill, M., and Williamson, T., 'The Promise of Pre-distribution', *Policy Network* (2012a). www.policy-network.net/pno_detail.aspx?ID=4262&title=The+promise+of+pre-distribution.

—, and Williamson, T. (eds), *Property-Owning Democracy: Rawls and beyond*, Oxford: Wiley-Blackwell, 2012b.

Ostrom, E., *Governing the Commons: The Evolution of Institutions for Collective Action*, Cambridge and New York: Cambridge University Press, 2015 [1990].

Paine, T., 'Agrarian Justice', in *The Life and Major Writings of Thomas Paine* (ed. P. S. Foner), New York: Citadel Press, 1974 [1791], pp. 605–23.

Pateman, C., 'Democratizing Citizenship: Some Advantages of a Basic Income', in E. O. Wright (ed.), *Redisigning Distribution: Basic Income and Stakeholder Grants as Cornerstones for an Egalitarian Capitalism*, London and New York: Verso, 2006, pp. 101–19.

Pérez Orozco, A., *Subversión feminista de la economía: aportes para un debate sobre el conflicto capital-vida*, Madrid: Traficantes de Sueños, 2014.

Pettit, P., *Republicanism: A Theory of Freedom and Government*, Oxford: Oxford University Press, 1997.

—, *A Theory of Freedom: From the Psychology to the Politics of Agency*, Oxford: Oxford University Press, 2001.

—, 'Freedom in the Market', *Politics, Philosophy & Economics*, 5(2), 2006, pp. 131–49.

—, *On the People's Terms: A Republican Theory and Model of Democracy*, Cambridge: Cambridge University Press, 2012.

—, *Just Freedom: A Moral Compass for the Modern World*, New York and London: W. W. Norton, 2014.

Piketty, T., *Capital in the Twenty-First Century*, Cambridge, MA: Harvard University Press, 2014.

Pinto, J., 'Green Republicanism and the Shift to Post-productivism: A Defence of an Unconditional Basic Income', *Res Publica*, 26(2), 2020a, pp. 257–74.

—, 'Environmentalism, Ecologism, and Basic Income', *Basic Income Studies*, 15(1), 2020b, pp. 1–12.

Pisarello, G., *Un largo Termidor: la ofensiva del constitucionalismo antidemocrático*, Madrid: Trotta, 2011.

—, *Procesos constituyentes: caminos para la ruptura democrática*, Madrid: Trotta, 2014.

Pizzigati, S., 'The Corporate Pay Gap: Do We Need a Maximum Wage?', *Perspectives on Work*, 12(1–2), 2009, pp. 40–2.

—, *The Case for a Maximum Wage*, Cambridge: Polity Press, 2018.

Polanyi, K., *The Great Transformation: The Political and Economic Origins of Our Time*, Boston: Beacon Press, 1944.

Pradel Miquel, M., and García Cabeza, M., 'Innovación social en las ciudades españolas: la centralidad de la gobernanza local y ciudadana', in M. Pradel Miquel and M. García Cabeza (eds), *El momento de la ciudadanía: innovación social y gobernanza urbana en Barcelona, Bilbao, Madrid y Zaragoza*, Madrid: Los Libros de la Catarata, 2018, pp. 13–31.

Raes, K., 'Basic Income and Social Power', in K. Widerquist, J. A. Noguera, Y. Vanderborght and J. De Wispelaere (eds), *Basic Income: An Anthology of Contemporary Research*, New York: Wiley-Blackwell, 2013 [1988], pp. 246–54.

Ramonet, I., 'Las cuatro cosas que el papa Francisco les dice a los pobres', *Le Monde Diplomatique* (Spanish edition), 254, 2016, pp. 1 and 12.

Ramos, F., 'Políticas activas de empleo y renta básica: ¿soluciones sustitutivas o complementarias?', in D. Casassas and D. Raventós (eds), *La renta básica en la era de las grandes desigualdades*, Barcelona: Montesinos, 2011, pp. 137–67.

Raventós, D., *El derecho a la existencia: la propuesta del subsidio universal garantizado*, Barcelona: Ariel, 1999.

—, *Las condiciones materiales de la libertad*, Barcelona: El Viejo Topo, 2007 (in English: *Basic Income: The Material Conditions of Freedom*, London, Pluto Press, 2007).

—, *Renta básica contra la incertidumbre*, Barcelona: RBA, 2017.

—, and Casassas, D., 'Republicanism and Basic Income: The Articulation of the Public Sphere from the Repoliticization of the Private Sphere', in G. Standing (ed.), *Promoting Income Security as a Right: Europe and North America*, London: Anthem Press, 2004, pp. 229–51.

—, and Wark, J., *Against Charity*, Petrolia, CA: AK Press & Counterpunch, 2018.

Raventós, S., 'Crisis, salud mental y renta básica', in D. Casassas and D. Raventós (eds), *La renta básica en la era de las grandes desigualdades*, Barcelona: Montesinos, 2011, pp. 236–59.

—, 'Desigualdad socioeconómica y salud mental: la propuesta de una renta básica para proteger y promover la salud mental', *SinPermiso*, 2016. www.sinpermiso. info/textos/desigualdad-socioeconomica-y-salud-mental-la-propuesta-de-una-renta-basica-para-proteger-y-promover.

Rawls, J., 'The Priority of Right and Ideas of the Good', *Philosophy and Public Affairs*, 17, 1988, pp. 251–76.

—, *Justice as Fairness: A Restatement*, Cambridge, MA: Harvard University Press, 2001.

Revelli, M., 'La prima generazione arrabbiata del post-crescita', *Democrazia nella Comunicazione*, 2010. www.megachip.info.

Rey Pérez, J. L., *El derecho al trabajo y el ingreso básico: ¿cómo garantizar el derecho al trabajo?*, Madrid: Dykinson, 2007.

Riutort, S., *Energía para la democracia: la cooperativa Som Energia como laboratorio social*, Madrid: Fuhem Ecosocial and Los Libros de la Catarata, 2016.

Roberts, M., 'Basic Income – Too Basic, Not Radical Enough', *The Next Recession*, 2016. https://thenextrecession.wordpress.com/2016/10/23/basic-income-too-basic-not-radical-enough/.

Roberts, W. C., *Marx's Inferno: The Political Theory of Capital*, Princeton: Princeton University Press, 2017.

Robeyns, I., 'Having Too Much', in J. Knight and M. Schwartzberg (eds), *NOMOS LVII: Wealth Yearbook of the American Society for Political and Legal Philosophy*, New York: NYU Press, 2016, pp. 1–44.

Rodríguez López, E., *La política en el ocaso de la clase media: el ciclo 15M-Podemos*, Madrid: Traficantes de Sueños, 2016.

Roemer, J. E., *A Future for Socialism*, Cambridge, MA: Harvard University Press, 1994.

Russell, B., *Roads to Freedom: Socialism, Anarchism and Syndicalism*, London: Unwin Books, 1966 [1918].

—, *In Prise of Idleness: And Other Essays*, London and New York: Routledge, 2004 [1935].

Samuelson, P., 'Wages and Interest: A Modern Dissection of Marxian Economic Models', *The American Economic Review*, 47(6), 1957, pp. 884–912.

Sandel, M., *What Money Can't Buy: The Moral Limits of Markets*, New York: Farrar, Straus and Giroux, 2012.

Santens, S., 'How to Calculate the Cost of Universal Basic Income (Hint: It's Not as Easy as You Might Think)', 2022. www.scottsantens.com/how-to-calculate-the-cost-of-universal-basic-income-ubi/.

Sculos, B. W., 'Socialism and Universal Basic Income', *Class, Race and Corporate Power*, 6(1), 2018, pp. 1–6.

Sempere, J., 'Trabajo y medio ambiente: tensiones y oportunidades en la transición verde', in D. Casassas (ed.), *Revertir el guion: trabajos, derechos y libertad*, Madrid: Los Libros de la Catarata, 2016, pp. 161–71.

Sennett, R., *The Corrosion of Character: The Personal Consequences of Work in the New Capitalism*, New York and London: W. W. Norton, 1999.

Shadab, M., and Koshy, T., *Understanding the Characteristics of the Sumangali Scheme in Tamil Nadu Textile and Garment Industry and Supply Chain Linkages*, Washington, DC: Fair Labor Association, 2012.

Simon, W. H., 'Social-Republican Property', *UCLA Law Review*, 38, 1991, pp. 1335–413.

Skinner, Q., 'Meaning and Understanding in the History of Ideas', *History and Theory*, 8(1), 1969, pp. 3–53.

Smith, A., *The Theory of Moral Sentiments*, (ed. D. D. Raphael and A. L. Macfie) Indianapolis: Liberty Fund, 1976 [1759].

—, *Lectures on Jurisprudence* (ed. R. L. Meek, D. D. Raphael and P. Stein), Indianapolis: Liberty Fund, 1978 [1762–6].

—, *An Inquiry into the Nature and Causes of the Wealth of Nations* (ed. R. Campbell and A. S. Skinner, 2 vols), Indianapolis: Liberty Fund., 1981 [1776].

Sorscher, S., 'We All Do Better When We All Do Better', *Huffington Post*, 3 May 2012. www.huffingtonpost.com/stansorscher/we-all-do-better-when-we-all-do-better_b_1469635.html.

Sousa Santos, B. de (ed.), *Another Production Is Possible: Beyond the Capitalist Canon*, London and New York: Verso, 2006.

—, 'Constitución y hegemonía: Luchas contra la dominación global', in *Chasqui: Revista Latinoamericana de Comunicación*, 136, 2017, pp. 13–31.

Srnicek, N, and Williams, A., *Inventing the Future: Postcapitalism and a World without Work*, London: Verso, 2015.

Standing, G., *Beyond the New Paternalism: Basic Security as Equality*, London and New York: Verso, 2002.

—, *Work after Globalization: Building Occupational Citizenship*, Cheltenham: Edward Elgar, 2009.

—, *The Precariat: The New Dangerous Class*, London: Bloomsbury, 2011.

—, *A Precariat Charter: From Denizens to Citizens*, London and New York: Bloomsbury Academic, 2014.

—, *The Corruption of Capitalism: Why Rentiers Thrive and Work Does Not Pay*, London: Biteback, 2016.

—, *Basic Income: And How We Can Make It Happen*, London: Penguin, 2017.

—, *Plunder of the Commons: A Manifesto for Sharing Public Wealth*, London: Penguin, 2019.

—, 'The Case for a Basic Income', *Resilience*, 2020. www.resilience.org/stories/2020–11–24/the-case-for-a-basic-income/.

—, *The Blue Commons: Rescuing the Economy of the Sea*, London: Penguin, 2022.

Stern, A., *Raising the Floor: How a Universal Basic Income Can Renew Our Economy and Rebuild the American Dream*, New York: Public Affairs, 2016.

Swaton, S., 'For an Ecological Transition Income', *Green European Journal*, 2018. www.greeneuropeanjournal.eu/for-an-ecological-transition-income/.

Szreter, S., 'How Seriously Should We Take Universal Basic Income?', *The Political Quarterly*, 93(3), 2022, pp. 517–23.

Taylor, R. S., 'Market Freedom as Antipower', *American Political Science Review*, 107(3), 2013, pp. 593–602.

—, *Exit Left: Markets and Mobility in Republican Thought*, Oxford: Oxford University Press, 2017.

Taylor-Gooby, P., 'Why Do People Stigmatise the Poor at a Time of Rapidly Increasing Inequality, and What Can Be Done about It?', *The Political Quarterly*, 84(1), 2013, pp. 31–42.

Tena Camporesi, A., *Los orígenes revolucionarios de la renta básica. Textos de Thomas Paine y Thomas Spence del último tercio del siglo XVIII*, Madrid: Postmetropolis Editorial, 2021.

Thomas, A., *Republic of Equals: Predistribution and Property-Owning Democracy*, Oxford: Oxford University Press, 2016.

Thompson, E. P. *The Poverty of Theory and other Essays*, London: Monthly Review Press, 1978.

—, *Customs in Common: Studies in Traditional Popular Culture*, London: Merlin Press, 1991.

—, *La formación de la clase obrera en Inglaterra*, Madrid: Capitán Swing, 2012 [1963].

Tierney, B., *The Idea of Natural Rights. Studies on Natural Rights, Natural Law, and Church Law 1150–1625*, Grand Rapids, MI and Cambridge: William B. Eerdmans, 1997.

Toledano, D., 'La larga marcha por la renta garantizada de ciudadanía', *Viento Sur*, 25 August 2017. http://vientosur.info/spip.php?article12942.

Torrens, L., and González de Molina, E., 'La garantía del empleo libre: desempleo, robotización y reducción de la jornada laboral', *SinPermiso*, 2016. www.sinpermiso.info/textos/la-garantia-del-tiem¬po-libre-desempleo-robotizacion-y-reduccion-de-la-jornada-laboral-parte-1.

Tuck, R., *Natural Right Theories: Their Origin and Development*, Cambridge: Cambridge University Press, 1979.

Van der Veen, R. J., and Van Parijs, P., 'A Capitalist Road to Communism', *Theory and Society*, 15, 1986, pp. 635–55.

Van Parijs, P., 'The Second Marriage of Justice and Efficiency', *Journal of Social Policy*, 19, 1990, pp. 1–25.

—, *Real Freedom for All: What If Anything Can Justify Capitalism?*, Oxford: Oxford University Press, 1995.

—, 'A Basic Income for All', in J. Cohen and J. Rogers (eds), *What's Wrong with a Free Lunch?*, Boston: Beacon Press, 2001, pp. 3–28.

—, 'Basic Income: A Simple and Powerful Idea for the Twenty-First Century', in E. O. Wright (ed.), *Redesigning Distribution: Basic Income and Stakeholder Grants as Cornerstones for an Egalitarian Capitalism*, London and New York: Verso, 2006, pp. 3–42.

—, 'Political Ecology: From Autonomous Sphere to Basic Income', *Basic Income Studies*, 4(2), 2009, pp. 1–9.

—, 'De chacun (volontairement) selon ses capacités, à chacun (inconditionnellement) selon ses besoins. Propos recueillis par Baptiste Mylondo et Simon Cottin-Marx', *Mouvements*, 73, 2013, pp. 155–74.

—, 'Basic Income and Social Democracy', in P. Van Parijs (ed.), *Basic Income and the Left: A European Debate*, London: Social Europe, 2018, pp. 12–20.

—, and Vanderborght, Y., *Basic Income: A Radical Proposal for a Free Society and a Sane Economy*, Cambridge, MA and London: Harvard University Press, 2017.

Vanderborght, Y., 'Why Trade Unions Oppose Basic Income', *Basic Income Studies*, 1(1), 2006, pp. 1–20.

Varoufakis, Y., *The Global Minotaur: America, the True Origins of the Financial Crisis and the Future of the Global Economy*, London and New York: Zed Books, 2011.

—, 'When Does a Society Become Social?', lecture presented at the 'Future of Work Conference', organized by the Gottlieb Duttweiler Institute, Zurich, 4 May 2016.

Vercellone, C. and Harribey, 'Quelle place pour le travail?', *L'Économie politique*, 67, 2015, pp. 62–75.

Virno, P., *Gramática de la multitud: para un análisis de las formas de vida contemporáneas*, Madrid: Traficantes de Sueños, 2003.

Vrousalis, N., 'Workplace Democracy Implies Economic Democracy', *Journal of Social Philosophy*, 50(3), 2019, pp. 259–79.

Wacquant, L., *Prisons of Poverty*, Minneapolis and London: University of Minnesota Press, 2009a.

—, *Punishing the Poor: The Neoliberal Government of Social Insecurity*, Durham, NC: Duke University Press, 2009b.

Weeks, K., *The Problem with Work: Feminism, Marxism, Antiwork Politics, and Postwork Imaginaries*, Durham, NC: Duke University Press, 2011.

White, S., *The Civic Minimum: On the Rights and Obligations of Economic Citizenship*, Oxford: Oxford University Press, 2003.

—, 'The Republican Critique of Capitalism', in *Critical Review of International Social and Political Philosophy*, 14(5), 2011, pp. 561–79.

—, 'Property-Owning Democracy and Republican Citizenship', in M. O'Neill and T. Williamson (eds), *Property-Owning Democracy: Rawls and beyond*, Oxford: Wiley-Blackwell, 2012, pp. 129–46.

—, 'Freedom, Exit and Basic Income', in A. Eleveld, T. Kampen and J. Arts (eds), *Welfare to Work in Contemporary European Welfare States: Legal, Sociological and Philosophical Perspectives on Justice and Domination*, Bristol: Bristol University Press, 2020, pp. 307–30.

—, 'Labour, Capital and Commons: Three Sites of Predistribution', forthcoming.

Widerquist, K., *Independence, Propertylessness, and Basic Income: A Theory of Freedom as the Power to Say No*, New York: Palgrave Macmillan, 2013.

—, *The Problem of Property: Taking the Freedom of Nonowners Seriously*, New York: Palgrave Macmillan, 2023.

Willetts, D., *Civic Conservatism*, London: The Social Market Foundation, 1994.

Winters, J. A., and Page, B. I., 'Oligarchy in the United States?', *Perspectives in Politics*, 7(4), 2009, pp. 731–51.

Wray, L. R., *Understanding Modern Money: The Key to Full Employment and Price Stability*, Cheltenham: Edward Elgar, 1998.

Wright, E. O., 'Compass Points: Towards a Socialist Alternative', *New Left Review*, 41, 2006a, pp. 93–124.

—, 'Basic Income as a Socialist Project', *Basic Income Studies*, 1(1), 2006b, pp. 1–11.

—, *Envisioning Real Utopias*, London and New York: Verso, 2010.

—, 'Sociology and Epistemology of Real Utopias: A Conversation with David Casassas and Maciej Szlinder', *Theoretical Practice*, 2016. www.praktykateoretyczna.pl/sociology-and-epistemology-of-real-utopias/.

—, *How to Be an Anticapitalist in the Twenty-First Century*, London and New York: Verso, 2019.

Young, I. M., *Responsibility for Justice*, New York: Oxford University Press, 2011.

Zelleke, A., 'Wages for Housework: The Marxist-Feminist Case for Basic Income', *Política y Sociedad*, 59(2), 2022, pp. 1–14.

Zimmermann, R., *The Law of Obligations: Roman Foundations of the Civilian Tradition*, Oxford: Oxford University Press, 1996.

Zunz, O., Schoppa, L. and Hiwatari, N. (eds), *Social Contracts under Stress: The Middle Classes of America, Europe, and Japan at the Turn of the Century*, New York: Russell Sage Foundation, 2004.

Index

Thanks to our Patreon subscriber:

Ciaran Kane

Who has shown generosity and comradeship in support of our publishing.

The Pluto Press Newsletter

Hello friend of Pluto!

Want to stay on top of the best radical books
we publish?

Then sign up to be the first to hear about our
new books, as well as special events,
podcasts and videos.

You'll also get 50% off your first order with us
when you sign up.

Come and join us!

Go to bit.ly/PlutoNewsletter